Letting Go of Stuff®

Powerful Secrets to Simplify Your Life

Darren L. Johnson

Part of the *Letting Go of Stuff*® Series
Published by InsideOut Learning, Inc.

Published by InsideOut Learning, Inc.
P.O. Box 281048, Nashville, TN 37228
www.insideoutlearning.com

ISBN 0 9652307 2 4

Letting Go of Stuff® is a registered trademark
of InsideOut Learning, Inc.

Cover design by Claudia Smith.

Dedication

This book is dedicated to the memory and in honor of my parents, Alva Marie Lewis Johnson and Dr. Thomas Walter Johnson, Sr., and to their parents, grandparents, and ancestors.

Thank you!
I love you—forever.

Sawu Bona!

Acknowledgements

I would be remiss if I did not give credit to those who have provided support for and believed in me along the way. To Claudia Smith for the cover design, as well as the design of all of the flyers, booklets, and other related material, you are the best! Thank you Gayal for your support, love, and belief in me as a person. Thank you Indira Belizaire for the countless reviews of the book and scheduling all the book signings and radio/TV interviews. You made it look effortless. Patricia Carter, thanks for your review and suggestions for the second printing. Thanks Amy Lee and Elisha Vernon for the review and input before our second printing. Thank you Jenna Anderson for the great last minute proofing. You saved the day! Angela Robinson, your referrals and support were priceless. To the countless many who provided input and perspective along the way, thank you so very much.

Letting Go of Stuff®

Powerful Secrets to Simplify Your Life

Table Of Contents

"WE SHALL NOT CEASE FROM EXPLORATION,
AND THE END OF ALL OUR EXPLORING
WILL BE TO ARRIVE WHERE WE STARTED
AND KNOW THE PLACE FOR THE FIRST TIME."
—T.S. ELIOT, *LITTLE GIDDING*

Introduction

This book provides the tools and information needed to live life to the fullest. You'll learn to focus on loving life, learning lessons, and sharing those lessons with others.

The concepts, strategies, and techniques are referred to as "secrets"—not because we don't know about them, but because we don't apply them. They reflect years of research and study and my personal approach to life. I practice them on a daily basis because, like you, I am constantly learning, growing, letting go, and moving forward in life. For example, I use the Self-Managing Grid® in Chapter 8 to help me stay focused every minute of every hour. Also, I am constantly recording my thoughts, dreams, and goals to help me design and redesign my life.

I have learned where to look for the key to my success. Looking inside and searching your soul is where the key exist. Everything you need to become the person you want to be exists within you. Many people spend years trying to find themselves, moving from city to city and bouncing from job to job. It is important to slow down long enough to figure out who you really are on the inside and to learn how to let go of things from the past that keep you stagnant.

To make a positive, long-lasting change, you must **focus on your essence**, not your surroundings.

Many people either don't know how or are afraid to look inside themselves. Do you constantly blame other people and situations for your circumstances, mistakes, and shortcomings? Do you find yourself feeling angry with people for no apparent reason? Do you often feel frustrated and tense without knowing why? Are you unable to get along with your spouse, children, and friends? If the answer to these questions is "Yes," then it is time to make a change. It may not be easy, but it certainly is necessary!

You might ask yourself, "Why should I make a change?" I ask you, "Why not?" Let the exercises in this book challenge you to look inside your soul and make positive, lifelong changes.

An additional question you should ask yourself, regardless of your religious practice or spiritual beliefs, is "What have I done for my faith lately?" I encourage you to recommit yourself to your spiritual purpose. If you don't have one, then I suggest you begin the journey. I challenge you to spread your light. Don't allow it to be overshadowed by the impact of procrastination, fear, confusion, dishonesty, gossip, disrespect, and the like. Learn to let go so you can move forward toward the light God has placed in your heart, soul, and spirit.

There are exercises in this book to assist you in the process of *Letting Go of Stuff.*® You also will read about my personal life experiences—my own journey of "letting go" and moving toward success. Each date accompanied by the words "Personal Journal" is an excerpt from the journal of my experiences. I have kept a personal journal for more than twenty years and share these experiences to help bring clarity to some of the concepts discussed in the book.

Challenge yourself by putting all of you into the exercises, which will allow you to go through the process of letting go on a conscious level. After repeating the Seven Secrets continually, you will develop "new habits." Eventually these "new habits" will become second nature, and you will be able to let go on purpose.

I wish you well with your endeavors. Don't forget: *Long-lasting change only happens when it is made from the InsideOut.* Knowing how to let go is one major key to success.

Letting Go of Stuff®

Sometimes in life we feel there's never enough.
And in our quest to accumulate,
We make the road seem rough.

We even masquerade and try to be very tough.
Yet, when it comes right down to it,
You'll eventually have to let go of some stuff.
Letting go is easy to say, but hard to do.
If you've ever had to do it, you understand, too.

But if you can, just let yourself part.
Then you will feel much better
Through your soul, right to your heart.
Learn to let go by reading this book.
And when you see yourself again,
You'll have a different look.

Face the fear, and step out of your facade.
And please remember the old expression,
Let go and then let God.

Darren L. Johnson 1996

Chapter 1
Stuff & Letting Go – Defined

Have you ever lain awake at 2:00 in the morning, feeling stressed and overwhelmed, because your dreams are not being accomplished? Do you constantly remind yourself you have made mistakes in the past? Do you worry about whether or not you are making the right decisions and choices in your life?

You can spend hours writing down your desires and wants in life. You can also tell your friends about your dreams. But until you change your internal conversations and create a clear picture of your future, the outcome will remain the same.

Many of us think changing hairstyles, clothes, and jewelry will make a significant difference in our habits. Some people believe making new friends, moving to a different city, and constantly changing jobs will bring about a long-term internal change. Those kinds of activities will make some difference, and they are easy ways to begin making changes in your life. However, the impact is temporary. Long-lasting change that will help you create new habits and actions requires an inside-out approach, as well as two very important tools: the mirror and time.

In order to change unwanted habits and actions, it is important to take the time to get to know yourself. These learned habits and thoughts, whether good or bad, are what got you to this point in life. Until you take a good look in the mirror, you will not be able to truly let go and move forward with your life.

This chapter will provide a context in which to understand the *Letting Go of Stuff*® process. It will explain the various terms that will be used throughout the book. These terms include the following: stuff, letting go, and internal conversations. We will also explore assumptions about letting go.

What Is Stuff?

One of the challenges of making a positive change in life is learning to manage the stuff in it. I don't know about you, but, to me, stuff seems to be everywhere.

Stuff seems to find its way into the middle of all of our lives, no matter what! Everyone has stuff. There is closet stuff, desk stuff, garage stuff, car stuff, storage stuff. There's your stuff, my stuff, their stuff, our stuff, his stuff, her stuff, and the notion that everyone else's stuff is worse than your stuff. There is also religious stuff, work stuff, financial stuff, and, often the most challenging of all, relationship stuff.

If you look up "stuff" in the dictionary, you often find words like "belongings," "heart," "materials," "nonsense," and "timber," as well as phrases such as "supplies or equipment used in various activities," and "writing, discourse, or ideas of little value."

My favorite definition comes from *Webster's Ninth New Collegiate Dictionary*, which describes "stuff" as "a matter of a particular and often unspecified kind; something introduced into the body by humans; a group or scattering of miscellaneous objects or articles."

The "stuff" discussed in this book is not necessarily visible to the naked eye. It is the unspecified, intangible, negative elements we introduce to our minds, through thoughts or some outside stimulation. When you do not know how to focus your thoughts effectively, they can become scattered, miscellaneous, and fixated on "stuff"—negative notions, toxic relationships, and situations from the past.

An InsideOut Approach
In *A Course In Miracles* (1996), the author writes of two inner creations within each of us. One is the *spirit*. The spirit is God-given and everything that is true and real. The other creation within us is the *ego*, which is created by us.

The ego constantly competes with the spirit for control over your inner voice. Although the ego is within you, it is separate from your spirit. The internal struggle between your ego and your spirit can help create the stuff in your life.

This internal struggle depicts the age-old fight between good and evil in which the ego represents evil and the spirit represents good. If that is the case, then I have experienced that battle many times in my life. The first step to dealing with this struggle is taking a hard look at yourself, being brutally honest, and becoming inspired.

An inside-out approach requires commitment to your dreams, proper goal setting, and trust in your inner spirit, as well as consistency, perseverance, courage, hope, forgiveness, and love. It's difficult work, but it can be fun, exciting, and character building. This approach requires listening to, trusting in, and taking action based upon your internal guide.

Another key component to an inside-out approach is your internal dialogue. We all talk to ourselves. A major key to success exists in what we say to ourselves, which helps to shape our attitude and mindset.

The mindset is the place inside you that determines your reality and view of the world. It also determines your way of being, which is how you interact with the world around you (Anderson and Anderson, 2001). Some of it begins with your internal conversations, the dialogue that takes place in your head.

For the purpose of this book, there are two categories of stuff: good and not-so-good. The next few pages provide a broad explanation of both categories using excerpts from the personal journal I have kept for the past twenty years.

The Good Stuff

The good stuff includes love, forgiveness, healthy self-esteem, confidence, and happiness, as well as past achievements, successes, positive thoughts, joyous events, and tender moments with family and friends, including life events such as graduations, birthdays, and weddings. Usually these experiences create the stuff we want. The following excerpt from my personal journal is an example of what could be categorized as good stuff.

Personal Journal – July 3, 1994

As I stand in the room filled with my wonderful aunts, uncles, cousins, brothers, sister, and father, whom I lovingly refer to as "T," I am overwhelmed with a feeling of love and understanding of my destiny. As I watch everyone laughing, talking, and enjoying each other's company, I get a definite sense of what family is about. [End]

I know family has different meanings for different folks. For me, family reunions are filled with nothing but "good stuff"—fun, love, hugs, good food, laughter, great stories, and more love—just like real homemade chicken soup. It all leads to a content and happy soul.

I was raised around this kind of good family stuff, which is so powerful and wonderful that it is easy to take for granted. Taking things for granted is part of the not-so-good stuff. I took a journey that led to the center of my soul during the 1994 family reunion. That journey helped to change my life forever. There were many new events in my life at the time. One night, I listed on paper all of the new events in my life. Below is the actual list:

Personal Journal - July 22, 1994
New Stuff in My Life
- *New life without Mom (she transcended in December 1992)*
- *New business (began June 1994)*
- *New feeling of fear for all the new events*
- *New at taking such a risk with my career*
- *New experiences being Darren, the adult, around family and relatives*
- *New feelings associated with realizing the importance of family.* [End.]

Each new event brought about new outcomes for my life. Because I wanted only good stuff happening in my life, I began the new journey in a way that helped determine the full impact of these new outcomes.

Ultimately, your state of mind determines your circumstances. To realize the outcomes you want, it is critical to recognize and experience the transition from our present thoughts, habits, and actions to new thoughts, habits, and actions. Doing this on a conscious level will help you continuously to have "good stuff" occur in your life—on purpose.

The Not-So-Good Stuff

I refer to the outcomes we don't want in our lives as the "not-so-good" stuff. It can be a combination of emotions sparked by anger, frustration, depression, humiliation, and past experiences, such as being laid off from the job after twenty years; going through a messy divorce; feeling dissatisfaction with your body because it is too fat, too small, too short, or too tall; living in a high-crime area; etc. I could go on and on. Sometimes these elements interfere with our ability to maintain a healthy mental environment.

This not-so-good stuff, combined with our internal thought process, prevents us from growing and keeps us stuck in a rut. To illustrate how the not-so-good stuff can impact our lives, here is another excerpt from my personal journal:

Personal Journal – February 2, 1996
As I jogged past a woman and her car, I could feel the woman's pain. With several inches of snow on the ground, the temperature at 30 degrees Fahrenheit, and more snow falling, I turned around and went back to the car to see if the woman needed any help. There was a young man standing next to her car who had also stopped to help.

As I approached the woman, I asked, "Are you okay?" She responded, "No. I have run out of gas, and I don't have any money." Then after a long pause, she continued, "I am homeless and have been living in my car. I used to have a job, but they laid me off. I never thought I'd end up living in my car. I never thought I'd end up homeless."

She began to pound on the steering wheel with frustration and anger, saying, "It makes me so angry." I responded to her by saying, "You know what? It is okay for you to be angry." She began to cry. Her frustration had festered in her soul and she, without even realizing it, had provided the necessary ingredients for the seed of hopelessness to grow. Perhaps she had given up on seeking other opportunities. After the other young man and I pushed her car out of the street, we wished her blessings and went our separate ways. She really seemed to have been dealing with some not-so-good stuff.

As I resumed my jog, I could feel a difference on the inside. First, I wondered what had happened to her. My thoughts then shifted to how my inner spirit led me to give her aid. I wondered if anyone had ever told her it was okay to be angry and that she had a right to be frustrated and disappointed. She seemed to have been holding on to a lot of pain.

My appreciation for life was taken to another level by that one small experience. I began to think about how good it felt to do something for someone without expecting anything in return. I wanted to do more for her, to help her, to give her some money, or just listen to and console her. So after finishing the jog, I got into my car and drove to the street where her car was stuck, but she was gone. [End.]

She seemed to be fully immersed in the no-so-good stuff. In my past, I have seen—and have been—this person many times. There have been times in my life when I have felt abandoned or angry about a situation. There have been times when I was scared or disappointed in myself and wanted to lash out at anyone who was near.

Imagine a spiral spinning downward in a counter-clockwise direction. On each rung is a negative thought or experience you have had that has led to some unwanted outcome. There are people whose lives are in a constant spin downward toward a pool of nothingness.

In dealing with my not-so-good stuff, I have experienced this downward spiral in my life. After going through a series of unfortunate experiences in 1988, I filed bankruptcy. There was a series of thought patterns that helped create the actions that led me to the bankruptcy. The challenge I faced was changing the internal mental processing about how I lived the rest of my life. If something had not changed, I may have ended up in the same situation. In relation to stuff—especially not-so-good stuff—if you think the way you have always thought, you will act the way you have always acted. Part of letting go is to change the way you think.

The not-so-good stuff keeps us from moving forward in life the way we could or should. It is also what we tend to focus on most of the time. Not only do we focus on it, we hold on to it, as if we really need it to survive. Often you may find yourself spinning around and around in circles because of the not-so-good stuff in your life, and you seem never to get ahead. The problems of yesterday seem never to go away, and they become more complicated by the problems of today. Sometimes you worry the problems of today will still be there tomorrow. As a result, you keep going around and around in an endless cycle of worry, almost feeling out of control.

When you learn to let go, you can actually see yourself growing. I don't mean to imply you can simply release the stuff in your life without going through changes, or that you will wake up tomorrow morning and the stuff will be gone. One good option, however, is to learn how to manage the stuff. Experience is not what happens to you; rather, it is what you do with what happens to you. How you manage yourself as you deal with stuff in your life largely determines the quality of your life.

What Is Letting Go?
Letting Go of Stuff® is a lifelong process of learning, changing, growing, and becoming better by thinking differently about yourself. It is about loving, caring, forgiving, and understanding your self.

The process outlined in this book will guide you along the path of letting go by helping you identify what may be holding you back. Chapter 7 is specifically dedicated to letting go. It will provide a process to work through the "stuff" you identify in Chapter 2 and create goals that will give you a foundation for whatever your definition of success is.

A big part of letting go is recognizing when it is time to stay in a situation and when it is time to move on.

Each time you let go, you create a new beginning and ending. William Bridges (1980) wrote about the importance of beginnings and endings and how they play out in our lives. In order to realize the outcomes we want, it is critical for us to recognize and accept the transitions from old to new thoughts, habits, and actions. *Letting Go of Stuff*® helps to create new beginnings, which also happens with acceptance of self. Accept your own strengths and shortcomings; and embrace the ups and downs, losses and discoveries, lessons and missed learnings as being a part of your life journey as you grow through the various phases of maturity.

According to Bridges, we grow and develop through the "ending-then-beginning" patterns in our lives. These patterns represent the way we grow and change as we move from one phase of life into another. Regardless of how you have learned to transition, every phase of life represents an ending and a beginning. The ending provides closure, and the beginning provides an opportunity for new growth and learning.

We often do not want to let go of a particular phase in our life, even though all the signs indicate it is time to move on. I can remember how difficult it was when my parents took me to Atlanta for college. After they had gotten me settled in the dormitory and said their goodbyes, they were ready to head back to Tennessee.

I never will forget how much I wanted to be in the car with them, how I wanted to go back home the very moment they were driving off. I can remember not wanting to leave the sidewalk where I was standing and feeling stuck to the cement. I didn't want them to leave, yet I knew they had to go.

In that instant, watching them drive away simultaneously represented the end of my total dependence on my parents and the beginning of becoming independent of them. Some of us hold on to this ending-then-beginning phase, getting stuck between leaving and staying home. We stay stuck there for a long time. For me, leaving home represented the end of my childhood and the beginning of my time as a responsible adult. In order to let go of my parents, I had to accept the notion of being a grown up.

EXERCISE 1-1
Before we move on, refer to the grid below and answer the questions by placing a check mark in either the "yes" or "no" columns:

QUESTION	YES	NO
1. Have there been significant, unwanted changes in my life?		
2. Am I still dealing with the same issues I dealt with one to ten years ago?		

Question	Yes	No
3. Am I still angry with the same folks I was angry with one to ten years ago?		
4. Am I still making the same promises I made one to ten years ago?		
5. Am I still facing the same challenges I faced one to ten years ago?		
6. Am I still "working on" the same things now as I was five or ten years ago, such as losing weight, quiting smoking, increasing my exercise, being on time, telling the truth, being a good friend, etc.?		

If you answered "yes" to any of these questions, then it may be time for you to make a positive, uplifting change in your life. Do you really want to take the same ten-year old "stuff" into your future?

Three Assumptions About Your Success

Your progress in this wonderful journey toward letting go is based on three assumptions, which are grounded in Gestalt Theory (Nevis, 1987). The first assumption is that if you decide to read beyond this point, you are aware that there is a need to make a change in your life—to let go of some stuff—and that this awareness has stimulated a need to do something about it.

The second assumption is that you have an inherent desire to make changes in your life and that you will succeed in this endeavor. Third, it is assumed you will learn from the process of letting go as outlined in this book. There are definite lessons you will learn as you complete and participate in the exercises in this book. Those lessons will become the foundation of a new, redesigned self. This is a small investment of your time, energy, and spiritual resources that will pay off in a big way.

The interesting thing about the previously mentioned two categories of stuff is that we tend to focus on the not-so-good stuff rather than the good. Ironically, it is not until we are prepared to let go of something that we can really enjoy it. This idea can sound complicated at first, but it is made clear with the following example.

Is growing older something you worry about? If it is, then it's reasonable to conclude you probably think about not being as young as you used to be some years ago. By not being able to let go of the notion of not being as young, you will hold on to the worries associated with getting older. Until you let go of the fact that you are not as young, you will not be able to enjoy the process of getting older. Make sense? As Ramona S. Adams said in her book *Letting Go: Uncomplicating Your Life*, "It is one of life's paradoxes that you can fully enjoy only those things you are willing to let go."

This book will introduce seven strategies (referred to as secrets) that, if applied, will lead to the *Letting Go of Stuff*® in your life. Many times, we are not sure how to truly let go of certain things in our lives. Unhealthy habits and toxic relationships developed in the past are among the most difficult to let go of and change. First, we must realize what letting go is all about and then fully participate in the process.

EXERCISE 1-2
The following questions are designed to put you on the path of *Letting Go of Stuff*® and moving forward.

List below what is "new" in your life:

_____   _____
_____   _____
_____   _____
_____   _____
_____   _____
_____   _____

List the outcomes you want as a result of these new events or situations in your life. What must you do to create the outcomes you desire?

_____   _____
_____   _____
_____   _____
_____   _____
_____   _____
_____   _____

Chapter 2
Letting Go & the Seven Secrets

"AND NOW HERE IS MY SECRET, A VERY SIMPLE SECRET; IT IS ONLY
WITH THE HEART THAT ONE CAN SEE RIGHTLY, WHAT IS ESSENTIAL
IS INVISIBLE TO THE EYE."

— ANTOINE DE SAINT-EXUPÉRY

An Attitude of Letting Go

Letting go is synonymous with acceptance. It is about taking responsibility for your actions, accepting your faults, and moving forward—all at the same time. Let me share some incidents from my past that help illustrate *Letting Go of Stuff*.®

After graduating from high school, I left home to pursue a college experience in Georgia. My intent was to graduate from college and perhaps become a doctor. Well, after one and a half years of confusion, I chose to drop out of school. Of course, in my mind, dropping out was not my fault—it was the professors' fault.

Soon after, I began working as a soccer coach for the YMCA in Atlanta. Then I had an extraordinarily eye-opening, near-death experience. One morning while driving, I approached a four-way stop intersection on a street behind Morehouse College. Upon entering the intersection, I looked to my left and immediately saw the approaching grill of a 1972 Plymouth, the width of which was equal to the length of my car. In less than a second, I felt the impact of the collision.

As it turned out, the person behind the wheel was learning to drive and had confused the brake with the gas pedal when approaching the stop sign. She smashed into the driver's side of my car, ramming it to the other side of the street, shattering all of my windows, and somehow knocking me into the passenger's side of the car. I ended up curled in a ball under the dashboard, face buried in my knees, arms wrapped tightly around my knees, and my hair glistening with pieces of shattered glass.

The police officer who arrived on the scene asked me the name of the hospital where the driver of my vehicle was taken. When I told him I was the driver, he said only one in every one thousand people survive an accident like this one. He then looked at me and said, "Son, you are here for a reason."

The Downward Spiral Had Begun to Spin

As a result of the accident, I lost my job—not because I was too hurt to work, but because reliable transportation was a requirement for the job. Even though I nearly starved and couldn't pay my rent, I refused to call my parents for help. Not calling home was my choice, but I wrongly blamed my parents as if it was their fault I didn't want to call home.

Finally, my car was repaired, and I got a job as an assistant manager at a convenience store. Now I felt things were starting to look up. It was the beginning of a new career. It was exciting to have the responsibility of an entire store. I dreamed of being manager one day and of maybe having a store of my own. Wow! Life was beginning to get back on track.

Some months later, on a Sunday afternoon, I was in the store by myself. Two men in three-piece suits walked into the store. I was watching a football game on the store television, munching on potato chips, and gulping down orange juice. Thinking nothing of the two customers, I continued to watch the game as they walked about the store. Suddenly, one of the two men ran down the middle aisle, jumped over the counter, and put a gun to my temple. He forced me back up against the wall, then placed the cold barrel of the gun on the back of my neck, telling me over and over again he was going to blow my head off. In the meantime, the other robber loaded beer and cigarettes into my car.

Long story short, the robbers decided to let me live and drove off in my car. As the downward spiral continued to spin, I got fired. The convenience store owners considered me a risk to their operation because I did not get hurt and my car was later found trashed on the side of some road. So, once again, I found myself without an income with no place to live and no job in sight. Something had to change.

Shortly after that experience, I entered into a management trainee position at a fast-food restaurant, Church's Chicken. One day, during a management meeting, I looked across the room at a guy, whom I later learned was 55 years old. I asked myself two questions that absolutely changed my life.

Question one: "Do I want to be where he is when I am his age?" The answer was an emphatic "No!"

Question two: "What can I do right now to keep that from happening?" The answer was simple: go back home, go to college, and major in business management. Within two weeks of my revelation, I had returned to Nashville and was back in college.

The Steps Toward Life Change

What did I do to turn my life around? Asking questions internally about my life was nothing new. However, the conscious decision I made to trust my answers was. It was the first time I realized that the answers I needed to design my life were inside my heart and soul. I had been searching everywhere for the answers to my problems, but God had already given me what I needed. I just needed to look inside myself.

Like me, you have everything you need to design your life to be the way you desire. Most of us dream of a new life and believe in the dream as long as it is in our mind's eye. We may even write it down, but we don't believe we have what it takes—the innate faith in our abilities—to make our dream come true.

In praying, many people ask for faith, but faith is already there; you were born with it. You just have to *believe* you were born with it.

The events I have shared really happened, and it is important to know I never lost hope. I refused to believe I was supposed to end up lost and frustrated with my life. I never imagined myself staying in any of those situations for long. My choice was to keep moving forward, which I did with great energy. I never determined the outcomes of any of those situations as being negative. I only saw them as temporary setbacks that would not last long. William Bridges (1980) would say I was transitioning—preparing the way for new growth and new activities.

I believe those experiences were the universe's way of saying, "Darren, it is time to move on with your life; I have something bigger and better in store for you."

As a result of my hope, which shaped my attitude and vision, I moved through these experiences knowing in my soul that somehow everything was going to be all right. The hope within your heart is powerful. Whatever happens, you cannot afford to lose hope in your dreams, goals, and desire to make your life better.

You cannot afford to lose hope in your ability to do the things you know in your heart you are destined to accomplish. Do not lose hope in what the universe has placed you here to do. Only when you plant in your heart the seeds of belief, hope, and faith, rather than anger and heartache, will your dream garden grow.

Making the Choice to Change

You have choices to make about what you do with the rest of your life. My choice is to view the outcomes of yesterday's experiences as positive, motivating lessons to be applied to tomorrow's challenges—nothing more, nothing less. Just as you choose to get up every day, go to your job, and drive the same car, you decide how much of an impact your past has on you today.

It is your choice whether or not to be happy. Applying the Seven Secrets detailed in the next seven chapters of this book will make a huge difference.

I stumbled upon these secrets one at a time throughout my life. Applying them on a daily basis has absolutely changed my life for the better.

They have had a profound impact on my outlook and have helped me to make wiser, more appropriate life choices. They can do the same for you. Whatever you do, do not be fooled by the seeming simplicity of the Seven Secrets. Their very power lies in their elegance and simplicity.

Next is an exercise that will allow you to begin the process of letting go according to the Seven Secrets. This exercise is most important as it sets the tone for your redesign as you complete the rest of the activities and exercises in this book. Have fun as you learn about yourself!

EXERCISE **2-1**

What you write in this section will be used throughout the rest of this book, particularly in Chapter 9. Please respond to all of the following statements before going to the next section of this chapter. Fold the top outside corner of this page so you can easily flip back to it.

List at least five things that constantly cause you to worry, stress you out, and/or otherwise frustrate and bother you.

1. _____
   _____
   _____
   _____

2. _____
   _____
   _____
   _____

3. _____
   _____
   _____
   _____

4. _____

   _____

   _____

   _____

5. _____

   _____

   _____

   _____

Write down your ultimate life dream goal—
something you have always wanted to do, or have
dreamt of doing. Perhaps you should find the dream
you laid aside years ago when you got caught up in
life's stuff. Pull the dream out of your mental closet,
and write it down.

_____

_____

_____

_____

_____

An Overview of the Seven Secrets

The remaining chapters are devoted to the Seven
Secrets and to the understanding of the Self Managing
Grid®. The first of the Seven Secrets for *Letting Go of
Stuff*® is to *accept and acknowledge the fact there are
things you need to let go*. As simple as this may sound, it
is a very big step for most people. Chapter 3 expounds
upon this statement: Acknowledging the need for change
leads to acceptance, and letting go is synonymous with
acceptance.

Chapter 4 explores the second secret: You must *realize change is necessary,* and you will experience changes throughout the entire process of **Letting Go of Stuff.**®

Although many resist, change is the only real constant in our lives. Without change, your body would not be able to carry out the necessary functions that keep you alive. Without change, we wouldn't grow. Dennis Kimbro said, *Resolving the issues that face us almost always means changing something in ourselves.*

Many people don't like to change. Some of us are afraid of the unknown future that may result from changing. Others of us are worried about changes that may never come to pass. Still others are buried by events and situations from the past. In either case, Chapter 4 discusses how, regardless of our perceptions of the unknown or the past, we must realize change is necessary.

Chapter 5 focuses on the third secret, which is to *manage the unconscious internal conversations* taking place in our heads. Do you talk to yourself? Of course you do. The more important question is "What do you say to yourself?"

We develop habits in every area of our lives. Habits are developed from a belief and a value about something. Your beliefs manifest in some action representing your value about that belief. Finally, the action, once repeated over and over again, day after day, month after month, year after year, is carried out on an unconscious level, which leads to the development of a habit, often without you realizing it. Your internal conversations are developed in the same way. When you are confronted with having to make a change in your life, whether it is changing a habit, accomplishing a goal, or becoming better as a person, the first thing that must be changed is your mind.

It is important to initiate internal conversations that create pictures and vivid thoughts in your mind that represent what you want the change to be. In other words, visualize yourself being the way you want to be. See yourself walking, talking, and functioning as the person you want to become. This age-old visualizing process is used by many professional athletes, speakers, actors, sales people, entertainers, and others. It is a process that works well when used properly and consistently.

Chapter 6 introduces the fourth secret: *have the right attitude* while going through the process of **Letting Go of Stuff**.® Attitude is more about how you respond to situations than the situations themselves. Most of us believe outside situations shape our attitudes when, in fact, it is our view of the situations that shape our attitudes. This notion has been around for thousands of years, since the beginning of African cultures (Browder 1992).

In Chapter 7, the fifth secret teaches you to *focus on what you can control*. According to Earl Nightingale, most people focus 70 percent of their time, energy, and worries on things that either have or never will happen. That is a big percentage. Ask yourself how many times you have gotten upset about something you cannot control. How much simpler would your life be if you did not put any energy into a situation or person over which or in whom you have no control? Think about it!

Chapter 8 explores the sixth secret: *make a choice to let go of the things you cannot control* using the Self Managing Grid.® The Self Managing Grid® examines four choices we can make every day of our lives:

- **Choice 1–** *Over-control.* Often we attempt to over-control some situation or person in our lives. Over-control occurs when you attempt to act on something that simply cannot be controlled, regardless of the situation.

- **Choice 2–** *Let go.* When you accept the fact you have no control and choose not to take any action, you are letting go.

- **Choice 3–** *Set positive goals;* as opposed to negative goals. This occurs when you decide to take action on something you can control.

- **Choice 4–** *Under-control.* Constantly giving up on people and situations can lead to long periods of depression and much anxiety.

It is psychologically and physiologically healthy to put more time and energy into letting go of what you cannot control and taking positive action on things you can control.

The seventh secret is to *create a personal plan of action* that will help you develop the art of **Letting Go of Stuff**® in a healthy, proactive, positive, and winning way. In Chapter 9, you will design your plan of action, which includes a personal mission statement and *BE Statements*. The *BE Statements* are positive phrases you will create about yourself. These statements represent your "new" internal conversation and should be read every day. Your plan of action will also include a description of what you will be like after you have let go of stuff. In other words, you will create a new picture of yourself—a new *YOU*—that will result from implementing your plan of action to let go.

Use the exercises in this book to jump-start making your dreams come true. Your dreams are the only thing you can create, share with others, and yet still keep 100 percent for yourself. So, why not give yourself an opportunity to live according to your dreams? The Seven Secrets are a series of steps that, when applied, can lead to greater happiness and more focus on what is truly important in your life. There are more people walking around today who are mad, frustrated, worried, ashamed, and feeling guilty and/or afraid to make decisions about their life. Getting better at letting some things go in your life will make a world of difference in the way you see your world. Remember, "If you want to grow, you must learn to let go."

More and more people want to learn about how to manage change and stress. The more complicated this society becomes, the greater the need is to simplify your life. If you never learn how to manage change and stress properly, you will continuously feel out of control. Letting go is a process—one that if learned well, can add great value and longevity to your life. If you develop the art of *Letting Go of Stuff,*® you will be able to propel yourself forward and become who you want to be—on purpose.

Chapter 3
Acknowledge the Stuff – Love Yourself

"YOU CANNOT BE SAFE FROM TRUTH, BUT ONLY IN TRUTH.
REALITY IS THE ONLY SAFETY. IN THE SECURITY OF REALITY,
FEAR IS TOTALLY MEANINGLESS…TRUTH CAN ONLY BE IN YOU."
— FOUNDATION FOR INNER PEACE (1996)

In this chapter, we will examine forgiveness, aging, relationships, and the complications of having stuff in our lives. The *first secret* to *Letting Go of Stuff*® is the following:

Acknowledge that you have stuff.

According to *Webster's Ninth New Collegiate Dictionary*, "acknowledge" means "to recognize the rights, authority, or status of; to own or admit knowledge of or agreement with; to express gratitude or obligation for; to take notice of; to make known the receipt of; and to recognize as genuine or valid."

Acknowledgment leads to acceptance. Only after you accept something as it really is in your life will you be able to let it go and begin to make some kind of change. This holds true whether your "letting go goal" involves getting out of a toxic relationship, losing weight, moving to another city, becoming a non-smoker, increasing your fitness level, becoming a better spouse, or even learning to wake up 10 minutes earlier in the morning. No matter what habit or behavior pattern you want to change and let go, you must first identify where you are "now," known as the "present state."

Personal Journal - March 4, 1996
For the past two nights, I felt as if I was being dunked in my own thoughts, fears, inhibitions, and worries—drowning in them as if in a pool unable to swim to the surface. The first night, Saturday, March 2, I tossed and turned as I struggled to stay above the surface of the pool of negativity. I kept thinking, "What if I become bald?" "What if I get sick?" "What if I begin to look old?" "What if I don't sell my tape programs?" "How can I let my company grow?" "What will my tax bill be?" "Am I a good husband?"

Suddenly, I remembered Louise Hay's advice in You Can Heal Your Life *(1984) about accepting and embracing your fears. I realized I needed to love myself more. I revamped my internal dialogue, saying to myself: "Stop focusing on what you don't want and concentrate on what you do want. You don't deserve to feel resentful, uptight, scared, sad, unhappy, hesitant, angry, worried, frustrated, burdened, or any of that stuff. Just love yourself."*

The next night, my thoughts were different. Led by my inner spirit, I woke up in the middle of the night, and the answer to the previous night's questions came to me. It was as if God was whispering, "Don't worry, I am here with you. You have come a long way. I know you are tired. I'll take it from here, even though I have been here all along."

My entire body relaxed. I was freed. [End.]

I realized while writing that journal entry the Universe doesn't burden us—we burden ourselves. We are made to be wonderfully happy, beautiful, loving, and learning creatures of this world. We are loved, many of us just do not realize it. I felt touched by God the second night. Not only was He there those two nights, but I realized He was with me always.

I learned then to acknowledge how I feel, embrace it with love, stay focused on loving, and let the rest of it go. My thoughts continued: "Take care of yourself, and you will be able to influence others in a loving, positive way."

The next morning, I felt as light as a feather—free in a way I felt as a child, when loving came easily. Learning to love yourself is a worthy endeavor. The ability to love is a God-given gift. It is free. To refuse to love is like returning that gift, and saying, "I don't want this gift."

That is why it is important for us to want love, accept love, give love, and become love. Acknowledging and accepting whatever stuff you may have to let go comes easier when you love yourself. Only when you acknowledge the gap between what you want and what your current reality is will you be able to begin the work necessary to close the gap. For example, my goal was to create a more pleasant internal conversation about my life. The previous excerpt from my personal journal depicted an internal dialogue of fear, hesitation, and worry. The gap that existed between that internal conversation and the one I wanted needed to be closed. However, not until I acknowledged the fact there was a gap could I begin to close it.

Right now, as you read this message, there may be something in your life which you want to let go of or change. Only you know. Only you can acknowledge it. Only you have what it takes to let it go and make the change. The question for you becomes "Are you willing to acknowledge it?" Take a moment and reflect on this notion.

If you realize you have been in denial, now is the time to begin the process of letting go by first acknowledging what you need, and want, to change in your life, regardless of what it is. If there is a gap between who you are today and who you want to be tomorrow, now is a good time to begin closing the gap.

Sometimes there are other elements to become aware of prior to acknowledging what we really want to let go of. There are various unhealthy habits we all have developed. One of the most common is smoking cigarettes. Prior to changing the habit of smoking and acknowledging the need to change the habit, you may experience many other levels of heightened awareness.

You may be faced with health challenges as a result of smoking. You may go through a period of denial, during which your internal conversation will convince you your health is not in danger right now. This conversation will go something like this: "I will die of something anyway" or "My doctor hasn't told me to quit yet, so I guess I'm okay."

In an attempt to share how important it is for you to quit, the people closest to you might have to intervene, risking their relationship with you. The loss of those closest to you also may increase your willingness to acknowledge the need for change. You will encounter many other challenges as you acknowledge the need to let go of unhealthy habits, relationships, jobs, and anything else.

What are your internal conversations regarding the things you want to let go? The key is to become very aware of those conversations. Heightened awareness will increase your ability to change those conversations into powerful thoughts to propel you toward your goals. Internal conversation is covered in detail in Chapter 5. It plays a major role in the process of *Letting Go of Stuff.*®

Theologian Martin Luther is credited with saying, "Faith is permitting ourselves to be seized by the things we do not see." Here, he is not referring to the things we cannot see in the darkness, but the things we fail to recognize in the light—the symbol of knowledge. Often before we can see the light, we must walk in the darkness. Unfortunately, darkness has become a symbol for lack of knowledge, also known as ignorance. You can place your faith in either darkness or light. The difference is that in the darkness, you naturally look for light. The challenge is being able to see when you are in the light—that is, being able to acknowledge the thing you know you need to change and let go.

In *You Can Heal Your Life*, Louise Hay (1984) wrote the following:

> *Now is the time to acknowledge our responsibility in having created the situation or condition. I'm not talking about having guilt, nor about being a bad person for being where you are. I am saying to acknowledge the power within you that transforms our every thought into experience.*

Acknowledging there is something to let go is the first step to realizing you have the power to make a change. That power lies, to a great extent, in your ability to consciously control your internal conversations.

When you become aware of something you need to let go, you have moved from darkness to light. Once you see the light and acknowledge your stuff, it is like the first ray of sunlight in the morning—so revealing, good, warm, invigorating, and enlightening. Once it dawns on you that you need to make a change, you can acknowledge it, and eventually you will be able to accept it.

Letting Go of Stuff® Includes Forgiveness

Acknowledging and accepting your stuff can lead to forgiveness. Being forgiving frees your mind, spirit, and body. It allows you to truly let go. The first person you must forgive is yourself. The key to forgiveness is being able to identify the perpetrator and the victim. They often are one in the same because sometimes we're our worst enemy. Walt Kelly in a 1970 Pogo comic strip said, "We have met the enemy and he is us." The person we must first learn to forgive is who we see in the mirror.

Making real life changes is based on your ability to let go and accept truth without ego. It is important to become very aware of your ego because it can prevent you from forgiving yourself. It often becomes a shield against the emotions and inner spirit that allow us to love and, in turn, forgive those around us. You must become very aware of your ego. It is the one force you have created that will stand up against your inner spirit and get in the way of your ability to truly love, which means it can interfere with your ability to forgive.

In *Beyond Blame: Race Relations for the Twenty-First Century*, Michael Grant (1995) writes the following:

> *We must forgive after we have come to know who we really are and after we have been made whole and responsible through reality... Forgiveness, that marvelous, purging, resent-less, purifying act of magnanimity soothes the souls of both the perpetrator and victim. Forgiveness cleanses. Forgiveness renews. Forgiveness uplifts, removes burdens, unclogs the machinery, and allows the natural order of good will to be reestablished.*

Forgiveness leads to love, and love leads to forgiveness.

EXERCISE 3-1
How easy is it for you to forgive? If it is not easy, what is the benefit of not forgiving? Who benefits from you not forgiving? Is there someone you need to forgive?

Below is an exercise to help begin the process of forgiving, which is important in letting go. This entire process may take two days, six months, or even two years. What is most important is for you to get started now and complete each step for each person you forgive.

Here are the steps/actions listed in detail:

1. Make a list of those you need to and would like to forgive in your life. Include your self on the list.

2. Give yourself permission to forgive by making a statement or claim that you can forgive those listed above.

3. The process of forgiveness must begin with you; therefore, forgive yourself first.

4. Contact each person on your list and genuinely forgive each one by saying to them, "I forgive you for...."

5. Ask them to forgive you, but not until you love yourself enough to truly accept their response no matter what it may be.

This process of forgiving may not be easy, but it is definitely necessary. You will find your soul will be positively and spiritually fed when you take yourself through this process of forgiving. As a matter of fact, you may not be able to internalize fully the process of letting go and its benefits if you don't first learn how to forgive yourself and others. Forgiving allows you to let go and move forward.

In his discussion of forgiving one's self in *Tough Minded Faith for Tender Hearted People* (1983), Robert Schuller wrote, "Hidden hurts in the heart can nurture and nourish negative thinking. Often the most painful wounds are not the scars that are outwardly seen but the hidden wounds deep in the heart."

Forgiving yourself is crucial to the forgiveness of others. It is the element that lies between acknowledging and accepting, which only you can control. As Harvey Mackay (2000) explains in *Pushing the Envelope All the Way to the Top*, "The best way to get even is to forgive." So if you really want to get back at someone who has offended you in some way, forgive them. Forgiveness allows you to begin to move from a place of pain and suffering to a place of peace and harmony.

Our ancestors have created a wonderful way for you to know when to forgive. For example, the Christian Bible advises readers to "get rid of all bitterness, rage and anger, brawling and slander, along with every form of malice. Be kind and compassionate to one another, forgiving each other..." (Eph. 4:31-32, NIV).

As I learn more about my physiological responses to the world around me, I am constantly amazed. For example, if I don't forgive someone, even when I know I should, I become overly stressed and the muscles in my chest tighten and remain that way until I think of a way to resolve the situation. It is like having a built-in alarm in my body that goes off when I need to do the right thing and do not do it. If we do not forgive, the result can show up physically as well.

Knowing you possess a built-in mechanism for survival is one thing; recognizing it is another. Those mechanisms will help you realize it is time to begin acknowledging the fact you may need to let go. Listening to your body is so crucial to the process of forgiveness and to your overall success in life.

Barring any unusual circumstances, learning how to know your body is an important component to your success. Your body is the vessel you will use to carry out your purpose. You must take care of that vessel if you want your life journey to be successful. If your body breaks down because you have developed a habit of ignoring it, then your ability to succeed will be challenged, as will your ability to forgive.

Aging
We are aging every moment we live. Deepak Chopra (1993) explains, however, that even though aging is inevitable, we can have an impact on how our body changes over time. He said, "To gain control over the aging process you must first become aware of it. Awareness is one of the first important steps towards positive change. And no animal besides man is consciously aware of aging. Once the techniques of

awareness and control have been mastered, amazing effects can be achieved. The mind-body system reacts to every stimulus as a global event."

To begin to believe you can reduce the effects of aging, you must first let go of the belief that you can not reduce the effects of aging. Once you become aware of needing to let go of or change something, you can then begin the process of changing. All of your actions are a result of thought patterns or choices—from the time you were born until today, every decision you make is a result of thought patterns or habits you have internalized. To let go and change undesirable habits or beliefs, you must create and develop new habits to replace them.

It is the pursuit of making a change to create a new habit that will give you a sense of hope and fulfillment. Moreover, striving toward a healthier existence will make it easier to give up the old habit. Keep in mind that you will go through changes once you begin.

The impact of the aging process has a lot to do with the thought patterns or habits of thought you develop between the ages of 21 and 46. There have been numerous studies done on aging. Most of the conclusions are similar. In order to age the way you want, you must let go of many of the notions that your body is supposed to do certain things at certain times in your life. How many of us believe that at age 40 we will have trouble losing weight and that by age 50 we will have trouble with memory? Do you believe that at a certain age your body will change? If you do, then you may have been programmed to believe your body will change. Once programmed, you will unconsciously begin to develop behaviors that will make these beliefs a reality.

Because of these habits of thought, you will act accordingly. It can become a vicious cycle ultimately leading to early and unnecessary aging. Through acknowledging unwanted beliefs and notions about aging, you will become more aware, which will lead to acceptance—and from there, you can begin to let go. Only then, will you begin to grow and change. Change itself brings about planned and unplanned outcomes. Either way, you must realize change is necessary in order to effectively change your belief about aging.

Relationships

I called my friend in California one day to see how she was doing. During the conversation, she asked my opinion of the direction she was going with her life. She said she was up for a new management position, but neither she, nor some of her friends, thought she was ready for it. She was bored because she was not in a relationship and had no one to occupy her time. She really wanted to "find a man," but in her spare time had started reading philosophical books.

As she continued, I listened intently. Eventually, she asked, "What do you think? Should I take the position or not?"

I asked, "Are you sure you want to hear my honest response to your question?"

"Yes!" she replied.

So I responded with three questions that would help her reflect on her own situation:

1. What do you really want to do with your life?

2. When was the last time you truly answered question 1 for yourself?

3. When was the last time you dreamed about your future?

"Because you are not involved with anyone," I continued, "I would spend this time doing some real soul searching."

I gave her the name of some good self-help books and suggested she spend her free time "getting to know herself" instead of looking for a man.

You've got to get to know yourself first, set your goals, and live your dreams. Otherwise, when you meet someone, you will end up following that person and living his/her dreams instead of your own. Develop a relationship with yourself—learn to love you.

Some people are so afraid of getting to know themselves that they live and define their lives through the dreams and goals of others. How can a person be truly happy living someone else's dream? My suggestion is to take the time to know you and to know what you want and then develop relationships with others.

In a later chapter, you will complete the PZT Test®, which will help to release you from toxic relationships. The test shows how each of us is an amalgam, an average, of the seven people with whom we spend the most time. If you are spending time with someone you truly dislike, then the person eventually will become a part of who you are, and you could end up not liking yourself.

When dealing with this sort of situation, you must first examine why you are spending so much time with the person and determine what value they add to your life. From there, you have to decide what role, if any, you want them to play in your life. Becoming aware of and acknowledging the fact you are involved in toxic relationships is an important first step toward positive change in your life.

Relationships are so important to success. If you are thinking you don't really need people, think again.

Look at your life right now. How many times today have you relied on others? I don't know of any business person who can survive and be successful without the development of relationships, and I don't know of any religion or faith that doesn't encourage followers to foster relationships. There are very few roads in life you can take that do not in some way involve others. Even monks have to learn to get along, albeit in silence.

The kinds of people with whom you begin relationships are important, and learning how to relate effectively is critical to success.

The following poem (author unknown) is good to keep in mind as you choose new friends and decide which friends to have as a part of your closest circle:

A friend should be radical:
Love you when you are unlovable,
Hug you when you are unhuggable,
And bear you when you are unbearable.
A friend should be fanatical:
Cheer when the whole world will boo,
Dance when you get good news,
and cry when you cry too.
Most of all, a friend should be mathematical:
Multiply your joy, divide your sorrow,
Subtract the past, and add to tomorrow,
Calculate the needs deep in your heart
And always be bigger than the sum
of all your bad parts.

Fear and Letting Go

Della Reese once said, "Fear is a thief. It steals all of your today by making you afraid of your tomorrow." I believe this is true for many. Sometimes we are totally consumed by fear. Many people are too afraid to let go and admit they have issues and challenges they must face. Being afraid is a natural part of life. Being afraid is not a negative response and does not mean you are less of a man or woman. It means you are human. Fear stimulates us to take action and can be our friend, but if you act as though fear is not there—if you deny it—it will build and create barriers. For instance, I am a professional speaker, a career many people consider frightening. There was a time when more people reported being afraid of speaking in public than of dying. Because I love public speaking, I move toward the anxiety with a different perspective. I see speaking as a way to be of service to many, rather than as something to fear. To paraphrase Robert Schuller (1983), if you have a problem or a fear of something—like public speaking—learn to manage it. Years ago, I created the habit of managing fear by interpreting its impact on me as positive energy. This process is called channeling. Once I got into the habit of channeling, it became an unconscious act.

You, too, can create good habits on purpose in your life. It begins when you acknowledge and accept your fears and remember it is natural and okay to be afraid. The following is a poem I wrote titled

Afraid to Be Me. Written in 1994, it represents a realization I came to about accepting and acknowledging fear in my life.

As I face my destiny,
I am so afraid.
As I reflect on my past,
and wonder whether or not I am going to succeed,
I am so afraid.
As I turn to my life partner to reassure her,
I am so afraid.
As I wake up each morning,
and struggle for a feeling of worthiness,
I am so afraid.
As I move toward my goals
and visualize myself accomplishing them all,
I am so afraid.
As I think about putting great faith in God,
I am so afraid.
As I learn more about life while living it to the fullest,
I realize that there is an element that will always exist.
"I am not afraid to be so afraid."

The Complications of Stuff

The following is a true situation I experienced in 1995. After the experience, I wrote it down in my personal journal and here it is, word for word—only the names and a few details have been changed. This story demonstrates how complicated our life can become when we focus on other people's stuff.

Personal Journal - November 11, 1995
In a living room filled with cigarette smoke,
negativity, and other stuff, Joe and Mary were venting
about issues they deal with in their marriage. They
are both constantly bothered with colds and other
small physical ailments. During the conversation,
they would complain about each other to me, and
now and again speak directly to one other. Then
they would both light up cigarettes. The following
situation is also a continuous cycle for their family.

Joe has one child, and Mary has two, all from
previous relationships. Joe's family did not want him
to marry Mary, and Mary's family did not want her
to marry Joe. They loved each other, however, and
married anyway. Since the marriage, Joe's family
members have been civil to Mary. Unfortunately,
Mary's family constantly has voiced their dislike for
Joe. Mary's mother always has something negative to
say about Joe. When Joe speaks to Mary about her
mother, it is always negative. Her family is constantly
in the middle of their business, creating even more
challenges in their marriage.

Joe's child lives in a nearby city with his ex-wife, and
Joe feels guilty about this because he lives with Mary
and her children. Joe's philosophy on raising children
can be depicted in two phrases: "Do as I say, not as I
do" and "Do it because I am the adult, and I said so."

Needless to say, these phrases don't go over well with
Mary's children. When the children get upset with

Joe, they call Mary's brother, Chad. They tell Chad Joe is mistreating them. (Keep in mind the children know Mary's family does not like Joe.)

Eventually Chad calls Mary to ask about the treatment of the children. Mary then gets upset with Chad and the children and takes out her anger on Joe.

In the meantime, Chad calls Mary's mom to tell her what the children shared with him. The mother then calls Mary, and they argue. Mary again takes out her anger on Joe, and the cycle continues. [End.]

Joe and Mary's saga continues today. Life is not going to improve for these two until they decide to stop pointing fingers at each other. They must seek to learn and understand themselves first, and then seek to understand each other (Covey, 1990) or this cycle will continue.

Unless they acknowledge they have relationship issues and deal with the fear and other barriers preventing them from addressing those issues, the cycle will continue. Individually, Joe and Mary must be willing to see the world through the eyes of the other. They need to listen to one another, as well as demonstrate mutual understanding, empathy, selflessness, forgiveness, trust, and loyalty toward each other, in order to effectively let go of and break their cycle of stuff.

This recycling of stuff goes on in many people's lives. As I watched, observed, and listened to Joe and Mary, I could not help but feel compassion for them. I wanted to snap my finger and make it all okay for them. Knowing I could not, I continued to observe, listen, and ask them reflective questions as part of the coaching process.

There are those who are fortunate enough to rise above Joe and Mary's situation and similar cycles of stuff, not because they are better than Joe and Mary, but because they have different expectations of themselves and others.

If Joe and Mary could raise their level of expectations, they may have been able to at least recognize the cycle. If they could find reasons to be grateful for life—for having food on the table, for waking up in the morning, for being able to walk, and for all the things we often take for granted—perhaps they would develop a different perspective of themselves and the world around them. One thing about stuff is it doesn't care how good you look, how much money you make, who your parents are, or where you live. It will interfere, at any given moment, with the connections between your mind, your heart, and your dreams. These connections determine the level of integration of your goals and dreams into your daily life. We must learn to integrate new, positive, and uplifting bits of information into our cycles of stuff. This will free us from recycling the same old stuff.

Recycling old stuff creates barriers to growth, which can lead to an unhealthy emptiness. In order to grow, you must learn to let go and strive toward something greater.

This process can only begin when you acknowledge you have stuff to let go which is the first of the Seven Secrets.

After applying the techniques in this book, Joe and Mary have been able to dramatically improve the quality of their relationship. Don't worry! They'll be fine.

Chapter 4
Realize Change Is Necessary

"CHANGE BEGINS WHEN THE REALITY OF YOUR MINDSET MERGES
WITH YOUR EXTERNAL ACTIONS, TRIGGERING INTERNAL ACTIONS,
SUCH AS STIRRED EMOTIONS, SENSATIONS, AND MENTAL ENERGY."
— ROBERT DEBOARD

Two Midwestern Boy Scouts, headed for an African jamboree, stood at the ship's rail staring at the limitless expanse of ocean. "Just look at all this water. I didn't dream it would be this large!" exclaimed the first Scout.

The other responded, "And to think all we see is the top."

Acknowledging, identifying, and listing the stuff you want to let go is just the "top." The *second secret is the following*:

Realize change is necessary.

This secret will take you below the surface, and the process of changing will take you to an even deeper realm. Deciding to make a change is one thing; experiencing the change as it happens is another. Just knowing this will help you to manage change better as you experience it.

All books of ancient philosophical writings are about change. The writings and paintings on the walls of temples created by indigenous Egyptian cultures thousands of years ago depict making internal, value-based changes. As a matter of fact, regardless of whose version it is, the creation of this world is all about change. Your body is a major change machine. You live and breathe because of the cycle of change. The cycle of life and death is also about change. The ability to choose to change is God's gift to humankind. In return, changing, growing, developing, and loving yourself and others can be your gift to God.

If you look up "change" in the dictionary, you will find many words and phrases to define this six letter word, such as "switching, shifting, transforming, undergoing, modifying, phasing in, inchoate, phasing out, malleable, plastic, yielding, substituting, transitioning, incipient, and being changeable." There is also, "changeful, changefully, changeling, changeless, change off, changeover, under change, interchange, and exchange." Some of us may experience a "change of heart, change in life," or a "change of pace."

As you read over the words describing change, did you notice not one of those words was negative? Not one.

Change, in and of itself, is neither good nor bad. It is simply a cycle of building up and breaking down something. This cycle is inherent to the human experience. The outcome is determined by the labels we place on the cycle; we either like the change, or we don't. We either accept changes, or we resist and label them.

Realizing change is necessary in our lives is the second secret to letting go and is a natural extension of the first secret, which is acknowledging you have stuff to let go.

Change is inevitable, which is why changes will occur in your life whether you like it or not. Changes will occur in your body, whether you like it or not. As humans, our entire body changes constantly, and thank goodness. Without constant change, we would not survive. Seasons change. You change your clothes, change your hair, change diapers on the baby, change oil in the car, and change positions. How many times have you changed positions since you began reading this book? Just like you can change all of those things, you can also change your mind, which can change habits. According to Norman Vincent Peale, if you change your thoughts then you will change your world. One of the first choices you must make is to accept change as being an inevitable constant in your life.

This may sound simple; however, you would be surprised at how much energy people put into resisting change. We sometimes become so comfortable with our lives that the mere thought of change zaps our energy and puts us to sleep. Do you know anyone like that? Of course it's not you, but I bet there is somebody you know who does not like change, someone who really enjoys things remaining the same. The only thing you can depend on is the fact that eventually everything must change. Accepting the notion that change is inevitable, however, is your choice.

Another choice involves how you react to significant change in your life, such as the death of a loved one, the break up of a special relationship, or the loss of a promotion. Perhaps you recently got married or divorced, started a new career, or relocated for your job. Maybe you just found out you are pregnant.

EXERCISE 4-1
Whatever change you are experiencing right now, take a moment to reflect on how it has impacted your life. Once you're done, write down your responses to the following questions:

1. How did you respond to the situation that brought about a change?

_____
_____
_____
_____

2. Was your response emotional, physical, spiritual, or a combination of all three?

_____
_____
_____
_____

3. What changes resulted from this significant event in your life?

_____

_____

_____

_____

4. Did you resist the change, or did you readily accept the change?

_____

_____

_____

_____

Resisting change is natural. We will talk about resistance in detail later in this chapter. Most of the time, human beings tend to resist change, especially when it hits close to home. There are many reasons for resistance, including what we say to ourselves as we go through change. In other words, what you say to yourself about yourself determines how you react in various situations. This internal conversation has been called many things: self talk, the chatterbox, internal tape recorder, brain talk, internal chatter, and more. Any time you talk to yourself, whether out loud or not, it is internal conversation, which we'll discuss in greater detail in Chapter 5.

It is one thing for me to tell you about making a change and another for you to choose to make a positive, long-lasting change in your life. I believe everyone can always improve and learn; thus, constant change is inevitable in all our lives. You must learn to make positive changes if you want to grow and continue to succeed in any of your life's endeavors, but making a change is a choice.

You may ask, "How can I make a change?" It is simple in that you control whether or not you choose to let go and change. Yet, it is complicated. Because when you decide to let go and make a change, the following action must be consistent, persistent, and purposeful. In five seconds you can buy something over the telephone from a city 6,000 miles away using a credit card, but when it comes to changing something inside of you, something you have complete control over, it may take a lifetime. That is why many people first make changes on the outside. It can be easier, quicker, more superficial, and less threatening to our existence. If you want to make a long-lasting change that will allow you to build character, esteem, confidence, hope, faith, and purpose in yourself, change must be made from the inside out.

Changing Your Mindset

Once you make a decision to change something about yourself for the better, there are many things that begin to take place inside of you. These internal processes take place in your mind and are what lead to specific outcomes and behaviors.

In *Beyond Change Management: Advanced Strategies for Today's Transformational Leaders* (2001), Dean and Linda Anderson define mindset as "one's worldview" (p. 80) and as a place in which a person forms and experiences a perception of reality. When your mindset deems either an experience or event to be valuable, you have "expanded emotions—confidence, excitement, happiness, pleasures—and the body responds accordingly" (p. 81).

Your reality of who you are, this worldview of self as held in your mind, is a combination of what you see in the physical world around you and your internal conversation. In order to make long-lasting changes for the better, you must not only change your external environment, but also change your mindset. Over time this will lead to a change in behaviors and habits.

What leads to the change? Robert DeBoard explains in *The Psychoanalysis of Organizations: A Psychoanalytic Approach to Behaviour in Groups and Organizations* (1978) that change begins when the reality of your mindset merges with your external actions, triggering internal actions, such as stirred emotions, sensations, and "mental energy" (p. 130). This creates an internal state which precipitates an external behavior representing the emergence of emotions and mental energy. That behavior leads to activities, which lead to the development of habits over time. This is evidence that in order for you to execute a plan to change something about yourself for the better, it must begin on the inside.

My theory is the implementation of any plan begins inside of us long before we take any external action.

This inside-out approach is true for people as well as organizations.

Two Key Environments

It is important for us to create the kind of environment that will lead to success. We live within two environments: one is physical and surrounds us, the other is mental and is inside of us. Both can be designed to support your success.

The physical environment, which you have some control over, is simple to create. Surround yourself with people who will be supportive as you let go of old habits, toxic internal conversations, and other negatives. Do not frequent places that stir up harmful emotions that impact your self-esteem. Listen to uplifting music or change the pictures on the wall; do whatever makes you feel good about yourself. The ideas for positive change are endless, but these few suggestions are physical environmental changes that are fairly easy, effortless, and inexpensive to make, yet can help facilitate your new life.

The mental environment, which you totally control, requires a different kind of approach. It is determined by your mindset, what Kurt Lewin (1948) describes in *The Dynamic Theory of Personality: Selected Papers* as a "life space...the person and the psychological environment as it exists for him" (p. 210).

In doing his work and research on field theory, Lewin examined methods for analyzing the causal relations relative to change. He proposed that one's capacity to change at any given time depends on many variables, one of which is the person's present situation rather than his/her past. He wrote about the importance of creating extinction. A habit becomes extinct when there has been a change in the conditioning of one's formed habits. As an example, you may be conditioned to eat lunch at noon every day. After repeatedly eating at noon over a period of time, your body will be conditioned to display physiological symptoms of hunger around that time, whether it needs food or not. If you begin to do something different around noon, such as workout, then, over time, the need, or habit, of eating at 12:00 p.m. will become extinct, and you will be conditioned to working out instead.

We are conditioned in many ways we often do not realize. For example, we are conditioned to believe after a certain age certain things will happen to our body. As a result, we begin to do and say things supposedly indicative of our age, which represent this conditioned belief. For example, I have heard many people say they do not need to stop smoking because "I'm going to die of something. It may as well be this."

This form of conditioning can lead to more smoking as well as other health challenges, but this thought pattern can be changed and even become extinct over time.

Changing Habits

Our habits, which are learned on a conscious level, eventually will become subconscious activities. For example, maybe you've developed the habit of frowning when you hear certain words and phrases or eating when you feel a certain way. Perhaps you light up a cigarette during certain activities or say things to yourself supporting other unwanted habits when you make a mistake. Whatever your habits, the actions that form those habits begin with conscious thought. Over time, however, and through repetition, those conscious thoughts become the foundation for unconscious habits. So, if you want to change your existing habits and attitude, you must change your current picture. For example, if you want to stop smoking, you must picture yourself living as a non-smoker. If your goal is to lose weight, one strategy for beginning is to replace the current image of yourself with a picture of you being the weight you want.

When you look at it from that perspective, it may not seem as complicated. What I try to do is to break things down into their simplest elements and proceed from there. Every action you take and every thought you repeat in your mind is the result of a habit developed long ago through repeated behaviors and words.

Changing habits is challenging because your habits are a part of the mental self image, or picture, you have developed over the years. The subconscious holds on to that current picture; its job is to make the picture come true. When you try to develop a new habit or do something new, your subconscious says you are stepping outside the frame of the current picture that maintains your self-image.

Here's The Challenge!
When you set a goal to be a different person, or to change a current behavior pattern, your subconscious will feed you constant messages to support your current state of being. It does this because it believes in the picture you have created over the years, so it will continue to send messages to your brain to support the current picture. When you act differently than your current picture depicts, it creates internal stress, which makes the body respond in defense. As a result, you will end up convincing yourself not to make the change by defending the existence of the current picture of your self.

In other words, an intellectual decision to change creates a ripple of chemical changes before any physical action is taken. It primarily is due to the current picture (image) you have of yourself, and how entrenched it has become in your subconscious. It probably took years for you to develop this current picture and may take a while for you to redesign it. It may be a challenge, but it is possible. Remember your levels of confidence, happiness, satisfaction, or contentment are all based on your internalized self-image.

Not only must you decide how you want to be, you must also believe you can become the person you want to be. Additionally, you must have faith in your ability to transform into this newly redesigned person. I always say if there is just one person out there who has done what you want to do, then you can do it, too. If there is no one doing what you want to do, therein lies a great opportunity. There are thousands of people making personal, inside-out transformations every day.

Understanding how habits form and how to change them is not a newly explored topic. In 1942, Kurt Lewin researched and wrote about the development and changing of habits. He suggested two ways to bring about a desired change. One is when a person chooses to change a habit because of his/her own needs and interests. The other way is by force, meaning change occurs as a result of some unwanted or unintended situation or circumstance. Forced change can occur when you have to make a decision to choose one option over the current state with no other available options. In other words, if one wants to quit smoking, which is the current option, the other option may be to eat more sweets instead of smoking. Both options are unhealthy; however, picking the lesser of the two evils becomes the motivation, which must also be combined with some other action to effectuate the change. This forced choice will create a forced change. In either case, there is internal resistance.

As I studied Lewin's work, I realized motivation alone will not bring about a change in habits. Action is also an important aspect of successful change.

The action must be in the direction of the desired result. Here's a simplified example illustrating what I mean.

Let's say I want to let go of the habit of eating six or seven oatmeal cookies every time I celebrate good news or feel great about my day. To accomplish this goal, I will have to do something different. First, I will need to recognize the habit and current picture exists. Then, I will need to set a specific goal and new picture of what my actions will look like if I stop eating those cookies. Focusing on my weight by looking in the mirror may create some motivation to want to change this habit, but if I do not take some specific action to change the habit, the motivation will cease as soon as I step away from the mirror. Specific action is the key, which will be discussed in very specific terms in Chapter 9.

According to Lewin (1948), successful change includes three steps or aspects:
1-unfreezing of the present state of existence;
2-moving to the new state of existence;
3-refreezing the new state of existence.

Lewin's work was done at the organizational level; however, I have extended his ideas to the individual level, as organizations are composed of people. Expanding on the simplified oatmeal cookies example, let me briefly explain how Lewin's three steps of change can assist in the process of changing a habit.

Unfreezing

The current habit of eating oatmeal cookies every time I have a good day is an example of my present state of existence. It is what I am doing right now and also is what I want to let go. In order to let go of this habit, I must unfreeze it by creating a vision of a different, healthier kind of habit.

Moving to the New State - Taking Action

Rather than eating cookies to celebrate good days, I may choose other activities, such as riding a bicycle or taking a long walk in the park. I must create this new reality by consciously making the effort to see myself doing this new activity to celebrate a good day. I must make this part of my everyday vision of myself and move toward this new state by taking some kind of specific action. First, I could not purchase cookies and instead drink water. Then, I could plan bike rides and tell my friends I need their support as I attempt to make this change.

Refreezing

Once I have successfully begun to take long walks and bicycle rides to celebrate a good day, via repetition, I can refreeze this new state of existence. This now will become my new way of acting when I celebrate, and eventually, it will feel as comfortable to me as eating those cookies.

Although this oatmeal cookies example is a simpified version of these three steps, it depicts the unfreezing-moving-refreezing process for changing a habit. A big part of the process is in recognizing what you want to let go, realizing you will go through changes when you decide to let it go, creating a plan to integrate something new to replace the old thing, and then begin to do that new activity over and over again. The key is to begin by taking small steps.

Below is an exercise to help keep you on the path of *Letting Go of Stuff.*® The word *BE* is capitalized because these two letters are the first two letters in the words "belief" and "being." There is no greater level and form of belief than believing in yourself. The power of believing in one's self has been celebrated in cultures around the world. There are songs written about finding the hero in yourself and overcoming obstacles in life. If you don't believe in yourself, then it will be difficult for anyone else to do so.

As for the word "being," it is integral to our success. The combination of your inner spirit, state of mind, emotions, and behavior is the essence of your being. How you express this combination of components is your choice. Dean and Linda Anderson (2001) define being as a "powerful force in human interaction" (p. 82). If one is aware of his/her way of being, then it puts the person in better control of their life at that point in time, allowing them to have greater impact on others. Believing in who you are is a major part of a powerful combination for success.

EXERCISE **4-2**
In this exercise, you will write two things: The way you are at this moment and the way you want to *BE* as a person. Below, write the words you would use

to describe who you are today, the current you. This can also be called your present state of being.

1. Who I am now—my current state of being

_____
_____
_____
_____

2. Designing who I want to *BE*—Unfreezing

Next, write adjectives describing who you want to *BE* as a person. This is your future state of being. Take your time and really reflect on the kind of person you want to be. Perhaps you have a role model you know well who possesses characteristics you admire and want to adopt in your person.

Make sure this list of adjectives and descriptive phrases describe how you want to *BE*, such as loyal, honest, trustworthy, patient, understanding, open-minded, and compassionate. Use the space below.

_____
_____
_____
_____

Now that you have defined your present and future states of being, we need to see what exists in the gap between the two and begin to fill this gap with the right stuff to close it. The exercises in this chapter and the rest of this book are devoted to moving from your frozen, present state of being, to unfreezing you to the future state of being, and refreezing yourself at the new state. What will get you from one state of being to another is movement or action (Chapter 9). This is exciting, isn't it? Okay, let's begin!

The answer to one question will begin closing the gap between present and future states of being. "What must I do to let go and transform myself?" Asked another way: "How can I let go and become the person I want to become?"

Ancient writings offer this insight into personal transformation from present to future states of being. This quote from Colossians 3:8-10 of the Christian Bible supports the importance of creating new activities that replace the current ones: "But now you must rid yourselves of all such things as these: anger, rage, malice, slander, and filthy language from your lips. Do not lie to each other, since you have taken off your old self with its practices and put on the new self, which is being renewed in knowledge...."

Have, Do, and Be
I first learned about the notion of "have, do, and, be" in church as a young child. I understood it but never really gave it specific thought until, as an adult, I began to read other ancient writings and philosophical musings from African and Asian cultures. One day, it was put into clearer perspective for me when I co-facilitated a workshop with David L., an effective trainer at one of the companies

for which I worked. He shared his perspective on "have, do, and be."

Most people usually believe it is better to decide what you want to "have," believing that what you have will make you the person you want to be. According to David, this thought pattern is backward. He says people need to reverse the "have" and the "be." Be who you want to be, do what it takes to be that way, and in time, you will have what you want in life. Although David did not originate this notion, when I heard him say it on that particular day, it hit home. You see, there is nothing new under the sun, but you can always create a new perspective on old stuff.

In order to either make a change or let go of stuff, you must search the very core of your being, your core value system. Your behavior is based on your beliefs, and what you do and say, over and over again, helps develop your habits. This means your habits are based on your beliefs. Your beliefs and your value system are intertwined. If you change what you believe about yourself, you can reshape and change your habits, and your destiny ultimately.

I consider this to be a big part of what life is all about—gaining new insights into what already exists in the world. It is called learning. Your growth ends the day you believe you can no longer learn, or when you believe you know everything about everything. This attitude can stagnate you and is another form of resisting change because it blocks learning.

Resistance to Change

Resistance to change manifests itself in many ways and has always been a challenge for us. The following quote is from a writer who struggles with doing what is right and wrong according to the law: "I do not understand what I do. For what I want to do, I do not do, but what I hate, I do." The author goes on to describe this internal strife and confusion: "For I have the desire to do what is good, but I can not carry it out. For what I do is not the good I want to do...the evil I do not want to do, this I keep doing" (Rom. 7:15-19, NIV).

Everyone experiences this internal struggle. It becomes prevalent, especially when they decide to change something inside themselves. Once you develop a high level of comfort with being a certain way, it may take some time to undo, but if someone else can do it, so can you.

In his book, *See You At The Top* (1981), Zig Ziglar wrote about his theory that indicates hope is the fundamental quality of all change, and encouragement is the fuel for hope. I encourage you to make the changes you want in your life today. Be driven by the hope that you can be the way you want to be. Do not wait until tomorrow to change your life because it may never get here for you. One way you may resist making this change is to create all kinds of internal conversation to convince yourself not to change.

When I lived in California, I had a dear friend living with Lupus who used to talk about feeling free in the Caribbean. One conversation we had about being free in particular stands out in my mind. She explained she could be herself in the Caribbean. She didn't feel compelled to wear wigs to cover the baldness caused by her chemotherapy. She could walk around with no hair, and people seemed to respect her. No one there knew about how she used to look before the chemotherapy; therefore, no one could compare her old self with her new bald self. Moreover, she said she never felt angry, hurt, or ashamed of herself while in the Islands.

She talked a lot about changing her career and being more compassionate about the people in her life. She also talked a lot about living in the Caribbean.

Unfortunately, she never took action toward making any of those changes. She never took the time to look for that home in the Caribbean, and she did not get a chance to become more compassionate. As the Lupus progressed, she began to focus all of her energy on her health.

In 1995, the physiological complications of Lupus took her away. She took the dream of moving to the Caribbean, being more compassionate, changing her career, experiencing what she believed to be true freedom, and probably many other dreams and desires to her grave. She resisted making the changes during the years before she was consumed by her health challenges. I know she would be happy to have others learn from her experience, which is why I shared this story.

One lesson learned from my dear friend is not to wait to make changes in your life because tomorrow definitely is not guaranteed. This lesson has been repeated for me many times in my life. I finally learned to live in the present and focus only on what I want rather than what I don't want.

EXERCISE 4-3
How do we resist? One answer: We resist with our thought patterns. Below is a list of what I refer to as change resisters. They are phrases that represent feelings and thoughts that could keep us from letting go and making changes in our lives. Identify your change resisters by checking the box next to those that represent your current state of being.

What Is Your Change Resister?
(place a check by all that apply to you)
❏ Waiting for the right time to make a change
❏ Fearing the unknown
❏ Knowing all about everything so change is unnecessary
❏ Worrying about events, situations, or people in the past
❏ Focusing on past events, situations, or people
❏ Living in the past
❏ Being so comfortable with the present that change is not necessary

- Feeling unworthy and undeserving about having a new outlook
- Feeling unwanted
- Lacking motivation
- Not knowing how to change
- Knowing how to change, but not applying the knowledge
- Fearing success
- Fearing failure
- Inability to forgive self and others
- Being unsure of how to forgive one's self (see Chapter 3)
- Being afraid to forgive one's self and others
- Being unable to break or change old thought patterns
- Being too comfortable with existing thought patterns
- Believing not enough other people are changing
- Believing too many other people are changing
- Believing changing takes too much time
- Not finding the right time to change
- Believing there is not time to change
- Believing I can change when I want, but declaring a state of unreadiness
- Believing I can change when I want, but trying to change another person first
- Believing I can change when I want, but first trying to change the world
- Believing I tried changing and that it didn't work because I changed right back
- Believing I tried changing, but it was too difficult for a person like me

No Matter Where You Go...

While employed at a major automotive manufacturing company in Michigan in the mid-1980s, I worked with a gentleman who, regardless of what I was doing, where I was going, who I was talking to, or what was going on around us, would walk up to me, put his arms around my shoulders, look in my eyes, and say, "Son, no matter where you go, there you are."

I didn't really understand the statement at the time. I thought he was just a kind old man who simply needed to retire. Later on in my career, while co-facilitating another workshop with David, he told a story about an old guy in his home town in Kentucky. This old guy would say this same phrase to David all of the time, "No matter where you go, there you are."

Once again it was not until David told his story that the meaning of the phrase really hit home with me. That statement is simple, yet it is profound.

Think about the phrase for a moment. No matter where you go, there you are! You bring your current state of being into every situation. This means all your thoughts, stereotypes, past experiences, understanding of the world, hang-ups, beliefs, misconceptions, interpretations, feelings, and fears go with you everywhere. As a matter of fact, the one commonality between you and all of your experiences is...Guess who? Therefore, change must begin with…Guess who? That's right, the answer to both those questions is: You!

No one can change you but you. When you don't like something about another person, guess what? It could be a reflection of you! When you get upset with another person, it means there is something about you that is out of control, not the other person. That is why it is so important to focus our energy on only changing ourselves.

While in Memphis, TN, I was a guest on the Bev Johnson Radio Show, and someone called in to the show for my advice. The caller's husband had walked out on her and their children. She said the relationship was abusive, and she was glad he had left the family. Though it was unexpected and hurtful, she decided to believe his departure had happened for a good reason. She experienced the relationship as being toxic. I suggested she celebrate her new life without toxicity and celebrate the opportunity to live as she wants—without a person who makes her feel guilty and bad about her current state of being.

The husband's departure initiated a forced change in the woman's life from the inside out. She chose to embrace the new life that was ahead. She felt as though she deserved something better in a relationship. She knew there was much more in store for her, especially now that she did not have to deal with her husband's stuff. He was the one with the internal challenges, and she refused to allow his stuff to become her reality. She made the change, adjusted her attitude, and moved on.

Another caller, a grandmother, shared how she had spent her life "being there" for her family, even though no one was ever there for her. She was tired of it and wanted to make a change. I asked her what she wanted to do, and she said, "I want to have some time for myself, but I keep getting caught up in everyone else's problems. People tell me that trouble finds me. It seems that everywhere I go, there is always some negativity." The challenge she faced was she had bought into what everyone was saying about her, and her internal conversation supported the thought pattern, which was that trouble finds her.

Sometimes the change we need to make is with our internal belief system. If our core belief is based on what other people think, then we eventually will allow their opinions to become our reality. In every city I visit, whether it is to conduct a seminar or to be a guest on a talk show, I meet people just like you and me, who are trying to make positive, uplifting, and inside-out changes in their lives. I applaud them! It takes courage, tenacity, a fearless attitude, and love of oneself to truly change one's life and begin moving in a completely different direction toward a new vision. These are the kind of people who believe in themselves, or some higher power, more than they believe in others' opinions. The key is having something greater than yourself to strive toward. Having a greater sense of purpose and meaning will take you a long way when times get tough. I love the title of Robert Schuller's (1983) book, *Tough Times Never Last, But Tough People Do!* If you stop and think about it, you can find power in the title alone.

You may be saying to yourself, "Well, Darren, that is fine and dandy, but how do I get started on making my change? How do I let go?"

The answer is "Take Action!"

The next exercise can help you continue the journey of personal inside-out change.

Exercise 4-4

When completed, this exercise will provide you with a tool, a blueprint of what the "new" you is going to be like. Once you have decided to make a change from the way you are—your current state of being—to a new you—your future state of being—there must be some movement in order to close the gap between the two.

As you attempt to close the gap, you will need a method for keeping focused on the future while living in the present. Consider this to be your reference guide to this wonderful transition upon which you are embarking. Based on the "have, do, and be" concept discussed earlier in this chapter, please complete the next two sections.

Write three to five statements, in present tense, which you can use as your positive internal conversation.

Use the adjectives you wrote in exercise 4-2 to form the *BE Statements* you write below.

1. _____
   _____
   _____

2. _____
   _____
   _____

3. _____
   _____
   _____

4. _____
   _____
   _____

5. _____
   _____
   _____

After you have written your *BE Statements* you must develop the habit of saying them to yourself on a daily basis. You also have to begin to do what it takes to be this kind of person. Start by brainstorming and making a list of what you need to do. Your list may include activities such as reading more, participating in exercise programs, changing your diet, watching what you say to others, and writing down your goals in specific terms.

Whatever it takes, you should write it down and take action. The key word is action. What is it you need to do to make your *BE Statements* a reality in your life?

Please take some time and list the "to do" items. Place your start and completion dates at the end of each action item.

Action	Start Date	Completion Date

Chapter 5
Manage the Internal Conversation

"SPEAK FREELY IN PRAISE FOR ALL YOU ARE. SPEAK CLEARLY WITH
PRIDE FOR ALL YOU MAY BECOME. SPEAK BRAVELY WITH HOPE..."
— EDWARD CUNNINGHAM

Do you talk to yourself? Of course you do. Everyone does! That is not the key question however. A more important question is, "What do you say to yourself?" An Egyptian proverb says, "The body becomes what the foods are, as the spirit becomes what the thoughts are." What are your internal conversations like? The *third secret* is the following:

Manage internal conversations.

One of the most powerful ways conversation impacts your life is through the internal discussions that take place in your mind. I have conducted hundreds of seminars on change and letting go. During these seminars, the audience participates in an activity on change that has consistently produced the same results regardless of the audience composition. Those results are that people will resist making a change when the change requires them to step too far outside their comfort zone. Interestingly, when a person is confronted with a major change, approximately 75 percent of his/her internal thoughts will become more negative than positive, and the internal conversation becomes more resistant.

When we experience a change, we really begin to speak to ourselves. The internal conversation is very powerful and represents our core belief system.

Collective Internal Conversation

Individuals have internal conversations, and groups have internal conversations. Because a group or organization is made up of individuals, the group is capable of having collective internal conversations. When a critical mass of people, who work in the same department, come together on how they feel about an organization, they form one voice. That voice represents the collective internal conversation of the individuals in the group. When you bring many groups (or departments) together, their collective voices become the internal conversation of the organization. These collective internal conversations are powerful and offer, among other things, insight into how employees feel about decisions made by leadership. Executive leaders must learn how to listen to the organization's internal conversation. If they do not develop the skill of listening to the organization, failure is almost inevitable. Listening is how you are able to tap into the internal pulse of any organization.

Figure 5-1 depicts the InsideOut Learning Organizational Diagnostic Model (Johnson, 2001),

which depicts the relationship between leadership
and internal conversation within organizations.

IOL MODEL
Figure 5-1

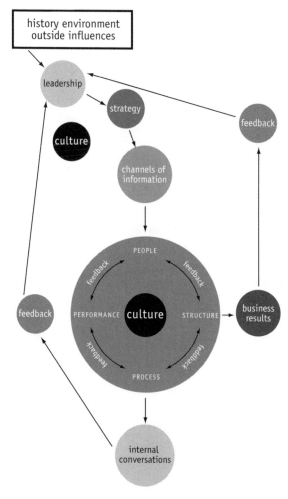

Supported by the same theory as Hanna (1988) and the Nadler-Tushman Models (1977), the IOL Model is the only one of the three models that specifically demonstrates internal conversation as an output of an open system. This unique output characteristic allows leadership to maintain a finger on the pulse of the organization, relative to how people are feeling about what is going on within the organization. This can offer opportunities for more effective leadership, which ultimately benefits the entire organization.

Being aware of what people are feeling and thinking helps leadership to make certain day-to-day and long-term decisions about the direction of the organization. Although the focus of this book is not on organization development and consulting tools, such as the IOL Model, it is important to stress the internal conversation, collectively and individually, is a powerful force.

Individual Decision Making & Internal Conversation
Have you ever made a decision about something and then changed the decision midstream? Did the changed decision result in an undesired outcome? After seeing the undesired outcome, did you say to yourself, "If I had only stayed with my first decision…?"

Well, if that has ever happened to you, it is because at first you were led initially by your inner spirit, then failed to trust its guidance.

On the other hand, have you ever made a decision and stayed with that first instinctive choice, which resulted in everything working out as planned? Everything clicked like clockwork. Meetings went well, deadlines were met, the necessary signatures were received on time, and everyone was happy with the outcome. That success might have been because you were led by your inner spirit, trusted its leading, and the outcome was awesome. Just think if you could do that every day and in every situation! What would happen if you could have awesome outcomes on purpose? It is possible to do that every day. The key is to listen to and trust your inner spirit. You must learn the process of being still and paying attention to your internal conversations.

Ego vs. Spirit

I believe there are two important components inside each of us. One is our God-given spirit, the other is our man-made ego. The relationship between the ego and the spirit can sometimes feel like there is an internal battle going on inside of you. It only feels that way, in reality—there is no battle. How can there be a battle when only one side is fighting?

The ego is constantly trying to figure out how it is going to survive. It uses strategies like control, guilt, anger, and shame to win its battles. Ego will build you up when you don't need building up. The spirit, on the other hand, has no need to respond to these strategies. Responding will only give the ego more power and control. Love is the best response to the ego, and the spirit is love. Since it is love, it has no need to respond.

The ego tears down others to build itself up. It will justify its existence by convincing itself no one else exists who is as powerful, beautiful, or intelligent as it is. The spirit has no need to respond to these strategies because the *spirit is love*.

The ego will use fear to try to justify its existence. It will create fear-based scenarios in your mind to keep you from moving forward. The ego uses fear to stagnate and stifle the soul. Fear can be used as a powerful method of control and will stop you in your tracks. The spirit has no need to respond to these strategies because the *spirit is love*.

The ego will always have a response for people, even if the response is not justified. The ego never wants to apologize because that is a sign of weakness. It never wants to do what is right, but it will do what is necessary to stay alive inside of you. The spirit has no need to respond to these strategies because the *spirit is love*.

Because you created your ego, this internal battle is not really going on between the ego and the spirit. It is between you and your self-made ego. The spirit never has to battle. The spirit was placed in you, with love, by your Creator. Therefore, it exists because you exist, or better said, you exist because the spirit in you exists. It is the universal voice of love—in you. If you had nothing else to listen to, no television, no radio, no other people, and if you never read newspapers, books, magazines, newsletters, etc., then all you would have left to guide you would be the spirit and your self-made ego.

The question then becomes, "Which one guides your life?" To answer that question, you must first discover how to tell the difference between the spirit and the ego. Actually, it is somewhat simple. I love this poem, which was e-mailed to me in 1999. Even though the author is anonymous, it hits the nail on the head when it comes to our listening and distinguishing between the ego and the spirit.

I whispered, "God, speak to me."
And a meadowlark sang. But I did not hear.

So I yelled, "God, speak to me!"
And the thunder rolled across the sky. But I did not listen.

I looked around and said, "God, let me see you."
And a star shone brightly. But I did not notice.

So I shouted, "God, show me a miracle!"
And a life was born. But I did not know.

So I cried out in despair,
"Touch me, God, and let me know you are there!"
Whereupon God reached down and touched me.

But I brushed the butterfly away,
And walked away unknowingly.

Your spirit is always there, but sometimes you do not recognize it when it speaks. When you overlook the spirit, there appears to be a struggle—not with the spirit, but between the ego and yourself. Anytime there is a struggle between doing what is actually right or doing what seems right, then your ego is interfering with your decision. Anytime you go back and forth between making a decision, but deep inside you know what the right choice is, you are struggling with your ego. It is trying to make you choose the alternative that will allow for it (your ego) to exist more prevalently in your life.

I realize this may sound like there are two people living inside of you; do not worry, it is just you. However, it is important to note your ego is there and can represent all that is fearful, threatening, controlling, guilt-based, and shameful. Also, remember you have created this ego. The universe gave us a spirit that is our internal guide, but we have created another version of the spirit to deal with all of the various forms of information. This is the ego, the facsimile of your universal spirit.

The spirit's focus is love. Love is the foundation from which your decisions about your life should be made. Instead, many of us have lost internal love in the midst of television/radio news and reading all kinds of other information that negatively molds our emotional state.

What can overwhelming ourselves with too much unnecessary information teach us about loving one another? Not a whole lot. If we need to be reminded to love one another, then we have already lost sight of the very essence of our existence.

Living a "spirit focused" life will also lead you to forgiveness. A key component for forgiveness is to love yourself enough to release someone else from your emotional stronghold, which ultimately releases you. Letting go of negative feelings toward another benefits you more than them. It makes them feel good to know you have forgiven them, but the real benefit is for you.

That is why it is so important for you to forgive everyone. Apologize to people you have crossed or hurt in some way. Let love be the basis for your actions and internal conversations. If you can do that, then you will always be led by your spirit because your spirit is love. If loving others is part of your belief system, then love will manifest itself in how you act toward others.

Do you need the media to tell you how to do that? Of course not. I am not suggesting you should never watch television, listen to the radio, or read the newspaper. I am simply saying to be selective about how much of it you allow into your internal thoughts. Make sure you take the time to feed yourself with what your spirit has to offer. Keep a nice balance between what is available to you from within and from without. In other words, maintain a balance between the external information to which you expose yourself and listening to your spirit internally. Let the spirit rule inside of you. Trust your spirit. Believe in your spirit. Once you begin to do this, your life will change.

The Power of Knowing

There are four combinations of consciousness and competence. They are listed below. I will explore the fourth category—unconscious competence—in more detail.

1. Unconscious incompetence—Not knowing what you don't know.

2. Conscious incompetence—Knowing what you do not know.

3. Conscious competence—Knowing what you know and what you don't know.

4. Unconscious competence—Knowing what you know so well you forget you know.

Have you ever been on the elevator when another person got on and greeted you by saying, "Good morning," and instead of returning their greeting, you said, "I'm fine, and you?" Even though the person did not ask about how you were doing, you unconsciously responded to them as if he/she did.

If that has ever happened to you, it is because you unconsciously and competently responded to the person. You never heard the person say, "Good morning;" all you heard was a greeting. The person could have moaned at you, and you still would have said, "I'm fine, and you?" I call this state of unconsciousness the danger zone. This is the zone in which we exist while being unconsciously competent. That is when you are so good at doing something, you could probably do it in your sleep.

However, being in the danger zone can create certain challenges to learning. At the unconsciously competent level, learning is stagnated without new information. Another good example of being unconsciously competent is driving from home to work in the morning and forgetting the drive. Has that ever happened to you? During this state of consciousness is when many people have accidents while driving.

To a certain extent, being unconsciously competent is a good place to be. The actions and habits you repeat and reinforce, over and over again, every day for months and years become second nature. You will be able to perform these behaviors without even thinking about what is required to do them.

Consequently, anything you say to yourself over and over again for months and years on end will become part of your unconsciously competent internal conversation. For example, if you constantly tell yourself you hate some aspect of giving presentations, you may never be a good speaker. Your subconscious belief will manifest itself during each public speaking performance. You will automatically be uncomfortable, perhaps sweating, shaking, and maybe even losing your voice. All of this will happen in an effort to confirm your belief of your dislike for giving presentations.

Using another example—if as a child you learned people whose skin color is darker than yours are not as important as those whose skin matches yours, then over time you may develop certain habits while interacting with certain people. You either may become comfortable with treating people unimportantly, or you may constantly struggle internally with that core belief. The challenge is that even if you are aware of having learned the belief as a child and attempt to be fair and non-judgmental to people regardless of skin color, non-verbally and unknowingly you may still treat people unimportantly. I could go on and on with examples, but the question is "How does one change unconscious thought patterns?"

It is important for us consciously to say, or claim, only the things we want rather than what we do not want. Using the previous example, instead of saying,

"I do not treat people unimportantly," say, "I treat everyone importantly." If your challenge is to lose weight, instead of saying, "I am not fat," say, "I am slim." Claim what you want, not what you do not want. The subconscious recognizes the positive, not the negative. "I am not fat" registers subconsciously as "I am fat." "I am slim" registers as "I am slim." Inevitably your subconscious will produce a picture in your mind of what being slim will look like. Eventually you will begin to manifest the belief in your actions. Over a period of time, those actions ultimately could lead to you becoming slimmer.

Another example of the power of this concept is if you constantly tell yourself you do not deserve something, inevitably you eventually will act undeservingly. How many times do you get up in the morning and consciously say to yourself, "I feel great?" How often do you look at yourself in the mirror and say, "I am great?" How often do you actually tell yourself good things about you? According to ancient writings, "An anxious heart weighs a man down, but a kind word cheers him up" (Prov. 12:25). Sometimes a kind word is difficult to come by, especially if you are depending on others to give it to you. That is why it is important for you to get in the habit of saying kind words to yourself. For this reason the *BE Statements* you created in Chapter 4 are very important. They provide you with *positive stuff* for your mind, spirit, and body. Once you get in the habit of saying good things to yourself, you will begin to believe in that great conversation, which will lead to great actions. The key is knowing how to listen to the greatness inside.

Being Still Can Lead to Being Congruent

If you learn to be still and listen to your inner voice, and learn to trust that voice, you will almost never go wrong with any decision you make about your life. In her book, *Lessons in Truth* (1903), H. Emily Cady wrote, "When you have learned to abandon yourself to infinite spirit…you will be surprised at the marvelous change that will be wrought in you… The wisdom and strength you seek await you in the silence within."

In order to find the power within, you must take the time to be still and go inside yourself with courage and a desire to learn.

I make a special effort to listen to my inner voice. I spend at least one hour each day being still. In order for you to listen successfully to your inner voice, you must first learn to remain still—to do nothing. Doing nothing means just that: sitting and listening only to what is going on inside of your head and heart. That means no television, no radio, no people, and no books. Sit and listen to the quiet. Sit and listen to your soul. Sit and learn about yourself.

Your thoughts will be reflective of your beliefs. Just like your success will reflect what you believe success to be, which is why success is relative. For me, success is about having an inside-out balance in life. What I mean is my spiritual, physical, and intellectual being must all be in sync and congruent with one another. Success is not about having a lot of money, although wealth does help, but that is not my focus. Success, for me, is being able to provide information that will help to change someone's life positively. This is congruent with my personal mission, which is to *provide methods and information to individuals and organizations to enable them to grow positively and develop from the inside out.*

Carl Rogers (1961) defines congruence as being in touch with one's self. His theory on intrapersonal and interpersonal relationships includes this paraphrased definition of congruence: Congruence is being real, genuine, and in touch with yourself and knowing what you feel physically and emotionally.

To be congruent is not an easy task. One of the challenges for members of many religious groups is the inability to live a life that allows for total congruence with the ancient philosophies and lifestyles of their chosen religion. For parents, one challenge is to act in a way that matches the philosophy and methods used to raise the children. Being congruent is a tall order, which can be filled but requires much effort and introspection. You have to find out what will work for you. What is your life mission? What is your purpose? What does God have in store for you? If you do not believe in God, what does life have in store for you? These questions are asked constantly, yet often seem to go unanswered. However, the answers can be found in the same source as the questions—on the inside. Perhaps we are afraid of the answer, or worse, we are afraid once we discover the answers, we may have to do something about it, like take action.

Many of us are too comfortable with our lives right now to make a change. But if you are looking for more out of life, then you must begin by being still and listening to yourself. You must trust what you hear and be willing to act on the information.

If there are things you want to change about your life, then you must reprogram your internal conversations with new information that represents what you want. You also must have faith and believe in your ability to reprogram yourself. It is also important to have a written personal mission with positive statements reflecting what you want and believe about yourself. As Robert Schuller (1966) wrote: "Faith must rise to the level of affirmations. You must always declare that you are succeeding, even when you can't see the success."

The following is a mission statement originally handwritten by Bruce Lee in January 1969. I discovered his statement framed and on the wall at Planet Hollywood (when it was open for business) in Nashville, TN.

I will be the first highest paid Oriental super star in the United States. In return, I will give the most exciting performances and render the best quality in the capacity of an actor. Starting in 1970, I will achieve world fame and from then onward till the end of 1980 I will have in my possession...ten million dollars. I will live the way I please and achieve inner harmony and happiness, which are my definite chief aim.
—Bruce Lee

Bruce Lee accomplished his mission. For those of you who are fans, you know how succsessful he was as an actor. He designed his life with this mission statement.

Now, it is time for you to do the same: *design your life*. Don't get too caught up in making money or having a job, get excited about the fact that you can design your life. Have you ever thought about it that way? You actually can design, create, carve out your niche, leave your legacy, institute your actions, and leave this world having had an impact on millions, if you so choose.

Think about how you approach your job. How important is it for you to be on time so you can get paid for what you do? For most people, it is very important. Why not approach your dreams and goals the same way—as if they are so important you will get paid well to achieve them? Although you may not get paid in dollars, what you do get is priceless. There is no amount of money to compare to the successful fulfillment of a dream, and the outcome is the redesign of your life.

All that having been said, to truly redesign your life it is important to take yourself through a process, which involves deciding, then describing, what kind of person you want to be, from the inside out. You must reprogram yourself by creating positive mental pictures of yourself, being the kind of person you really want to be. These positive mental pictures, along with your written *BE Statements*, create a powerful combination that will inevitably manifest in new pictures for your subconscious and an expanded belief system.

Please refer to the written *BE Statements* you created in Chapter 4. These statements will help you create a new daily internal conversation and will be a major part of the the foundation for the redesign of your life.

Below is what I read every morning upon rising and every night before going to sleep. I created my original "*BE* statement" in 1995 and since have revised it twice.

I, Darren Johnson, am articulate, honest, teachable, optimistic, laid back, and smart-working. I am loving, caring, conscientious, understanding,

*compassionate, humble, and patient. I positively
impact the people in my life, and I give my best
in everything I do. I am healthy and take pride in
my appearance. I see myself as positive, good, and
always getting better. I am motivated, confident,
assertive, have a good sense of humor, and I love
adventure. I honor my ancestors and I am a child
of God.*

As I change and grow, I adjust my *BE Statements*.
The same will happen with you.

Once you have completed this next exercise (5-1),
you will have created a personal "*BE* statement"
that reflects your essence, expectations, values, and
personal convictions. It is also very important for
you to believe in the "*BE* statement" you create,
otherwise it will be a waste of time. You must learn
to treasure this statement, for where your treasure is,
there will be your heart, also.

As you read it, you also should visualize yourself
being this person. See yourself doing what is
necessary to be the person you really want to
become. Picture yourself, in your mind's eye,
interacting with co-workers, friends, and family
members as this newly redesigned person.

1. Use the area below, and re-write the *BE Statement* from Exercise 4-4.

_____

_____

_____

_____

_____

_____

_____

_____

_____

_____

2. Re-read your *BE Statements*.

3. Use the *BE Statements* to create a two- or three-sentence paragraph that best describes the new, redesigned you.

4. Make sure they are real and you can believe in them.

5. Do what is necessary, each day, to make them a reality in your life. Allow the *BE Statements* to function as a guiding force in your life.

6. Read these statements before you lay down to sleep every night and when you wake up every morning.

7. Share the *BE Statements* with those closest to you.

8. Have endearing discussions about the *BE Statements* with co-workers and friends, and encourage them to do the same thing.

9. Ask your significant other to remind you to read your *BE Statements* prior to going to bed and when you first wake up in the morning.

Chapter 6
Adjust Your Attitude

"WE DO NOT SEE THE WORLD AS IT IS, WE SEE THE WORLD AS WE ARE..."
— ANAIS NIN

It was a beautiful morning in mid-August. The sun was just beginning to emerge over the top of the trees, and the birds were singing. There was a nice, cool breeze blowing gently, and the light was glistening off of the dew on the grass and tree leaves. This morning was meant for joggers.

As I began my jog, I was feeling good because this was the morning I would begin to write this chapter of this book. As I jogged through the neighborhood, I noticed the variety of new homes being built and thought about how nice the neighborhood would be once they were completed. I thought, "This is a great neighborhood!"

I then approached a home with a flag flying in front. As I got closer, I realized it was a Confederate flag. This flag reminded me of a diversity class I attended at a small, local church in Franklin, Tennessee. The minister, who facilitated the class, came into the session wearing a Confederate flag bandana wrapped around his head and a Black Power T-shirt. His wardrobe was meant to get a reaction from the audience and initiate an open discussion about diversity. During the class, many students expressed the idea the Confederate flag represented racism in America, and many were offended by his bandana.

As I continued to jog, I thought about how the flag would make other people feel as they drove through the community. Would the flag offend my neighbors in the same way the minister's dress offended the students in class? What impression would this flag have on visitors of our beautiful southern Tennessee community? I also thought about the impact the flag may have on people of color who may want to move into the neighborhood. The more I thought about the potentially controversial presence of this flag flying on the porch of my neighbor's house, the more offended I became.

My thoughts shifted to the action I could take to voice my opinion about the flag. I thought about writing a letter to the owner, asking him/her to remove the flag. Then I thought about writing a letter of complaint to the president of the homeowners' association. I began to imagine all kinds of other creative ways to remove the flag.

Eventually I was fixed on the flag and its impact on me. As my attitude spiraled downward and changed for the worse, I began to get even more irritated with the fact the flag was flying on a neighbor's porch.

After the irritation was a feeling of anger. Finally, I decided to knock on the door and let the owner know how I was feeling, but something inside me kept saying, "Don't do it," so I did not knock.

As I continued to jog and look around the rest of the neighborhood, I forgot about the flag for a moment. I began to realize the flag was not the real problem. The more I thought about it, the more I realized I had no control over the flag, the owner of the flag, where the flag was flown, or the homeowners' association's decision to allow it to be flown.

The true historical meaning behind the flag has nothing to do with racism. Although there has been a stigma of racism attached to the display of the Confederate flag, historically, the true meaning of the flag does not represent racism. Even if it did, why should I allow it to control my attitude? Why should the flying of this flag control how I feel about myself? Why should this flag determine my level of self-esteem? Better still, why did I allow some inanimate object, blowing in the wind, to control any part of my attitude and feelings? The true answer to the last question is "Because I allowed it."

I gave control of my attitude over to the notion of a Confederate flag representing racism in America. As I continued jogging, I asked myself, "How important is this flag in the overall scheme of my life? Will it keep me from loving, caring for, and respecting myself and others?" The answers to those two questions, respectively, are "Not important at all" and "No".

In processing my emotions and thoughts about the flag, I realized I had, in a matter of five minutes or so, experienced a drastic shift in my attitude. I started my run with a great attitude, gave control of my attitude to a flag, then recaptured control of my attitude by asking the right questions of myself. In other words, I implemented the *fourth secret:*

Adjust your attitude.

Sometimes we give control of our attitude to someone else and may not always regain control. Some of us would have tried to control the owner of such a flag. Others would have tried to force the removal of the flag. Still others may have created an impression of the owner of the flag without ever actually getting to know him/her.

Most of us try to control everything that goes on around us—other people and their feelings, animals, plants, even the ozone. *Letting Go of Stuff*® also requires us to relinquish this quest for control. You may not like it, and your ego may not want to accept it, but the reality is you cannot control other people—not your co-workers, your significant other, or your friends, and you certainly cannot control what happened in your past.

There is one element of your life in which you do have 100 percent control—your mind. You shape your attitude and imagination, as well as the actions resulting from your thoughts. These are the things over which you have complete control. You control when and how often you make the journey between your heart and your mind. Believe me, it can be a wonderful journey!

According to Earl Nightingale (1990), out of 100 percent, about 8 percent of what most people worry about is legitimate. The remaining 92 percent is comprised of the following: 40 percent of what people worry about are things that will never happen; 30 percent are about things that already have happened; 12 percent of people's concerns are about health-related issues that may never exist; and the remaining 10 percent are worries about miscellaneous stuff. Therefore, approximately 70 percent of what people worry about either have happened in the past or will never happen at all. Another way to think of it is people spend about 42 minutes of every hour focusing their thoughts on what has been and what may never be. How does your percentage breakdown of worry add up?

The Imagination

Your imagination is a powerful tool that can shape your entire life. The scientist Albert Einstein has been credited as saying, "The imagination is a preview of what is to come in life." A big part of letting go is focusing on what you can control—your imagination and, more importantly, your attitude. You can change the pictures in your mind. By doing this you can actually manage the impact any situation has on you. For example, if you experienced the death of a loved one some years ago and are still holding on to the mental picture of the person in pain before dying, the picture can keep you feeling down and depressed. This could also keep you from fully enjoying your life today. You must change the picture you see in your mind about the lost loved one. I am speaking from experience.

My Mom transitioned in December 1992. I have a choice as to what I play back in my mind about my Mother before she passed away. I choose to remember the positive lessons and good times we had together. The great influence she had on our family will be alive forever in my heart and imagination.

Your imagination is one of the most powerful and beautiful tools God has provided for you. You can see the world through your imagination. You can go places you never have been and have experiences you never thought you would have with your imagination. It is truly powerful.

Your imagination is the tool over which you have complete control and literally can change your life. You can use it to envision and shape your future. In your imagination, you can take a journey to the center of your being, and no one can keep you from enjoying this journey but you. You already have what it takes to redesign and live your life the way you want, and to a great extent, it begins with your imagination.

Sometimes people go through the process of **Letting Go of Stuff**® and they are willing to share the experience. Here is an excerpt from a faxed letter from a client, who, with coaching and guidance, took herself through this process of tapping into the power of the imagination.

Everyone experiences some down time or may want to modify something about themselves in their lifetime. A few years ago I was grieving over the death of my father.

Depression had set in and was like a dark, inescapable cloud hovering over me. I learned about this method of mental processing, and it impacted my living. It moved me from gloominess to blissfulness. I actually experienced a transformation. I had to remember what was good about me. I could really be the person I wanted to be, a happy me.

During the session, Darren walked me through some steps that were simple—envision a pleasant "me" from prior years. Hear the laughter of my voice. See the beauty of nature, family, and friends. Experience the good times in my mind that have not long ago occurred. Actually relive them. It felt wonderful!!! So wonderful that I wanted to have it back.

So…that's what I did. I sought to rediscover and capture that part of me that was missing. I can now achieve my goals through mental imagery. The desire to change was the first step. The rest of the process flowed with ease. You can direct positive or negative energy.

The choice is yours. You must want to modify your behavior, then let the positive happen in your mind, and let it manifest itself into reality. I have adapted this behavior and use this concept to manage my life.
- KC (printed with permission from client)

EXERCISE 6-1
In this exercise there are five parts. If possible, complete the parts in the order given. First give yourself a few minutes to think about and write down your dreams—everything you have always wanted to be, do, and have. I believe dreaming is a great attitude adjustor. Imagine all the things you wanted to do when you were younger but have not gotten around to yet. Think about the dream that has fallen by the wayside for whatever reason and write it in this next section.

A. DREAM LIST

- _____
- _____
- _____
- _____
- _____
- _____
- _____
- _____
- _____
- _____
- _____

- _____
- _____
- _____
- _____
- _____
- _____
- _____

B. After writing down your dreams, get into a comfortable position, and, if you want, listen to soft instrumental music. Imagine yourself as you are right now. See yourself in the chair, or on the sofa, stretched out in your favorite lounge chair, in the office, or wherever you are while reading this book. In your mind's eye, hold that picture in full living color. Now open your eyes and look around you.

C. Now, close your eyes again. This time, imagine yourself living the dream(s) you just wrote in this exercise. See yourself successfully participating in your dream. Imagine yourself participating in the dream and loving it! Now, add some color to this picture—bold color—and make the picture brighter.

D. Pay attention to how you feel as you imagine this experience. Is it fun and exciting? Is it calming? Do you want to get started living your dream right now? If this process feels strange, that may be because you have not done this before. In time, you will get used to it. After all, it is your choice. Take a few moments and enjoy this activity, and remember how you are feeling.

E. Now it is time to write down, in detail, the feelings you experienced during this exercise. Capture the moment—this is important. By writing down what you experienced, it becomes embedded in your subconscious. Every time you read over this information it will trigger the feelings you just experienced. It also will help you to stay focused on accomplishing your dream goal.

My Feelings About Living - My Dream

Congratulations, you have just provided yourself with what it will feel like when you accomplish this dream goal. It is important for you to create a plan of action to make this a reality.

During one of my *Letting Go of Stuff*® seminars, a young lady confessed she never had participated in any kind of dream activity. As a matter of fact, she never had taken the time to dream; she was too busy making a living and raising her family. Many people often do not take the time to dream. They get used to living a dreamless life. If you are not careful, you can become proficient in having a dreamless life, like the lady in the following story who had lunch with her fortune-telling friend:

> *While sitting under an awning in front of a small cafe in downtown Burlington, Vermont, the friend leaned over the bistro table and said, "I have a gut feeling about your future." The lady, excited and giddy, asked, "What is the feeling?" The fortuneteller said, "You will be unhappy and dreamless until you are 46 years old." The lady asked hopefully, "Then what will happen?" The fortuneteller looked her in the eyes, took a deep breath, and said, "Then, you will get used to it."*

Without dreams, you don't have anything to move toward, and you may end up retired, looking back on your life, and saying, "I wish I had…" To avoid this, I urge you to dream. Allow yourself a chance to experience the joy of the process. If you do dream enough, and put the dream in a plan of action, the dream can come true.

A Positive Attitude - Your Choice

Please know you always have a choice about your attitude. Choosing to be miserable is an option, but not one I recommend. You can control how you react to people and/or situations. It may feel like other people or situations have control over your feelings, but the fact of the matter is they do not. Adjusting your attitude begins with recognizing only you can control it.

The exercise in Chapter 5, in which you rewrote the *BE Statements* is extremely important. It is designed to help you maintain, through repetition, a positive attitude. If you want to become unconsciously competent at having a great attitude, getting there begins with making your internal conversation more positive.

It is important to learn from your experiences and realize those lessons also can help shape your attitude. When something incredible happens to you, examine the entire situation and try to figure out the significance. Identifying the significance can help you discover the lesson(s). Sometimes an experience will help substantiate a belief. For example, if you have developed a certain attitude about a particular culture of people, then a bad experience can help substantiate the attitude. If you only focus on the substantiation, you may totally miss the lesson. It is always good to reexamine every learning opportunity and try to discover and learn the intended lesson. I do this because it keeps me in a perpetual mode of learning.

Over the years, I have always tried to think positively and live a healthy lifestyle so I can stand tall and feel good about myself. You read part of my story in Chapter 2. In less than 25 years, I experienced a near-death accident, was robbed at gun-point, was fired from one job and laid off from another, filed bankruptcy, and regained financial stability. So if you are wondering whether or not it is possible for you to do the activities in this book and change your life for the better, I am here to tell you it is very possible.

It took those kinds of experiences for me to realize I needed to heed the lessons presented to me by the universe, which led to a change in attitude about my life. We need to listen to our experiences. When something crazy happens, we should examine the entire situation and try to figure out the significance on a higher spiritual level.

If you have had experiences in the past that have caused you to rethink your life, but you did not make any adjustments, perhaps you should once again review the lesson(s) in those experiences. Reexamining those experiences today might help you change your attitude about something that happened to you yesterday, enabling you to enjoy fully the new experiences you will have tomorrow.

In 1991, during a conference, I had the distinct pleasure of meeting the great college football coach Lou Holtz. He gave a keynote speech about attitude. I took many notes, writing down some of his comments word-for-word. Below are excerpts from the notes I wrote during his speech:

The power to choose is the greatest gift God has given us. Here are some reasons why people don't have good attitudes: not handling adversity in life; not sticking to fundamentals; complicating everything and not keeping it simple; being too aggressive toward people; being withdrawn from people for long periods of time; having loss of discipline; having lack of confidence; blaming others for your shortcomings; having no sense of purpose; a weak self image…

According to my notes, Lou Holtz then said, "First be the best, then be the first." He also gave three simple rules to raising your self-image: "1) Be the best you can be; 2) Do what is right, avoid what is wrong; 3) Treat others as you want to be treated."

After his speech, he autographed my notes by writing, "Darren, you take great notes. Lou Holtz." I was thrilled about the experience and later realized nothing he talked about was new. It can all be found in any philosophical book. You can even read about attitude in the ancient Egyptian text, *42 Admonitions of Maat*, written thousands of years ago (Browder, 1992). Managing your attitude is one of the oldest and simplest activities in which you can participate, yet it is one of the most complicated. Your attitude can either work for you, or it can work against you. It can be either your biggest handicap of life or your most powerful tool for loving life. It all depends on what is going on inside of you.

What is inside of us is the awesome, powerful, wonderful, spiritual, and God-given ability to decide what kind of attitude we would like to have every day.

Our attitude can be positively powerful, inspiring of inner beauty, and a basic foundation for happiness and success. It also can be the largest, most negative, and self-destructive handicap some of us may ever confront. I say that because, for some of us, choosing a positive attitude is a challenge.

My Personal Challenge with Attitude

I once knew a lady who spent the first 50 years of life living the female American dream of the 1930s and 40s. She was a housewife and married to a successful doctor. Together they raised four successful children. Her inner spirit was so beautiful you could see it when you looked into her eyes. At age 50, she was diagnosed with multiple sclerosis (MS), which devastated her family. Nonetheless, with a positive attitude, she continued to laugh and smile as she courageously faced the challenges of MS.

From 1985 until about 1990, her youngest son dealt with her diagnosis differently. He had periods of depression. He prayed to God, asking, "Why is this happening? Why my Mom?" He felt guilty for being able to live a normal life, while, in his mind, his mother struggled. Though the mother was disabled by her condition, it was her youngest son who was handicapped by his attitude. It was not until August of 1990 that the son was able to change his attitude and recapture the loving spirit he inherited from his mother and father.

The lady was (and still is) my Mom, and the youngest son is yours truly. One memory I have of her is the way she accepted the daily challenges of her condition with zest, courage, persistence, a wonderful attitude, and best of all with a smile that came from within her soul.

On the other hand, I had the challenge of choosing whether or not my attitude was going to be a handicap. With her influence, I chose to not have the handicap. I remember walking into the hospital room to visit her and hearing the nurses laugh at something she had said as they stood around her bed. They enjoyed talking with my Mother; she was a delight. Although she was not able to move physically and had trouble speaking as a result of the impact of MS, she still could laugh. She was a strong person. It is difficult to believe someone can have a great attitude while having to lie in bed every day, not being able to control their own body while feeling the continuous loss of muscle control. However, people do it every day. There are people dealing with this kind of challenge and much, much more every day, but they CHOOSE to have a positive, upbeat attitude. You can make the same choice as well.

I also credit my Dad, known as "T," because he stayed by my Mom's side the entire time she was ill. He was a great example for his children and others. I honor and respect him for not allowing his attitude to be his handicap. He transitioned in July 2003, about ten and a half years after my Mom. He, too, walked his last walk with style, grace, and pride. *Here's to you "T"!*

All of us may be faced with challenges in life, but, no matter the degree to which we are placed in a situation in which we have no control, we must not allow, as I did, our attitude to become the greatest handicap.

We all must learn to dig down deep inside, trust that inner voice, and not be afraid to face and forgive ourselves. We must not allow our attitude to become the greatest handicap of our lives.

I challenge you! This challenge comes in the form of a simple question: "Is your attitude your greatest handicap?"

Chapter 7
Choose to Focus on What You Can Control

It was a chilly, overcast day when the great wise man encountered a little sparrow lying on its back in the middle of the road. With his wise eyes squinting from behind his small spectacles, the wise man looked down and asked the little creature: "What are you doing? Why are you lying on your back with your feet in the sky?" The sparrow replied, "I heard the sky is falling."

The wise man laughed and quipped, "And I suppose you are going to use your spindly little legs to hold up the sky?"

"One does what one can," replied the sparrow.

Though we can't save the world or stop the sky from falling, it is important that we do our part as we apply the *fifth secret* to letting go:

Focus on what we can control.

We spend a lot of time and energy trying to control stuff that isn't ours, stuff that we did not create, and stuff that someone else owns—but we have claimed as ours. We also hold on to other people's emotional stuff, even though it is not ours.

As Americans, we seem to desire control over all kinds of emotional and materialistic stuff that isn't ours. The media ensures that we hold on to stuff by repeating negative stories in the news over and over again. Even after almost a decade, news outlets still are reporting on the O.J. Simpson murder trial. During the ordeal, the media explored the story from every conceivable angle and perspective. On cable, you could learn about O.J. every hour, on the hour. Most of the reports were negative, forcing viewers to relive the painful events over and over again.

No wonder Americans have become adept at the art of holding on to stuff. I am not saying the media is the sole cause; however, media outlets do have a tremendous influence on our lives. They help create and perpetuate stereotypes, substantiate certain beliefs, and, in an effort to find news and information that sells, can bring about destructive outcomes.

There are other, more destructive factors preventing us from letting go. One is not knowing how to listen to our true inner voice. As we learned in Chapter 5, it is imperative for us not just to hear, but listen, trust, and believe in our true inner voice. It is just as important to know how to talk to yourself, to choose the best words to use during your internal conversations. If you were paid 10 cents for every kind word you ever spoke and had to pay a nickel for every unkind word, would you be rich or poor? Listening and talking to yourself are two important components of your being that you can control fully.

I believe focusing on what you can control is one of the best lessons one can learn. It is also a part of moving toward the future state or your dream goal, as discussed in Chapter 4. The first step in applying the secret of focusing is to identify what you can and cannot control. For example, you have full control of your thoughts and the words you speak. You have full control over how you react to a situation, person, or event. You have full control over what you do with your time, energy, and money. You have full control over whether or not you create, pursue, and accomplish your personal and career goals in your lifetime. Because these kinds of elements are what you can control, these are the elements you should put energy, effort, and, perhaps, money into making happen for yourself.

We really tend to exercise overcontrol in relationships. How many times have you attempted to change a family member or friend? Why do we want to change the other person? Because it makes us feel better, even if the change is not what they want. The truth of the matter is you cannot control another person, and the energy to change should be put into yourself. Change how you react to others. Maybe you need to be more understanding, flexible, and accepting of others. I am speaking from experience. I have had my share of relationships in which I focused my time and energy trying to change someone else. I finally realized the focus should be on managing my attitude and reactions, rather than theirs.

Without realizing it, we can sometimes alienate family members and those close to us by trying to control them and taking them for granted. Part of the reason is we tend to take for granted the fact they are going to be around, but nothing is so important that you cannot take a minute for someone else who cares about you or whom you care about. I remember reading somewhere that you have to take time to smell the roses in life. At first, I thought smelling roses meant taking long walks in areas where there were lots of flowers. Eventually I realized roses can come in many different forms. What you think is a rose may not be a rose at all to the next person. Roses are not just flowers; they are spending time with family, watching your children play, playing with your children, relaxing with your spouse or significant other, reading your favorite book, being in love, loving who you are, and much more.

A rose also represents taking time to be available for others when they really need you, even if it means not getting something done that is important to you. It means being there for someone you do not know, taking the time to learn about who you are and what your purpose is for being on this earth. A rose also refers to doing something you really love to do with someone you truly love, even if that person is yourself. Smelling the roses also means taking time to dream about the way you want your life to be, and imagining yourself working on your plan to make those dreams come true. The list could go on and on.

On our website, www.LettingGoOfStuff.com, you will find a game that hundreds of people have played. The game challenges you to choose three to five items from a list of about 45 ways to enjoy life. You are then challenged to spend a week making those three to five items happen. The goal is to accomplish three to five of the items listed each week until you have accomplished every one on the list. You would be surprised how often we walk past "the roses" in our lives without even taking the time to smell them. What we do with our time is something we can control.

A great lesson I learned in managing myself was initiated by a call I received from a sales representative from the Nashville Area Chamber of Commerce. He was calling to find out whether or not I had received and reviewed some membership literature he had mailed to me the week before. I could have been more polite when I informed him I was preparing for a workshop and did not have time to talk. However, I went on to let him know I had many important things to read, and though his information was among them, it was not a top priority. In retrospect, I probably did not even need to say that to him. You see, in an effort to tell him he had interrupted me, I tried to make him feel that what he wanted was not as important as what I was doing at the time. He had no idea I was entrenched in writing a speech. I could have told him about what I was doing, and still looked at his information later, as I did.

After I hung up the telephone, I began to feel very bad. The feeling was a weakening one, almost as though I had not eaten for days. When I finally did speak to him again, I apologized. I realized, however, I would not have had to play the "I'm too busy" game if I treated the caller fairly at the beginning. Most people are consumed with that particular game and play it all day, every day. Well, I stopped playing the "I'm too busy" game on that day.

I learned something about myself with this experience. I was growing and approaching another level of consciousness. If I had hung up the telephone and thought nothing of my actions, I never would have recognized the incongruent nature of my actions. The physiological reaction I had after hanging up the telephone was a very strong indication that I was not doing the right thing. It was this physical discomfort that helped me realize something about my mindset had to change. At the same time, the physical realization also indicated I was growing and learning, which was exciting because I knew it was all right for me to learn these lessons. I have applied what I learned every day of my life. Why? Because learning about ourselves and making adjustments in our *who-ness* is what we can control.

The Big Money Chase – A True Story and Great Lesson

How often have you spent time, energy, and money chasing after what you cannot control? Some years ago I had the experience of chasing someone else's dreams, only to realize that if I had trusted in my dream, everything would have been okay. In the end, that was a valuable lesson.

In 1996, I met a "business man" whose nickname was Woody. Woody told me about an opportunity that would make a lot of money in a short period of time. After having been associated with him for a few months and listening to him talk about his experiences making money in the network marketing industry, I began to trust him. He had long-term, non-specific, financial goals. He shared his dreams with me and anyone else who would listen.

Well, I learned something in dealing with Woody. *If one does not focus on accomplishing one's own goals, one will end up helping someone else achieve his/her, at one's expense.* At that time, I did not have any specific financial goals other than to make a lot of money. That meant I was willing to do just about anything legal to make money, except taking the time to do research, ask questions, do more research, and identify someone who had already made a lot of money who either could coach or mentor me. Woody was not in any of those categories. It was like the blind leading the blind. Needless to say, I lost a lot of money dealing with Woody. It was a painfully expensive lesson.

Woody had friends, Lou and Ken, and Ken had friends, Ed and John. Even though they were all very nice people, not one of them, I learned later, was truly successful in making large amounts of money over long (or short) periods of time.

Although Ken had never made a lot of money over time, he was a very good orator and shared great stories about overcoming obstacles. He always talked about God and how important is it to trust people. He was leading thousands of people down a path that was supposed to make all of them rich quick. To his credit, through his speeches, Ken could help you see yourself living your dreams. It seems he was also masterful at *using your dreams* to convince you to make decisions about *your money* that ultimately filled his pockets, and it was done legally.

Well, there I was, right in the middle of the pack, being greedy and trying to make a lot of money in a short amount of time. I put off my dream of being a nationally-recognized speaker and trainer, and began to focus on Ken's goals. I set aside money for his organization that I should have been using to invest in my company. After losing thousands of dollars reaching for Ken's dreams instead of mine, I finally awakened from this slumber.

What was the lesson? Once I figured out the game, I was angry at Woody. Then the anger shifted to Ken for telling all of his convincing stories and getting me to believe in him. However, the more

I examined the situation, the more I realized none of those people were responsible for the decision I made to get involved. Even though it seemed Woody initially was responsible for getting me involved, he did not control my actions. The decision to write checks was mine. I went to the meetings. I shared the opportunity with others, and I believed in Ken's pipe dreams more than my own.

The more I thought about it, the more I realized the only person I could be upset with was myself. That was a difficult, not to mention big, pill to swallow. In the process of trying to get rich quick I met some great people. I have since forgiven Woody and his band of business associates. More importantly, I have forgiven myself for having made a decision that led to an unwanted outcome.

I would not trade the experience; without it, I would not be the person I am today. It took me a while, but I finally learned financial independence must first exist in your heart and mind before it can exist in your bank account. Knowing and applying this philosophy in your life, my good friend, is what you can control.

That experience also reminds me of a Chinese proverb: "That the birds of worry and care fly above your head, this you cannot change. But that they build nests in your hair, this you can prevent."

Relationships and the PZT Test

How many close relationships are you in right now? What impact do you think your relationships have on your daily decisions and attitude?

Remember, you are influenced by the personality average of the five to seven people with whom you spend most of your time. For instance, if you are friends with people who gossip and are miserable, then you probably will spend some of your time feeling awful and gossiping about others. Conversely, if all your closest friends are happy, you will spend more time being happy. If you surround yourself with goal-oriented achievers, you probably will be influenced to set goals as well.

In the next chapter we will talk about our unconscious actions. For now, let me say that once you get in the habit of thinking certain thoughts and performing certain actions, those thoughts and actions become unconscious. Consequently, you may be influenced by your seven best friends and not realize their level of influence on your actions and attitude because you are unconsciously competent when it comes to performing those actions.

In other words, if you allow yourself to be influenced by people who believe the sky is falling, chances are pretty good you eventually will believe it, too. Focusing on your *who-ness* and your purpose will allow you to determine better who you allow into your life. If you have not identified a purpose, you will hang around with almost anyone.

People who have purpose in their lives are influenced by others only if they allow themselves to be, and only by those they believe will contribute to their purpose. Those with a purpose spend time with a chosen few, a select group of individuals who want the best for others and themselves.

It is important to surround yourself with people who are healthy for your life overall, people who accept your dreams, people who challenge your thinking and perspectives, yet respect your opinions and beliefs. If you have family members, friends, or associates who make you feel bad about yourself, then I suggest you reconsider the time you spend with them. Remember, part of your stuff is linked to theirs.

In order to fully let go of the stuff you identified in previous chapters, you will have to examine the relationships you have with others. You should reevaluate your relationships at least every two years or so, regardless.

Use the section on the next page to write how you feel as you complete Exercise 7-1. It is important for you to capture these feelings so you will be able to manage them better. Feelings of discomfort during this process are normal.

PZT CHART

NAME	P	Z	T
1.			
2.			
3.			
4.			
5.			
6.			
7.			
8.			
9.			
10.			
11.			
12.			
13.			
14.			
15.			

Here is a suggested method for evaluating the influential folks in your life.

A. First, list your closest family members, friends, and associates in the column labeled "Name" in the PZT Chart. These are people with whom you spend the most of your time every day. These are people who may feel they know you better than you know yourself.

B. After you have listed those closest to you, rate them according to the PZT descriptions in the next three sections and place a check in the column representing the category into which each person fits.

P = Positive

These are people closest to you who have a very positive influence and impact in your life. They are very nurturing. When you have a conversation with them, you feel good about it. You truly enjoy being with them. They consistently accept you as you are, love hearing about your dreams, share their dreams with you, and challenge you to make your dreams a reality. They respect your feelings, genuinely listen to you, and support your dreams no matter how far-fetched they may be.

People in this category are good for your soul. You feel connected to them in some deeper place of your heart. Although there may be times when you may have an altercation and disagree, in the long run you know they love you and want what is best for you, and it shows. These are people who, on an ongoing basis, provide love, support, and help to increase your self-esteem.

Z = Zero
Z represents those people closest to you who have a neutral impact on you. After being around them, you do not feel good or bad. They do not support your dreams, but they do not shoot them down either. These people do not really have an impact on you. They do not seem to have a strong opinion about you one way or another. They do not disrespect you, yet never demonstrate a high regard for your opinions. They are around you but are basically nonexistent in your life.

T = Toxic
These are people closest to you who consistently make you feel bad about yourself. The reaction can be physical; you might have tension headaches and stomach cramps or have trouble eating after interacting with them. These are people who, in the form of a joke or some sarcastic remark or quip, will ridicule your dreams.

These people really do not respect your opinions and are consistently trying to tell you how to live your life by making you feel bad about the way you do things. They continually disrespect you in the name of love. They make you feel bad about your decisions. They argue with you and are in your face about every little thing you do. They are threatened by your accomplishments and are on your back during the challenging times. Toxic people consistently give you compliments, which may begin with the following: "Your hair looks great today, but..." or "You look nice today except for...."

When you share your dreams, they might ask: "Is that your dream? Are you sure you really want to do that? It sounds silly, don't you think?"

Toxic people, over a period of time, will pull you down. They will consume you until there is nothing left, sometimes in the name of love. They are not bad people, but they are toxic to you. This means they can undermine your self-esteem and self-confidence, perpetuating negative internal conversations.

One caution about the T and the P categories: Sometimes people who truly care about you will challenge you to get better. Once challenged, you may temporarily feel uncomfortable and mistake the person for being toxic. Remember, a toxic person will not really challenge you to be better but only ridicule you and make you feel bad or worse on a regular basis. It may take very careful reflection to note the difference between the two. The thing to remember is how the people closest to you treat you on a regular, consistent basis. Consider this: Is it more important to have a toxic relationship or to feel good about yourself?

Categorizing the Names on Your List
Now it is time to determine who on your PZT Chart list is a P, Z, or T. I suggest you give this a lot of thought, and remember: Choose only one category for each name (for example, Jane Doe is either a P or a Z, but she cannot be both).

After you have made your choices on the PZT Chart about the names on your list, the next challenge is fighting the need, and the urge, to defend your decision. Even more challenging is not changing your decision about which category you placed someone.

A word of caution: This is not something you will want to run around and announce to everyone. You will need to have a conversation with everyone on your list about the impact they have on you. It may not be an easy conversation, but it is essential in the process of *Letting Go of Stuff.*® If you find it necessary to show your list and let them know which category they are in, be very sensitive about how you share this. This will also help you either to put closure on the toxic relationship or to manage better the kind of interaction you have with the person. Toxic relationships can be a big part of your personal stuff, and the toxicity often manifests in your internal conversation. Focusing on letting go of toxic relationships is something you can control, though it may be challenging to do.

Your *BE Statements*—Something Else You Control

As mentioned earlier in this chapter, we often allow other people's beliefs to become ours, just like we allow other people's conversations to become our own internal conversation. Take television and radio for example—many of us let the TV and radio be the foundation of our internal conversation. They are the first thing we turn on in the morning and the last thing we turn off at night, and sometimes the TV is on all night.

I Double Dare You!

In the morning, instead of turning on the radio, TV, or reading the newspaper, read the *BE Statements* you created in Chapter 5. You should read them at least three times before you leave the house in the morning and again each night before going to sleep. You really will begin to feel a difference once you get used to doing this on a regular basis. Trust me on this one!

What I refer to as *BE Statements*, Sue Hammond (1996) calls "provocative prepositions." She says these statements can help us to "keep our best at a conscious level. They are symbolic statements because they have meaning well beyond words, reminding us of what is best..." (p. 39). Although she is referring to a technique used by organization development consultants known as appreciative inquiry, for individuals the impact of using this process is just as powerful. Appreciative inquiry is used to assist organizations with creating a climate that fosters doing more of the activities that produce wanted outcomes rather than unwanted outcomes. It is also important for individuals to have the same focus.

I believe it is important for people to create a healthy mental environment in which to accomplish daily tasks. This can help them achieve outcomes and results related to accomplishing their dreams and goals. This mental climate is composed of thoughts, feelings, emotions, pictures of experiences, and words. It is the foundation for your actions. That is why the *BE Statements* are so important. By creating an internal conversation with words that increase your self-esteem, you actually begin to shape the mental climate into what you want—on purpose.

To paraphrase Jim Rohn, it is important to remember that in life you may not get what you want, but you will get what you are. This means that if you are being the person you want to be, then you will get what you want from life. Who is in charge of determining who you are? You, and only you. No one else should have enough power over your life to be able to dictate who you are; that is giving up too much of your personal power. You should have total control over that aspect of your *who-ness*. As a result of having that control, you can either design or redesign your life accordingly.

The challenge many of us face in today's society is we have never made a choice to design our lives. Somewhere along the way, someone told us where we needed to be and when and how to get there; subsequently, we took off in that direction. Perhaps we never took time to sit down, listen to, and follow our inner voice. I believe everyone needs to take the time to identify and follow their own path in life. You have a path that belongs exclusively to you.

Do you remember *Alice in Wonderland*? Alice reaches a point where she asks the Cheshire cat, "Which road do I take?" The cat responds, "Which road do you want to take?" Alice says she does not know. The Cheshire cat then says, "Then it doesn't matter which road you take. Any road will do."

Most of us never decide to take our own road. We often end up on someone else's path, not realizing we can get off their path and find our own.

It takes belief in one's self and requires specific action. You have to believe in you, because if you do not, no one else will. Your belief in yourself is also the one thing no one can give or take from you.

I once received a postcard from Joe Sabah that bore a simple riddle. It said:

Three frogs are sitting on a lily pad. One frog decided to jump. How many frogs are left? The answer is three. Remember: deciding to jump and jumping are two different things. Deciding is a thought. Jumping is an action.

Action is what counts! It makes the difference between those who succeed and those who only want to succeed! Chapter 9 is all about unfreezing and taking the positive action necessary to let go and move forward.

Today is your chance to begin the redesign of your life, to let go of stuff and put some pizzazz back into your life. Now is the time for you to unfreeze your current state, move toward your newly-designed future, and refreeze yourself at that new state of *who-ness* designed by you.

You will find your attitude will begin to change automatically as you take positive action toward the accomplishment of your dreams. It is amazing what the implementation of the exercises in this book will do for your life. You only have to be willing to take the first step of putting *all of yourself* into what you are doing and focusing on what you truly can control in your life.

Something amazing happens when you begin to focus only on what you can control. You feel more alive and energetic. By focusing only on what you can control, you will accomplish more in your lifetime than you ever dreamed. Getting focused on your dreams, goals, internal thoughts, and actions is going to be a most challenging and rewarding experience. If you remember to acknowledge the fact you want to get focused, accept the changes you will experience in the process, listen to and positively change your internal conversations, and continue to adjust your attitude along the way, then you will not go wrong. You may get sidetracked, but you must continue to come back to your plan, and eventually you will succeed.

Deciding to focus on what you can control is a choice; a choice you make by deciding to let go of all of the other stuff around you that has nothing to do with your goals and dreams.

The next secret is to choose to let go by using the Self Managing Grid® as a daily decision-making guide.

Chapter 8
Choose to Let Go

"IF WE TAKE CONTROL OF THE WORLD WITHIN OURSELVES, NO
CIRCUMSTANCE OUTSIDE OURSELVES WILL HAVE ITS WAY WITH US."
— SUSAN TAYLOR, *LESSONS IN LIVING*

Up to now, we have discussed where to put your
energy, where to focus your efforts, and how to
begin to let go of stuff that interferes with moving
forward. This chapter will provide a powerful tool
designed to assist you in *consciously choosing* to
change your life—*on purpose.* Your destiny is in
your hands, and creating the life you want is totally
up to you. Making a choice is one of the greatest
gifts given to us by God. Although many of us feel as
though we have no choice when it comes to creating
our destiny here on earth, I say, contrary to that
popular internal programming, we have many other
choices.

The *sixth secret* in developing the art of *Letting Go
of Stuff®* is the following:

Make the Letting Go of Stuff® Choice.

The Self Managing Grid® is a powerful tool that can
be used to help manage change and stress effectively

in your life and to help make the best choices about how you spend your time, energy, and focus. It is a decision-making grid used by individuals and organizations.

Many studies and much research have been done on the ways successful people focus their time and energy, as well as how they take action on the things they can control. We often focus and take action on elements in our environment we cannot control.

The process of *Letting Go of Stuff*® as I have emphasized throughout the book is a most revealing and empowering process. There are times, however, when Murphy's Law—whatever can go wrong, will go wrong—seems prevalent. Sometimes life gets tough and battles with change are lost daily. Sometimes your confidence level is low, and you feel down and out. Have you ever experienced the loss of a family member or best friend? Have you ever lost a job or been laid off? Have you ever ended a long-term relationship with someone special? Have you made a commitment or a promise, and broken it, resulting in the loss of a friendship?

If you have answered "yes" to any of the questions above or have experienced other types of difficult times, you understand it can be a challenge to make it through. It is during times like these that all of the written information about your goals, reading your *BE Statements*, managing your internal conversations, knowing what to expect of yourself, and choosing to let go of stuff on purpose becomes very important to your survival and state of being. It is important to realize you either can choose to let go and move forward, or you can choose to hold on and be stuck in a rut.

Choosing the latter eventually could lead to low esteem, depression, and poor health. In a way, it is like choosing between either life or death, whether it is death of a dream, death of hope, death of desire, death of faith, death of belief in yourself, or the death of a relationship. Refusing to let go eventually results in a death of some kind. Conversely, if you go after your dreams and desires with gusto, positive energy, loving thoughts, joyful activities, and an upbeat attitude, then you have chosen life.

Once you have decided to go after your dreams, the obstacle course of life gets filled with new kinds of creative challenges. As soon as you get enough money to open a savings account, your car breaks down. As soon as you decide to stay single and not date for a while, the person of your dreams shows up at the door. As soon as you get the car paid off and decide to invest your money in other opportunities, the landlord raises your rent. Although you cannot change the events as they happen, you can control and change how you react to them. To help make my point, let me share a quote from Dave Ramsey, author of *The Total Money Makeover*, "If you *will* live like no one else, later you *can* live like no one else." *Letting Go of Stuff*® is about daring to be **YOU**, which means living like no one else—on purpose.

I remember when I was laid off in the mid-1980s. I had an annual income of $68,000, but including credit card debt, I had annual expenditures of $80,000. You know how it is when you use credit cards; they can give you a false sense of confidence about your wealth. If you are not careful, you can end up living way beyond your means. I learned that the hard way. There I was, laid off from my job without a plan and with plenty of unfulfilled dreams about things I was going to do one day.

Everyone has those "One day I'm going to..." dreams. There is always something you are going to accomplish one day, but because we are so comfortable making a certain amount of money, or so comfortable in a certain kind of relationship, we never really put much energy into making positive changes that will create constant improvement. That false sense of comfort will keep you from going after what you really want out of life. That "one day" philosophy keeps you from living.

Over the years, I have adopted the "today philosophy" in my daily living. This means in my internal and external conversations I have replaced expressions that begin as one of the following: *One day I will...*; *I'm working on it...*; *Eventually I will...*

In place of those expressions I say: *Today, I will...*; and, *I am...*

As for you, today is the day you will make a change for the better. Today—not "one day"—you will love yourself better. Today—not "one day"—you will begin to let go of stuff.

Getting back to my story. I was comfortable in the mid-1980s, living according to the "one day" philosophy, until life changed my comfort zone. I was laid off and began to live in fear—fear of not knowing what the future seemed to hold for me. I eventually ended up filing bankruptcy. I was a living example of the adage:

If you don't move on life, then eventually, life will move on you.

That was in 1988. Ten years later, I had turned my life around by realizing I had choices to make about my lifestyle. I decided to strive to be happy and joyful and chose to have a positive attitude every day. I also chose to believe in and embrace the offerings of the universe, and through these offerings do my life's work. My choice led to the creation of the *Letting Go of Stuff*® seminar, which led to the audio book and, ultimately, to writing this book. I also chose to read my *BE Statements* every day and believe in them. I chose to surround myself with those who supported, cared for, and loved me. I chose to be trustworthy, caring, and loving to everyone.

Today, I am still making the same kind of choices. If I can turn my life around, so can you. It is a matter of effectively *Letting Go of Stuff*® that interferes with making the choice to move toward what you want.

There are two questions you can ask yourself to help you get and stay focused on what you really need to do to accomplish your goals. These two questions can, if you answer them genuinely and honestly, help you to remain focused throughout every day.

They can also keep you from spending time and energy on events, people, and situations you cannot control. These questions work in conjunction with the Self Managing Grid®.

The Self Managing Grid®

The Self Managing Grid® (Figure 8-1) is a decision-making model with four quadrants that represent four choices. They are as follows:

	CONTROL	NO CONTROL
TAKING ACTION	1 Setting Positive Goals	4 Overcontrol (wasted effort)
NOT TAKING ACTION	2 Undercontrol (giving up)	3 Letting Go (acceptance)

Figure 8-1

The Self Managing Grid®
©1998 All Rights

- Quadrant 1 - setting positive goals.
- Quadrant 2 - undercontrolling.
- Quadrant 3 - letting go.
- Quadrant 4 - overcontrolling.

Each quadrant represents the outcome of the combination of taking action, not taking action, control, and no control.[1]

Let's examine each quadrant in the Self Managing Grid®.

Quadrant 4: Overcontrol–Wasted Effort

Any time you take action on something you cannot control, you are wasting effort and time. Many people spend their lives chasing after unrealistic goals or holding on to emotions that resulted from a past event. As mentioned in an earlier chapter, approximately 70 percent of what people worry about, stay angry about, and/or are afraid of, has already happened or will never happen at all. That is why it is important to focus on the present—today—because in the here and now is when you can choose to change.

Let's first talk about what you cannot control. Here is a list of some of the things you cannot control. You cannot control your boss, significant other, friends, parents, in-laws, the changes your company makes about your job classifications, or the weather. You cannot control whether or not someone near and dear to you is going to pass on from a serious illness. You cannot control what happened yesterday or even one second ago, because it is in the past. In how many current situations are you trying to change or control another person? How often have you gotten involved in relationships thinking you could change the other person?

As far as your children are concerned, believe it or not, you cannot control your children. I know you are a good parent; however, you still cannot control your children. You can teach them, guide them, influence them, love them, and develop them, but you cannot control them.

People who are overcontrollers more often are prone to heart disease, high blood pressure, ulcers, prolonged frustration, and burnout. Overcontrollers tend to hold on to anger, guilt, frustration, shame, hostility, and feel anxious when even the smallest events do not go their way. They continuously tell you how to dress, what to say, when to say it, and how often to speak.

Overcontrollers enjoy having pity parties during which time they talk extensively about the stuff they cannot control. Overcontrollers use the word *they* a lot. For example, "I can't believe *they* are changing the rules again. *They* just changed the rules last year. Why are *they* changing the rules again this year?" Overcontrollers get together at water fountains, in rest rooms, in the halls, and in the parking lots and have mini-pity parties to talk about what they hate, what should be changed, and how unhappy they are about stuff in general.

Remember that being angry is an internal action. Feeling guilty or ashamed is an internal action. Having internal conversation is also an internal action, as is thinking. So when the overcontrollers continuously remain angry at someone for something that happened more than two years ago, they are taking action on something that cannot be controlled because it happened in the past. Forgiveness is the best action to take toward someone who did something to you in the past.

What can you control? How do you react to every one of the situations I just mentioned? You can control your attitude and manage the amount of effort you put into the accomplishment of your goals as they relate to your life. You can control what you think and what you say. You decide whether or not to remain angry, be sad, get happy, or experience joy. You and only you make those choices and can control the outcome of those choices through your actions. You control what you eat. You decide either to continue to smoke cigarettes or work out at the gym. Although most of us realize what we control and do not control, we live as though we do not really know, and in some cases we spend years focusing on things we cannot control.

There are many other examples of holding on to things. We hold on to guilt, shame, anger, and frustration. We remain in situations that are potentially destructive to our lives because we are afraid to make a change. Sometimes we overcontrol with the kinds of things we say to ourselves in our internal conversations and the kinds of pictures we hold on to and re-play in our minds.

Have you ever wanted to see a certain part of a movie you rented? You rewind to the part you want to see and play it back. You actually do this same thing with situations that happen in your life. You replay those situations over and over again in your mind. Part of the reason you are still angry at the person who upset you a year ago is because you replay, in your mind's eye, what happened to you a year ago, bringing about the same emotional and physiological results each time. As long as you continue to remain on playback, you will continue to be angry at the person, even if they have changed their ways, apologized, and bought you gifts.

You have to switch modes, fast forward to the present and deal with the person in the present. Look at the person with new eyes and with a renewed perspective. Perhaps they have changed, but you have not. Perhaps they have grown, but you have not. How do you change your reaction to them? How can you let go of your anger? One place to begin to change is by rearranging the pictures in your mind's eye.

Our minds communicate thoughts through pictures and words. When I say the word "love," you do not see the actual word. You see a picture of what love symbolizes for you, such as walking hand-in-hand in the park, enjoying a romantic candle-light dinner with someone special, eating popcorn and watching a movie together, or some other image.

Telling yourself you are depressed helps to create a picture in your mind of being depressed. Ultimately the picture manifests itself in some physiological way. You might mope, slouch, or lay on the sofa looking pitiful. The pictures in your mind help to determine your outward actions, and the pictures in your mind are a result of what you say to yourself.

The ability to let go of something is directly associated with the things you say to yourself and the pictures you see in your mind. If you are happy and excited right now about something in your life, it is because when you think about the situation, you see happy and exciting pictures in your mind's eye.

Another big part of letting go is consciously managing the kinds of pictures you choose to visualize as you talk to yourself. By changing the pictures in your mind, you actually can change the impact of any past situation. You also can create mental expectations of any future outcomes you want in life. Henry David Thoreau is credited with saying, "If one advances confidently in the direction of his dreams, and endeavors to live the life which he has imagined, he will meet with a success unexpected in common hours."

Focusing your time and energy on your own attitude, actions, reactions, thoughts, and dreams narrows the playing field, and keeps life simpler, easier, and uncomplicated. However, when you try to control everyone else's actions, attitudes, schedules, and thoughts, life not only gets more complicated, but will push away those who care for you.

You decide whether or not you are going to accept your dreams as being lost and unfulfilled. You decide whether or not to have a positive or negative attitude toward others. You are where you are at this point in your life because of your choices. It is not your parents' fault; it is not your spouse's fault; it is not your children's fault; and it is not the fault of your boss, your friends, your neighborhood, or society. It is because of you and your choices. You have the power to stop trying to control every person and situation around you. You have the power to let go and move forward with your life right now. Do not put it off any longer, because your life, family, and future depend upon it.

The following questions are ones I reflect on when I am in a situation I feel is getting out of control. Answering them helps me to slow down and re-examine my choices.

1. In how many of your current situations do you not have control but act as though you do?

2. How much time and energy are you expending, which ultimately will be wasted, because you have no control over these situations or people?

Quadrant 3: Letting Go–Acceptance
When you choose not to take action on something because you realize you have no control, this is letting go. Letting go can be challenging. Has anyone ever told you to just let it go and move on? Most of the time letting go is not that easy. It takes time to let some things go; it may not happen over night. As a matter of fact, it may not happen for many months,

sometimes years. Using the Self Managing Grid®, however, can reduce the amount of time and stress involved with letting go.

Letting go means that after you have done everything you can within your control to influence a situation or person, you must then move on. For example, if you feel as though you deserve a higher salary, there are certain things you can do and other things you must do. However, once you have done everything you can to influence the boss to pay you more, regardless of the outcome, it is important to shift your thoughts and energy to something else. Do not complain about a negative outcome to anyone or let it destroy the joy of doing your job. If you do not get the results you want, begin to plan to do something else with your life, such as finding a job with another organization where your unique talents will be appreciated. Always remember you have many options. Another example is learning to manage living your life after the loss of a loved one. This is a crucial area of growth; many people never really relearn to live after the loss of a spouse, child, or parent.

Jannie Coverdale lost her two grandchildren in the Oklahoma City bombing during the 1990s. During a televised interview in September 2001, she was asked how she was coping with her loss. Her response was profound. She said she never really got over the loss and had to create a new life, which is how she processed the loss and was able to let go. The life she lived with her two grandchildren was over. She had to create a new life without her two grandchildren. Learning a new lifestyle gave her a new goal to strive toward and kept her going.

There are two important elements necessary to let go successfully. One is to move toward something positive, something new, something exciting, something challenging, which will force you to take some sort of healthy action. The second is being willing to relearn how to live your life.

Does this mean Coverdale forgot her two grandchildren after they were gone? Of course not. Will it be painful to think about the fact they are gone? Of course it will. Will she be able to move on with her life? The answer is "Yes." As long as she sets positive goals, she moves forward on a daily basis.

Having baby-step size goals and claimimg what you want is important when you are trying to move forward after losing someone special. For example, you might repeat the following statement to yourself: "Today I can enjoy my life because I have the wonderful memories and lessons that resulted from having that person in my life."

How do I know this works? The use of the Self Managing Grid®, along with all the techniques in this book, are what got me through the loss of my parents and have since helped with countless other experiences. After the death of my Mother in 1992, I made a promise to myself; it was to share the Self Managing Grid® with everyone I could and whenever I got an opportunity.

On July 18, 2003, I lost my Dad to emphysema; thus, my siblings and I became parentless. The techniques in this book, eleven years after the loss of my Mom, are also what supported me through the loss of my Dad. *This stuff really works!*

Now my life has taken on a new dimension—being parentless. My choices are many in dealing with this new journey. The choice I have made at 40+ years of age is to redesign my life using the "today philosophy" I described in an earlier chapter. Every day I make a conscious choice to enjoy and learn from the wonderful journey of being a parentless sibling. I also realize in my heart and soul, I never will be parentless. Spiritually, both parents always will be with me in every decision I make and action I take.

I believe if you apply the *Letting Go of Stuff*® process in your life, integrate it into whatever you currently are doing for healthy living, then share it with someone else, you will contribute to the universal cycle of love and prosperity for all. For further clarity of quadrant three, here are some more examples of what letting go means, in the form of *BE Statements*:

I accept the fear of the unknown and am willing to move forward toward making my goals a reality by believing in myself and my ability to create a plan of action and to follow that plan.

I accept you as I believe you are and am willing to love you anyways, without judgment.

I will focus on being a better person by improving myself and will better manage my reactions to the way you are, instead of judging you.

I, as a parent, will not talk at my child but will talk and listen to my child with love and understanding as the underlying premise for my actions.

I will focus on trying to understand my boss and spend more time walking in his/her shoes, rather than complain about and convict my boss of being a poor manager.

I must accept the deadlines at work as a part of my responsibility and will figure out a way to meet them or accept the consequences.

I forgive the most important person in my life—me.

Within some of the above **BE Statements** there is the current action followed by an alternative. That is because you cannot let go of something without having something greater to strive toward. Goal-setting is a very important component in the process of *Letting Go of Stuff*® in your life, and knowing how to set goals effectively and stay focused on them is critical in moving forward.

Have you ever been in a city where someone begged you for money? People set goals that way; they either ask you for a dime or a quarter. Once a guy asked me to give him a dollar. I looked at him and said, "A dollar?" He said, "Yeah, I've got big goals!"

Everyone has to have something to reach toward. You can reach much higher if you are able to let go of stuff that interferes with moving toward the accomplishment of those goals. Trust me on this one. We will talk more specifically about setting goals in Chapter 9.

Sometimes, instead of moving forward, people get stuck in situations and lose all control, thus turning the control over to the situation. This choice, and it is a choice, is represented in quadrant 2 of the Self Managing Grid®.

Quadrant 2: Undercontrol–Giving Up

Giving up represents a choice you make when you decide not to take action on something over which you actually do have control. In the grid, there is a significant difference between undercontrol and overcontrol. When you let go of something, you are in control and being proactive. When you give up, the situation is in control of you, which leads to reactive behavior. People who undercontrol sing the "Woe is me" song. Their internal conversation may sound something like this, "Oh well, it is going to be this way no matter what I do."

Whatever you do, if you can help it, please try to avoid spending time giving up on yourself and others in your life, especially when you have control and influence to take some kind of positive action. When you become consumed by guilt, depression, helplessness, or some unhappy situation, do not allow the situation to control you.

According to Emrika Padus (1986), Dennis T. Jaffe, Ph.D. has written about how undercontrolling can make a person vulnerable to various diseases and infections such as cancer, various types of allergies, rheumatoid arthritis and much more. Padus included a quote from Jaffe, "A healthy person is one who practices optimal control, who acts on problems that are within his power to resolve and doesn't waste time worrying about those that aren't. To do otherwise is self-destructive" (p. 194).

With Jaffe's quote in mind, ask yourself, "Have I given up on a dream in my life that has fallen by the wayside?" As long as you are physically and mentally able to act on the dream and do not, you have given up not only on your dream but on yourself. I urge you to pick up your dream, dust it off, and place it back in the forefront of your heart and soul where you can, once again, see it every day. If you plan and stay focused, you can accomplish the dream or goal.

Years ago I had a client who had made some choices that resulted in adverse outcomes. Eventually he lost his business. Instead of apologizing to those who believed in him, dusting himself off, and moving forward, he withdrew from everyone. He disappeared from view and resurfaced in another city, using another name. During that time, there were plenty of opportunities for him to redeem himself, his reputation, and perhaps even his international business, but he chose to give up on those options and to this day continues to feel guilty, shameful, and embarrassed about his past decisions. However, he has opened a very small business in a totally different industry and is learning how to move forward with his life. He is taking small steps toward changing his life, but the shame from giving up weighs heavily on him.

This person gave up on the thousands of people who were impacted by his business and the small group of supporters who were closest to him. More importantly, *he gave up on himself.* Eventually the clients and other business associates lost confidence in him as a leader and became angry with him for giving up. Today, his is yet another story of one who has given up on a dream.

Quadrant 1: Setting Positive Goals

The final quadrant in the Self Managing Grid® is setting positive goals. When you have control over something or a situation and choose to take positive action by setting positive goals, it allows you to move forward with momentum and a new level of energy.

Remember, you can't fully let go unless you have something greater to strive toward. This quadrant represents a choice that is about taking action that will have positive effects on you and others. The key is to understand how to set goals effectively and stay focused on them in a positive way.

I describe the goals as positive because there are people out there who set negative goals. Think about people you know who seem to get up in the morning and get dressed just so they can go to work and make others angry. It seems they derive joy from bothering others. It is as if these people sit around trying to figure out how to make other people miserable. That is negative goal-setting. If you know such people, my advice is to stay away from them because they may influence you to be the same way.

The bottom line is it is important to keep a positive focus on your goals. According to the Center for Disease Control and Prevention, suicide rates are higher among people ages 65 and older and people ages 25 and younger. Suicide rates for ages 10 to 14 years have increased by more than 109 percent since

1980. Those ages are the times when positive goal-setting is very important.

After retirement, many people become depressed. Many retirees do not set *post-retirement* goals; as a result, their lives become stagnant. The same is true for people age 22 and younger. Young adults often are more inclined to get into trouble by following and accomplishing someone else's goals because they have not yet discovered what they want in life. For this reason, both age groups mentioned are often the target of people with goals that can lead to a life of crime and other social dysfunction. This is all the more reason why it is good to set your own goals, stay focused on them, and keep them positive.

Forming good habits, such as positive goal-setting techniques, is essential for getting a fresh start on successful living and for staying focused on your own path instead of the path of another.

The Self Managing Grid® is a personal decision-making model I use on a daily basis. I use these techniques to identify and put energy into what I can control and influence. I also make sure that when I do take action, it is positive and does not hurt anyone. The use of this simple, yet powerful grid has brought success in my personal and professional life.

Positive goal-setting is also a very important component for creating a plan for action. In Chapter 9, you will be asked and have a chance to answer those two important questions I have been referring to throughout the book. Additionally you will create a plan for action that will allow you to begin the redesign of your life in earnest.

FOOTNOTE:

[1] Psychologists have completed extensive studies on the physiological and psychological impacts of both overcontrolling and undercontrolling. In addition, the theory and research supporting the Self Managing Grid® can be found in the work of Kurt Lewin (1948), Dean and Linda Anderson (2001), and specifically Emrika Padus (1986). In addition to having done research to support the Self Managing Grid®, I would be remiss if I did not give credit to a very effective trainer who also used Padus' research in his training: David Logsdon, who worked with me in Tennessee used this research in his training sessions with managers and supervisors. Although during his presentations David did not give credit to Padus, he did a wonderful job of integrating the outcome of Padus' studies and concepts into his message. I am thankful to David for having shared his interpretation of Padus' work, and I appreciate his zest, knowledge, and creativity as a trainer.

Chapter 9
Plan for Action

"Success is the progressive realization of a worthy ideal.
If a man (or woman) is working toward a predetermined goal
and knows where he (she) is going, that man (woman) is a
success. If he (she) is not doing that, he is a failure... People
with goals succeed because they know where they are going."
— Earl Nightingale

Imagine you are driving a convertible down a long road on a mountain, winding alongside the ocean. You can feel the brisk breeze as it blows on your face. The sun is warm as it beams down from overhead. You look up, and as far as you can see, there is nothing but blue sky. You are in control of your vehicle and traveling down this road with a specific destination in mind. You are really enjoying this drive and not quite sure how long it will take to get there, so you do not know exactly what obstacles may exist along the way. Yet, you know you are headed somewhere and because of that you feel great. At different points during the drive you wonder if you are on the right road, but you do not want to stop to check, because it will interfere with the joy of your drive.

Located on the seat next to you is a map. This map is the only tool to tell you exactly where you are and the potential obstacles along the way, but because you are afraid taking the time to look at the map may interfere with your schedule, the map remains on your seat, unused. From time to time you glance at the map and say to yourself, "Soon I will take a look at that map. Soon, real soon!"

Though your inner voice constantly is telling you to look at the map, you never do. Without the map, your drive may be long, drawn out, and could become unbearable in time. On this road, you definitely will arrive at some destination, but without taking the time to look at the map, you will not know if it is the right road or the right destination.

It may seem as though looking at your map interferes with the journey, but, in fact, it is a major part of the journey. It will get you from where you are at this moment to where you really want to be.

In the above analogy, the drive is your journey through life. The road is the path to your purpose. You are the vehicle, and the map is the *seventh secret* in the art of *Letting Go of Stuff*® which is the following:

Create a plan of action.

This is known also as planned change (Cummings and Worley, 2001).

What Is Action?
Action is an important ingredient for letting go. Without action, the previous six secrets and the exercises related to them merely become intellectual

activities. Beginning the implementation of the seven secrets does not make sense unless you actively integrate all of them into your daily life while believing what you are doing is going to lead to the outcome you desire.

You will not be able to integrate the secrets into your daily life unless you consciously plan and execute the plan. The planning process requires taking action. From that action, you will get energy, and from the energy, you will create your desired outcome.

From my experiences and research, I have discovered three types of action that produce three effects. With no order of priority they are negative action, positive or desirable action, and neutral action. The consequences of each of these three actions are distinct.

Negative action produces suffering and pain. Positive or desirable action produces joy and varying states of happiness. Neutral action has a zero effect on our feelings, neither negative nor positive. We also have mental and physical action. Mental action requires no physical involvement at all but has chemical effects in our body. Physical action includes the body plus our verbal action. Verbal action includes internal conversation and what we say out loud to others.

Looking at action from this perspective allows us to examine it from three distinct modes—that of the mind, the body, and the speech. Each is distinct, yet each is a part of the whole, meaning that what you say and think are connected to what you do. Being able to break action down into simple components allows you to manage better and determine the outcomes of your actions.

We also can break a single action down into three stages of an act. There is the beginning, the execution, and the completion of a single act (Dalai Lama, 1997).

The beginning is defined as that which motivated the action. The intent for the action is what will create the need for action. Motivation and confidence create commitment. If one is highly motivated and confident, the person will be committed to creating a single act, followed by other acts. The next stage is the execution, which is the actual carrying out of the action. Performing the act is the execution. The third stage is the completion. The culmination of beginning and executing will create an opportunity for completion, which is the final outcome of the entire three-stage process.

In order for the three stages to be complete, there must be consistency through the entire act. The power of each stage of a single act is based on the intensity of the motivation and the execution. Weak motivation will result in the incompletion of all three stages of action. However, a strong motivation, followed by strong execution, will result in a strong completion.

A plan for action to let go of stuff only will be as successful as your level of motivation and execution. If you are highly motivated to execute your plan, then your execution will be successful, resulting in the stuff-free life you have planned to live. On the other hand, if you are only somewhat motivated, then your execution will reflect your level of motivation, and you will not have the outcome you planned.

When you take action, you should have faith in that action, and it should always be positive. Positive action means harm will come neither to you, nor anyone else by what you do.

Surviving in Crisis Mode

The process of letting go is like taking a journey to the center of your being. For many, this journey will be filled with excitement; for others it may be filled with trepidation and some anxiety. For the latter group it is important to remember sometimes we create stuff in an effort to keep us stuck in the same place. This is what I refer to as *surviving in crisis*. This mode describes what happens when we unconsciously resist making some kind of significant change in our lives by creating a crisis or some drama to shift the focus away from the goal. Whatever you do, do not let the *surviving-in-crisis* mode interfere with the execution of your plan.

Og Mandino is credited with saying, *Understand that all of us will live with crisis all throughout our lives. All of us are either approaching a crisis, in a crisis, or recovering from a crisis, and no one is immune.* We all must deal with crises. Please be careful not to let a crisis become your excuse for not accomplishing your goals.

Because the rest of this chapter is dedicated to exercises and information to assist in the creation of your plan for action to let go of stuff, here is a brief review. Remember stuff does not discriminate. It does not care where you live, if you are rich or poor, happy or sad, tall or short. Stuff thrives on your state of mind—your attitude, imagination, and internal conversation. Believe it or not, stuff will hang around as long as you let it. It will become comfortable, and make a place in your life, if you choose to allow it.

Letting Go of Stuff® is about making choices. These choices determine how well you deal with the vicissitudes of life. Where you are right now in your life at this very moment, you are here because of the choices you made. If you want a different outcome for your life, then you must choose to change. Also, remember once you make a choice to let go, you will go through changes.

You take your stuff with you into every situation and interaction. I often meet people who say they want to change from here (current state) to there (future state), and I usually let them know "here" is not going to be any better than "there," because when you get "there," you still will have the same tools as you did when you left "here." You have to use different tools when you go from "here" to "there" in order to achieve different results. You should use tools like the Self Managing Grid® and the secrets for *Letting Go of Stuff*® to help you to make make long-lasting, inside-out changes as you go from here to there.

The Components of Your *Letting Go of Stuff*® Action Plan

The action necessary to implement this plan requires the use of the information generated from the exercises in all the previous chapters of this book. The exercises you experienced throughout this book are designed to prepare you for this chapter. The following are the components for your *Letting Go of Stuff*® action plan.

- Chapter 2 - Work through the list of stressors.
- Chapter 2 - Turn your dream into a realistic goal.
- Chapter 3 - Forgive and love yourself and others.
- Chapter 4 - Read your *BE Statements* every day and night, and believe in them.
- Apply the 7 secrets over and over again in your life.
- Share the 7 secrets to *Letting Go of Stuff*® with others.
- Celebrate your journey and every goal you complete.
- Develop a relationship with God, Creator, Universal Power, or whatever name you use to describe a greater life source.
- Celebrate *Letting Go of Stuff*® every day.

The Power of Writing Your Action Plan

Writing your action plan is a big part of the success equation for *Letting Go of Stuff*.® It is powerful and therapeutic. According to an article published in the April 14, 1999, edition of the *Journal of the American Medical Association* (*JAMA*), people with asthma or rheumatoid arthritis who write about the most stressful experiences in their lives experience a reduction in symptoms. After studying 112 patients, researchers found that patients with mild to moderately severe asthma or rheumatoid arthritis who wrote about traumatic life experiences had clinically relevant changes in health status at four months compared to those in the control group. The researchers wrote that a growing amount of literature suggests addressing patients' psychological needs by having them write about their situation produces psychological and physical health benefits.

In the same issue of *JAMA*, Dr. David Spiegel of Stanford University wrote in his editorial, "Ventilation of negative emotion, even just to an unknown reader, seems to have helped these patients acknowledge, bear, and put into perspective their distress."

Writing goals and dreams down does make a big difference. The written creation of a plan for action is key. *Are you ready?*

EXERCISE 9-1
DEALING WITH THE "FIVE THINGS" IN CHAPTER 2

What about the things you listed in Exercise 2-1? Remember it dealt with the items that either stress you out, bother you on an ongoing basis, or you are constantly worried about? I bet you thought I had forgotten about that stuff. *No way!* These next steps will assist you in removing, or greatly reducing, the impact of that stuff in your life. Transfer the items from Chapter 2 to the section below:

ITEMS (1-5)	RATING (1-5)	CONTROL Yes	No
1.			
2.			
3.			
4.			
5.			

Rate each of these items above on a scale of 1 to 5, with 1 representing very little stress and worry and 5 representing the highest stress and worry.

Now transfer (by writing) the item with the lowest rating into the box below:

LOWEST RATED ITEM

The reason for focusing on the item that has the least impact is that it allows you to go through the process with fewer challenges. When you get to the more intense items on your list, you will need to have experienced some successes.

Below, list three specific, positive actions you will take to remove or reduce the impact of the item listed above. Also, list the dates you will complete each action.

SPECIFIC ACTION TO REDUCE/REMOVE IMPACT	DATE
1.	
2.	
3.	

Make sure you actually complete each of these specific actions. Once you have accomplished each task, go to the next prioritized item on the original list of five things that stress you out and repeat this exercise.

After you have done everything you can to influence positively each of the five things listed in Chapter 2, literally cross them off the list to let them go. Although it could take some time to complete this process, once you are finished, you definitely will feel more free and have more energy to pursue more rewarding activities.

The Two Important Questions

Every time you are confronted by a person or situation you believe causes you to get upset, feel frustrated, feel guilty, or whatever, there are two questions to ask yourself. The answers to these two questions will help you to manage those feelings effectively and determine the kind of action you should take. The two questions deal with the issue of control and focus. Edward T. Hall (1981) wrote, ...*many people's sense of worth is directly related to the number of situations in which they are in control, which means that many people have problems with their self-image because they are clearly in control of so little* (p. 6).

One key focus of this book is to teach **Letting Go of Stuff,**® and in the process allow one's self worth to be re-discovered from within, rather than from without. Realizing that only you can truly control your level of self-worth and self-esteem is key to the ongoing successful application of the techniques in this book.

Control

When you can control something fully, you can determine the outcome. If you could control how your boss talks to you and gives you assignments, you never would become upset with him or her. If you could control the deadlines for various reports due at work, you would not get stressed out because you would make sure you always met the deadlines. If you could control the company for which you work, you never would lay yourself off or anyone else for that matter. If you could control whether or not a customer liked a particular product, you would be able to sell to them all the time.

The fact of the matter is you cannot control these situations. Actually, there is very little we have full control over in this world, except how we act, what we do to move forward, and how we treat ourselves and others along the way.

EXERCISE 9-2
QUESTION 1 OF THE TWO IMPORTANT QUESTIONS

First, read over each of the "five things" from Exercise 9-1. After you read each, ask yourself the first of the two most important questions for letting go.

1. Can I control each of the items I listed?

If you listed a person, remember, you can not control other people, even if it is your own children or significant other. If you wrote down a specific action you seem to take in certain situations, it is within your control to change the action. No one else controls your actions, thoughts, and behaviors but you.

If you look to the right of your responses in exercise 9-1, you will see a column labeled "Control." If the answer to question one is "Yes, I can control this...," check "Yes." If the answer is "No, I cannot control this ...," then check "No."

Read over the dream goal you wrote in Exercise 2-1, and ask yourself the second question:

2. What does my dream goal have to do with these five things?

Usually the answer is **NOTHING!** The five things that constantly worry and stress you might interfere with the accomplishment of your goal, but they usually are not the same as your goal. Now answer this question:

2a. If you were to spend the same amount of time working on your dream as you do dealing with those five things, what would happen?

Enter your response in the box below:

Movement - Turning Dreams into Specific Goals

Walt Disney is credited with having said, *A goal is a dream with a deadline.* A goal also must be specific, clear, pertinent to your purpose, and measurable. You will discover that as long as you are pursuing a worthy goal, you always will have a feeling of worth and purpose. What you will not do is focus on other stuff that has nothing to do with the pursuance of that worthy goal. You also will discover that in the larger scheme of things, the other stuff does not matter anyway. It is a waste of your precious time and energy to focus on stuff that interferes with your dreams/goals. Once focusing only on your dream/goal is part of your unconscious behavior, you will be able truly to let go of stuff and move toward your dream/goal. Moreover, you will be able to do it on purpose.

There are three types of goals:
1. The goals you create to make personal dreams come true;
2. The goals that are given to you by someone else to make their personal dreams come true; and
3. The goals that do not belong to you, but that you end up unknowingly accomplishing for someone else.

The focus in this book is on the first type of goal. We often get caught up, however, in the second and third types of goals without even realizing it. This is why it is important to have a plan to which you can refer when you feel you have gotten off track.

I challenge you to begin focusing your energy and effort toward making the dream you wrote earlier a reality and to let go of the five items you listed in Chapter 2 and Exercise 9-1. You should take some small action every day to move you toward accomplishing your dream goal. This will get you started on the path to moving forward with your life.

Exercise 9-3
Turning Dreams into Reality

Transfer your dream from Exercise 2-1 (Chapter 2) into the box below:

┌───┐
│   │
│   │
│   │
│   │
└───┘

Ultimate Life Dream Goal
The next step is to brainstorm a list of things you must do to make this dream goal happen. Make sure the items on your list are specific, measurable, and reasonable. Do not be afraid to challenge yourself to step outside your comfort zone. This is key to *Letting Go of Stuff*.®

To Do List	Ranking	Completion Date

Now you must prioritize the items on your list, marking the first task as "1," the second as "2," and so on. The next step is for you to enter completion dates next to each item. These dates are deadlines for when you will complete each item. It may take you one, two, or maybe five years or more to accomplish each of the items on your list; it is up to you. Once every task on the above list is accomplished, you will have realized the accomplishment of the dream. Use the same process for the next dream, and the next, and so on. Whatever you do, never stop dreaming.

Once you have completed your plan and begin its execution, the fun and excitement can really begin. Knowing you are creating and designing your personal path to success, and that you have complete earthly control over your destiny, will put you pretty close to the feeling of true freedom.

There is a unique connection between all aspects of your life, just like your Creator has made connections between your body and the universe. Your body is made up of millions of various components, all designed to allow you to breathe, love, and live. Each component is linked to a greater purpose. Your tears taste just like the ocean; your cells look just like the galaxies of stars; your blood is filled with microorganisms just like the ocean and the rain. We are all infinitely connected, whether we like it or not.

In the same way you are linked to the universe, personal goals are the linking mechanism that keep you moving forward toward your purpose. Goals can help to create action; action creates energy; and energy is part of what is required for you to accomplish goals.

It is like one big chain linked together by a major component—*your purpose.*

One Final Challenge – The Future Is Now

Once you have made significant changes by *Letting Go of Stuff,*® you should repeat the process of applying the *Seven Secrets* over and over again. This repetition will create a refreezing effect (Lewin, 1948) of this new current state. Only through the repetition of the activities, exercises, and execution of your *Letting Go of Stuff*® plan will you create this new state of being. Basically, you are implementing a positive, planned change in your life using the *Letting Go of Stuff*® process. Planned change is good. It is being the best, giving your best, and doing your best—*on purpose.*

Now that you know where to put your energy, where to focus your efforts, and how to begin to choose to let go of the stuff that interferes with moving forward, I challenge you to use this book as a catalyst to begin to redesign your life. In order for you to be crowned with the life you want, you must be willing to fight for it, and you must finish the entire process as though it were your assignment. Also, you must keep the faith in your ability to redesign your life and remember Robert Schuller's words, "Today's decisions are tomorrow's reality."

Your destiny is in your hands. Creating the life you want is only, and always, up to you. Once you have begun truly to design your life, you can begin to help others by sharing the *Letting Go of Stuff*® process.

This book provides you with the information and methods to begin to get more focused on living life to the fullest. After all, isn't life about learning, loving life, and sharing those lessons and love with others?

Good luck with your endeavors, and don't forget long-lasting change only happens when the change is made from the inside out.

REFERENCES

Adams, Ramona S. (1980). *Letting Go: Un-complicating Your Life*. Los Altos, CA: Science & Behavior Books, Inc.

Anderson, Dean, Anderson, Linda A. (2001). *Beyond Change Management: Advanced Strategies For Today's Transformational Leaders*. San Francisco, CA: Josey-Bass/Pfeiffer.

Bridges, William (1980). *Transitions-Making Sense Of Life's Changes: Strategies For Coping With The Difficult, Painful, And Confusing Times In Your Life*. Boulder, CO: Perseus Book Publishing, LLC.

Browder, Anthony T. (1992). *Nile Valley Contributions To Civilization*. Washington, DC: Institute of Karmic Guidance

Cady, Emile H. (1903). *Lessons In Truth*. Unity Village, MO: Unity School of Christianity.

Chopra, Deepak (1993). *Ageless Body, Timeless Mind: The Quantum Alternative To Growing Old* (book on cassette). New York, NY: Random House.

Covey, Steven R. (1990). *Seven Habits Of Highly Successful People*. New York: Free Press.

Cummings, Thomas G. and Worley, Christopher G. (2001). *Organization Development And Change. (7th ed.)*. Cincinnati, OH: South Western College Publishing.

DeBoard Robert (1978). *The Psychoanalysis Of Organizations: A Psychoanalytic Approach To Behaviour In Groups And Organizations*. London: Routledge.

Foundation for Inner Peace (1996). *A Course In Miracles*. New York, NY: Penguin Books.

Grant, Michael (1995). *Beyond Blame: Race Relations For The Twenty-First Century*. Nashville, TN: Smithson-Berry Publishing.

Hall, Edward T. (1981). *Beyond Culture*. New York, NY: Bantam Doubleday.

Hammond, Sue Annis (1998). *The Thin Book Of Appreciative Inquiry*. Plano, TX: Thin Book Publishing Co. House.

Hanna, David P. (1988). *Designing Organizations For High Performance*. Reading, MA: Addison-Welsley.

Hay, Louise (1984). *You Can Heal Your Life*. Carlsbad, CA: Hay House.

International Bible Society (1984). *The Holy Bilble: New International Version*. Grand Rapids, MI: The Zondervan Corporation.

Johnson, Darren L. (2001). *The InsideOut Learning Model: An Organizational Diagnostic Tool*. Nashville, TN: InsideOut Learning, Inc.

Johnson, Darren L. (1998). *The Art Of Letting Go Of Stuff* (Revised Edition CD audio 2004). Nashville, TN: InsideOut Learning, Inc.

Johnson, Darren L. (1995). *Letting Go Of Stuff: Powerful Secrets To Simplify Your Life* (cassette). Nashville, TN: InsideOut Learning, Inc.

Kimbro, Dennis (1998). *What Makes The Great Great: Strategies For Extraordinary Achievement*. New York: Main Street Books.

Lama, Dalai (1997). *The Four Noble Truths*. Hammersmith, London: Thornsons.

Lewin, Kurt (1948). *Resolving Social Conflicts And Field Theory In Social Science* (1st ed.). New York, NY: Harper and Row.

Mackay, Harvey (2000). *Pushing The Envelope All The Way To The Top*. New York: Ballantine Books.

Merriam-Webster (1988). *Webster's Ninth New Collegiate Dictionary*. Springfield, MA: Merriam-Webster, Inc.

NLP Comprehensive (1994). *NLP: The New Technology Of Achievement*. New York, NY: William Morrow and Co., Inc.

Nadler, David A. and Tushman, Michael (1977). *Perspectives On Behavior In Organizations: A Diagnostic Model For Organization Behavior.* New York, NY: McGraw-Hill.

Nevis, Edwin C. (1987). *Organizational Consulting: A Gestalt Approach*. Cambridge, MA: GIC Press.

Nightengale, Earl (1991). *Lead The Field* [book on cassette]. Niles, IL: Nightingale Conant, Inc.

Padus, Emrika (1986). *The Complete Guide To Your Emotions And Your Health: New Dimensions In Mind/Body Healing.* Emmaus, PA: Rodale.

Rogers, Carl R. (1961). *On Becoming A Person: A Therapist's View Of Psychotherapy.* Boston, MA: Houghton Mifflin.

Schuller, Robert H. (1983). *Tough Times Never Last, But Tough People Do.* New York: Bantam Dell Publishing Group.

Schuller, Robert H. (1966). *The Inspirational Writings Of Robert H. Schuller.* New York, NY: Inspirational Press.

Segal, Morley (1997). *Points Of Influence: A Guide To Using Personality Theory At Work.* San Francisco, CA: Jossey-Bass, Inc.

Smyth, Joshua; Stone, Arthur A; Hurewitz, Adam; and Kaell, Alan (April 14, 1999). *"Effects Of Writing About Stressful Experiences On Symptom Reduction In Patients With Asthma Or Rheumatoid Arthritis: A Randomized Trial"* in Journal of American Medical Association (*JAMA*). 281:1304-1309.

Spiegel, David (April 14, 1999). *Healing Words: Emotional Expression And Disease Outcome* in Journal of American Medical Association (JAMA). 281:1328-1329.

Ziglar, Zig (1981). *See You At The Top.* Dallas, TX: Pelican Publishing Company.

NOTES

EMPOWERMENT IS BUT A WORD,
SOMETHING YOU THOUGHT ABOUT; SOMETHING YOU'VE HEARD.
NOW HERE IS SOMETHING TO KNOW,
TO BECOME EMPOWERED, YOU MUST LEARN TO LET GO.
ALTHOUGH, IN THE BEGINNING, YOU MAY NOT LIKE THE RIDE,
IT IS IMPORTANT THAT YOU START ON THE INSIDE.
ALONG THE WAY STUFF WILL HAPPEN
AND YOU MAY NOT KNOW WHAT IT ALL MEANS,
BUT KEEP THE FAITH AND REMEMBER,
SELF EMPOWERMENT IS ONE KEY TO FULFILLING YOUR DREAMS.

— DARREN L. JOHNSON

I AM WORKING TOWARD A TIME
WHEN EVERYTHING GIVES ME JOY.
— MAYA ANGELOU

To learn more about the other products and services
offered by Darren L. Johnson, including his seminars
and one-on-one personal development coaching,
visit http://www.LettingGoOfStuff.com.

About the Author

Darren L. Johnson, MSOD is an organization development consultant and personal coach on letting go. Having earned a Masters of Science in Organization Development (MSOD) from American University (AU/NTL), his specific areas of expertise are in team development, diversity, total system redesign, and personal one-on-one coaching.

With more than 25 years of combined managing, consulting, coaching, and speaking experience, Darren is a contributing author of *101 Great Ways to Improve Your Life* compiled by David Riklan. His client list includes more than 150 corporations and individuals. As a personal development coach, Darren has assisted athletes, celebrities, and others in effectively applying the secrets to *Letting Go of Stuff.*®

Darren has combined the techniques in this book with his true personal life stories, timeless philosophies, and the research and theory of theorists like Kurt Lewin, Carl Rogers, and Fritz and Laura Perls. The concepts and theories in this book are practical and have changed his life tremendously.

Known as the "Letting Go Pro," he created the *Letting Go of Stuff*® series, which includes a book, CD audio program, seminars, and a signature speech titled the same. He also offers free advice on his website. To learn more about *Letting Go of Stuff,*® visit http://www.LettfingGoOfStuff.com.

Business Week

Reinventing

Your

Career

McGraw-Hill, Inc.

New York   San Francisco   Washington, D.C.   Auckland   Bogotá
Caracas   Lisbon   London   Madrid   Mexico City   Milan
Montreal   New Delhi   San Juan   Singapore   Sydney   Tokyo   Toronto

another book from Affinity Communications Corporation

ISBN 0-07-009434-9

This book is printed on recycled, acid-free paper containing a minimum of 50% recycled, de-inked fiber.

Developed for McGraw-Hill by Affinity Communications Corp., 144 N. Robertson Blvd., Suite 103, Los Angeles, CA 90048

Designer: Janet Brandt
Developmental Editor: Melinda Gordon
Production Editor: Mari Florence
Copy Editor: Nancy McKinley
Front Cover Art: David Moyers
Back Cover Photograph: PhotoDisk
Photo Credits: page 138

Table of Contents

Introduction

The rules of success have changed. For people who don't practice the new rules and apply new thinking, work in the 1990s can be frustrating and disappointing. For people who do, however, work can be much more positive and rewarding than ever before.

Think back just a few decades. People often worked for one or two companies, and then retired on full pensions. This employment pattern was the norm; it's what people expected. But today, the average "up and comer" may change jobs a dozen times or may not have a traditional job at all. Now more than ever before, people are creating their own opportunities, crafting their own futures, and doing exactly what they want to do.

Part of this change stems from a new generation of individuals who are motivated in their careers, and also choose active family roles. Thus, necessarily, the careers of today have to include lifestyle components that were far less important when some had "careers" and others merely "held jobs."

Thus, there are two keys to success in the evolving world of work: one is understanding the new landscape; the other is knowing what is appropriate to best meet your individual needs. Only by integrating these two sometimes conflicting imperatives can you set your own optimum course toward success. We at *BusinessWeek* have created *Reinventing Your Career* with precisely this goal to help businesspeople at all stages of their career work themselves through this process.

Chapter 1 details five basic career-path options available to those with savvy and ability. Of course, any number of combinations of these paths exists in practice.

The next two chapters will enable you to focus on your own personal situation. Chapter 2 provides a career analysis tool to aid you in evaluating the current state of your career. Chapter 3 helps you identify personal preferences, strengths and weaknesses, preferred work environments, specific goals, mind-sets, unique characteristics, and family needs.

In chapter 4, we explore basic success principles and skill requirements related to attitude, decision making, health, interpersonal communication, and other crucial factors.

We put it all together in chapter 5, developing a personal strategic action plan for your career. We think you'll find this ongoing process flexible and dynamic.

You'll learn how to package and promote yourself in chapter 6. Whether you're applying for an executive position, seeking to build your career as an expert, or searching out investor funding for a new venture, you'll learn to market yourself as a desirable commodity.

With all of the new opportunities you've created for yourself throughout the first six chapters, you will need to review chapter 7 to learn how best to represent your compensatory and legal interests.

Finally, in chapter 8 we look ahead to the new millennium to consider how predicted changes over the next ten years will affect your career planning.

We believe this book will change your life. Applying its principles will enable you to progress as far and as happily as you can. Above all, it will help you get to where you *want* to go.

Chapter 1

Considering Your Career Possibilities

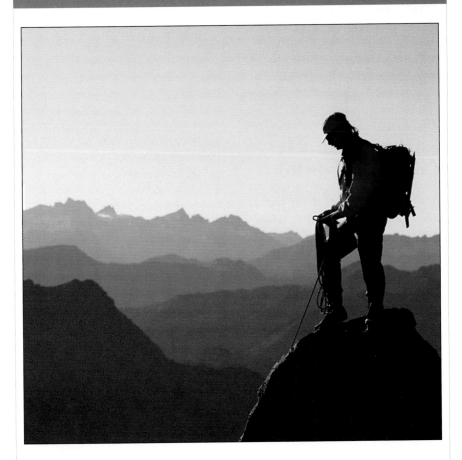

Recent economic shifts have transformed the world of work. Like a series of earthquakes, they have devastated entire industries. But, even more rapidly, these shifts have created new industries, jobs, and career paths. The first step to reinventing your career is to take note of the new landscape.

People's attitudes toward work have also dramatically changed. No longer do we feel forced to move whenever and wherever our employers ordain. No longer are we terrified of the "stigma" of being fired. No longer are we bound (or in many cases, enslaved) to our jobs. Today we are relatively free to choose our careers so that they mesh comfortably with our individualized, unique lifestyles.

In today's world of expanding options, you can craft a career that satisfies both your work needs and your personal desires. Of course, great success still requires great effort and great ability. But if you plan your career carefully, the effort can be expended on things you enjoy, and the skills needed for your career can be arranged to coincide precisely with your own strengths.

This chapter categorizes the major career paths shaped by today's trends, describing the personal characteristics and skills each path requires. It's designed to enable you to achieve the ultimate: career success coupled with personal satisfaction and quality of life.

Specifically, we begin by detailing five distinct career possibilities. Each is a discrete and full career path in its own right. However, most people will achieve optimal personal and professional success by combining several paths into a customized career plan uniquely appropriate to themselves. Let's examine each career path in detail.

Career Path #1: Climbing Up the Corporate Ladder

While working up through the layers of a large company is an old idea, the rules of what it takes to succeed have changed drastically. Just twenty years ago, college graduates would become new hires with the promise of steady, lifelong promotion. The old corporate code of contact went largely as follows: remain loyal to your employer; follow the corporate "procedure book"; work hard and responsibly; take on assignments without comment or complaint; and participate in company-approved social activities. The implication was that by simply adhering to this code, employees would be well rewarded,

regularly promoted *and never fired!* There are many prime examples of successful corporate climbers. George Weissman became president of Philip Morris in 1961 and Ed Harness became president of Procter & Gamble in 1974 largely because each man had spent many hardworking years on the job, proving, above all, their total loyalty to their respective corporations.

While a solid work ethic is still highly regarded, today a new attitude has emerged. Key corporate executives who make it to the top still have to prove themselves, as in the past. But they no longer have to demonstrate any great level of corporate loyalty. "Downsizing" has become so common that being fired is no longer a problem for future employment. In fact, switching jobs is often considered the norm. And the determination to take control of your corporate destiny rather than "doing what you're told" is viewed as a sign of competence.

On the other hand, modern career executives must possess some abilities that earlier generations did not much need. These days, many large corporations place a premium on executives who are flexible, innovative, and strongly motivated by challenge. Unlike their predecessors, who may have become blocked at a middle management level, today's executives cannot relax, "do a good

Executives who make it to the top have proven themselves in the corporate environment.

job," and wait for retirement. They must continually prove themselves indispensable within the context of a constantly shifting and expanding set of corporate standards. As we will discuss later, the up-the-ladder career path remains viable but requires a whole new set of skills and approaches.

Career Path #2: Creating Enterprises

The second new career path is to become one of a new breed of entrepreneurs. Past generations of entrepreneurs had the luxury of focusing on their trading and selling skills. As "middlemen," they bought groceries, hardware or some other staple and marked it up before selling it to their customer. Every other aspect of the business— manufacturing, technical innovation, financial manipulation, long-term economic forecasting, or legal advice— was a function they purchased from experts. Bottom line: Nothing was permitted to take their time away from the all-important task of making profits.

As a new entrepreneur, you are still choosing a career that requires traditional selling skills. But in order to stay viable in today's business environment, "salesperson" is but one aspect of the successful entrepreneurial persona. New entrepreneurs must possess the capacity to simultaneously see the big and small picture. They must demonstrate the detail-oriented capability it takes to run a business, along with the vision and creativity it takes to keep their business ahead of the pack. Microsoft's Bill Gates is a prime example of a successful new entrepreneur.

Of course, we're not suggesting that the great entrepreneurs of yore— men like Henry Ford, Henry Luce, or Henry Huntington—lacked vision. Quite the contrary. Yet they wouldn't have viewed entrepreneurialism as a career path to be studied, carefully planned, and logically pursued in and of itself. Although many such men earned MBAs, the new business school curricula has experienced a shift in emphasis. Today's MBA candidates learn to master the techniques of calculated risk taking, write business plans, forge relationships with investors, negotiate with suppliers, understand shifting markets, raise funds in both standard and creative ways, and plan how to exit from their businesses (plans usually best laid at the time of the business start-up).

Success for entrepreneurs remains in building their own ships and watching them sail. They still have to be energetic, optimistic, cunning, innovative, and as risk-averse as circumstances permit. But today's entrepreneurs are well-advised to plan their careers far more thoroughly and carefully than was necessary in the past. "Seat of the pants" intuition still plays a vital role, but a solid education in entrepreneurialism coupled with a carefully designed career plan, if not essential, is exceedingly helpful.

Career Path #3: Achieving Results

The achievers comprise a category of businesspeople whose career success depends exclusively on results. Until recently, only those on commission really fell into this category: If insurance, real estate, or Fuller Brush salespeople didn't sell, they didn't earn. These jobs still exist and are still judged by the same criterion. However, the achiever's sights have been vastly expand-ed. In today's world of business, many people live by results alone—not by management skills, team building, entrepreneurial venture creation, or any other form of performance competence. They include investors (whether running gigantic mutual funds or investing their personal fortunes); merger and acquisition experts; barter and countertrade facilitators; movie producers and music impresarios (both of whom are always only as good as their latest hit); direct mailers and TV pitchmen and women (whose results are virtually instantaneous); high-tech "inventors" of all sorts; contigency-fee lawyers; savings consultants who are paid a percentage of what they save; and, as previously mentioned, all the traditional commission salespeople, whether they're selling Mary Kay cosmetics to office workers or billion-dollar oil refineries to Arab royalty.

This achievement path to career success is, naturally, related in many ways to success in any career path. Its fundamental difference, however, is that it relies solely on results, which are often very sophisticated and require long-term planning to be successfully implemented. Any high degree of expertise in any skills other than those needed to achieve the results themselves is generally unnecessary, since achievers typically aren't interested in climbing the corporate ladder. They don't have time for total quality management or company politics. They feel they were put on earth to do one thing at a time and get visible results. Like Tarzan swinging from vine to vine, they move from one challenge to the next, getting paid for each success on the upscale and losing money with every failure on the down. To the achiever, everything else is viewed as an extraneous "clutter."

Career Path #4: Becoming an Expert

The fourth career possibility is the new world of expertise. In the "old" days until about ten years ago, such professionals as doctors and lawyers represented the main category of so-called "experts." Some tax experts, actuaries,

and management consultants also fell into this expertise-oriented classification. But most of the employees of the large consulting firms were not truly experts any more than most accountants were. They were simply temporary employees called in to do a job for which permanent management didn't have time. Success meant climbing the corporate ladder of the consulting or accounting firm for whom they worked, often followed by a move to the corporate ladder of one of their clients. Not infrequently, of course, "consultant" was just another way of saying "unemployed."

Today, an entirely new breed of expert exists in almost every area of modern industry. We see men and women in all fields who are in demand entirely because of what they know. They may or may not be permanent employees of a large corporation, but even if they are, they have no interest in being promoted up a ladder of any sort. Nor are they primarily motivated by the results of their expertise. Unlike the achievers, they devote themselves to the area of their expertise for its own sake. Experts' loyalty lies not primarily toward the client but toward their discipline and the other experts in it. People with expertise in such diverse areas as finance, management information systems, biotechnology, programming, editing, compensation, agricultural techniques, aerospace engineering, and organizational communication are today's experts as are, of course, doctors, lawyers, actuaries, and tax experts. The more arcane their specialties, the more their services are sought after.

Of course, experts have always existed. What is different today is that expertise can be a career path characterized by knowledge alone and unaffected by any other corporate hierarchical considerations. The route to the top—in other words, becoming a sought-after "expert"—involves building a network of people who can support your knowledge, participating in constant educational upgrading, and

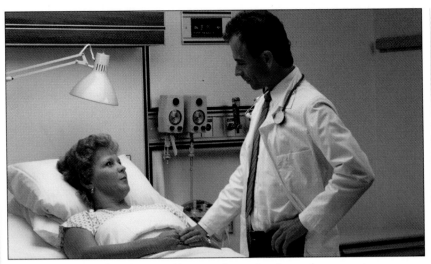

Today's experts range from doctors and lawyers to financial analysts and computer programmers.

building a reputation for expertise among your peer group.

A subcategory of expert is the management consultant whose expertise is "management" itself. Peter Drucker, John Naisbitt, Michael Hammer, and James Champy and their ilk earn huge consulting fees because of their reputation as experts in their fields. As such, they're different from those "consultants," mentioned above, who are re-tained as sequential employees to temporarily fill employee gaps that have sprung up as a result of either too vigorous or too sudden downsizing. "Temp" employment (whether at the consultant or the secretarial level) is only a long-term career if it is based on expertise. Although the ranks of full-time temps have experienced a dramatic upsurge in recent years, the nature of temporary assignments makes it difficult for these employees to follow a distinct career path.

Career Path #5: Facilitating Others

The fifth new career path involves the brokering of power, trust, and information. Such facilitators make a profit by

bringing together people who need each other's services, and by spreading information to people who can benefit from it. In a world filled with so many career options—some interlocking, others intersecting, still others separate but synergistic—people need a way to find each other and to gather data. Often people within the same conglomerate don't interact with each other or are totally unaware of each other's existence. Sometimes, different groups within a single company don't realize the beneficial impact that the exchange of their knowledge could generate. The facilitator is able to envision productive and beneficial interdepartmental and corporate unions—and possesses the skills, contacts and resources to bring these alliances about.

The huge mass of information available today often appears to breed ignorance rather than increase knowledge and awareness. From the morass of information and people, a new careerist has emerged: the person who knows and is trusted by virtually "everyone," the person who can quickly and reliably discover the facts about "everything."

Simply put, these information brokers maintain contacts, including people with needs and people with specific skills. They have access to data and know how to simplify it. Thus, they can make introductions, set up teams, and provide answers.

Brokers exist in almost every industry. They may work as executive recruiters, investment bankers, professional corporate directors, literary and show business agents, and "finders" of all sorts. At a lower job level, they may be librarians or computer experts. Some consultants are information brokers, as are some lawyers and even some salespeople. Indeed, many careers involve a large component of brokering. But a large number of successful people facilitate others through brokering—as a career in and of itself.

Brokers have to be trustworthy and politically astute. Because it's essential that they thrive in social situations, they should genuinely like people and be able to "work a room" with ease.

These, then, are the five basic career paths from a general perspective. From this overview, you probably already have some idea about which path—or set of paths—is right for you. Below we will explore each path in more detail and provide real-life scenarios in today's business world. As you read further, try to mentally keep your options open in context with the current state of your career, your personal preferences, and your skills and abilities.

Up the Corporate Ladder: Rising Through the Hierarchy

The dreams of many people working their way "up the ladder"—from entry-level to senior executive—are still very much alive despite changes in the economy. A recent poll of college students revealed that most still want their careers to be at a large company. Yet many who have actually worked for a large company are less optimistic about

"The Dream." Many start out at the bottom and tread water there indefinitely. Others, promoted once or twice, are still fifteen rungs down from the top of the corporate ladder.

It is possible, however, for today's corporate careers to be as lucrative and fulfilling as those of past decades. So what does it take to succeed in today's large firms? Research reveals that there are specific skills and concrete strategies you can use on this career path—if you decide that being a corporate stalwart is for you.

Bringing Something to the Table

The first skill involves your ability to add value in a variety of situations. Woody Allen's rule—"That 85 percent of success is just showing up"—doesn't work anymore. Today's executives can't just balance their budgets and expect to advance. In today's climate of merger-mania, they'd be lucky simply to survive. Consider Harry Mitchell's situation.

Harry was a promising young manager for a $200-million publisher in New York. Onlookers could see that he was a "player" to take seriously. Conscientious, dedicated, competent. He was all that and more.

But, like many others, Harry soon learned that there are many intangibles in climbing the next rung on the ladder. He eventually plateaued and a few years later resigned, feeling abandoned and disgraced. "I was loyal. I sacrificed. I gave them 60 hours a week! And for what?! I could've just stuck around like the other lifers, but it just wasn't worth it to me."

Amazingly, as Harry realized, even the progress he achieved over the years was incapable of sustaining his happiness. That's because he measured his success against continuous advancement. He wasn't able to cope with his failed expectations, so he packed up his family and withdrew to

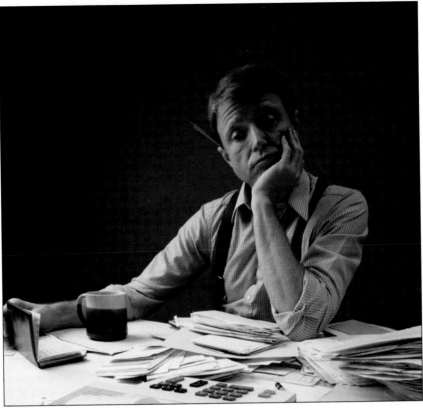

Modern managers must be gifted nonlinear thinkers.

a small Midwestern town. A broken man, he got a job at a local bookstore and forsook the corporate rat race. Harry didn't understand that you can't profess "unconditional love" and unwavering support to your company anymore, because the company won't love you back.

Today's successful executives view each moment as a chance to add value to their companies. In every meeting, while reading every report, in sending every E-mail message, in examining every budget item, they seek to make the company better, stronger, and more competitive.

The new way of conceptualizing a vital business requires a radical shift from a mindset like Harry's. Unlike the old model manager, in whom loyalty unquestionably preceded innovation and a rigid, uncompromising nature was consistently rewarded, new managers must be gifted nonlinear thinkers. They must possess the ability to strengthen their companies—and their own roles within them—by constantly seeing new opportunities and solutions all around them, rather than solely "upwards."

The executive landscape has changed dramatically. And though people who rock the boat may still be unpopular, their radical new thinking—with an eye toward the bottom line and a desire to make things better—has proven to generate success in the new climate.

Adding value often means challenging people who don't want you to succeed, who'd rather maintain the status quo, not only in the flow of business operations but in their attitudes toward the work itself. To succeed today, you need to add value and to master—with optimism—the next skill at hand.

Running for Office

Cynics say that executives are nothing but politicians who kiss babies, shake hands, and promise what no one can deliver. Today, even the word politics leaves a bad taste in many a mouth.

But, put simply, "politics" just refers to people. An executive, by definition, must be involved with people—both superiors and subordinates. The ability to effectively manage these relationships is the second trait of successful corporate stalwarts.

Being good at politics means knowing who is on your side and who would like to see you leave in disgrace. It means knowing who is "in" and who is "out," and how the picture is likely to change. And it means knowing what battles you should fight, which you can afford to lose, and which ones you absolutely have to win.

Evidence strongly suggests that being a good politician is both a science and an art. It's learned primarily from interacting with others and from reading about psychology and communication. Many people who lose their jobs in mergers, acquisitions, downsizings, and reengineerings were never really "in" at all. Their departure was inevitable. The merger or the reengineering was merely a catalyst.

Being able to utilize your inner voice—the voice of your intuition—is the key to political astuteness. Two psychologists, Myers and Briggs, studied the nature of personality and found that only certain people have a strong intuitive voice—perhaps as few as 25 percent of the population. Are you one of them? If so, surviving the political world of the big corporation will be much easier for you. Debra Chase used her intuition as a key to success in the corporate world.

Debra is a rising executive in Health Net, one of the largest publicly held managed-care companies in the country. When her firm's main competitor tried to acquire it, Debra quickly realized that her survival was tenuous.

Despite her success in managing 75 employees and her influence over a $100-million budget, she learned that her role in the organization was going to be divided between several directors and managers. Additionally, the new management had terminated nearly every major executive in her firm, eliminating several of her previous allies and information sources.

Debra's first move to salvage her position was to seek out advice from peers, subordinates, family, and executive coaches to determine her strategy and to realistically evaluate her chance for survival. Next she gathered additional data on the acquiring company, the key players, and, most specifically, her competition.

Debra reviewed and updated her written job description, emphasizing her department's progressive approach and its many accomplishments. She made sure key people in the acquiring organization understood that she was a results-oriented team player with compatible goals and values, and she made clear her commitment to the company's success and her crucial contribution to it.

As it turned out, the acquisition failed to materialize, but Debra had nonetheless developed some valuable skills that positioned her better within the corporate structure at Health Net.

Playing the political game well can be a life-or-death issue in your corporate career. And while some people enjoy "playing the game" of company politics, it's not a game to take lightly. One trait that corporate stalwarts share is their understanding of the sometimes dark and sinister nature of political games. Yet some people unwisely put playing politics ahead of adding value. They can become like bureaucrats in the old Soviet empire. Most of these people aren't respected and their positions soon vanish.

So what political traits should the ladder climbers possess? They must thoroughly understand the game, be strongly intuitive, and approach politics strategically. The successful executive knows how to play the game but sees politics as the means to adding value. Those executives who survive and

Maintain an active career strategy by keeping networks alive.

thrive don't think of the political game as an end in itself. Rather, adding value and being politically astute only make it easier to put the next trait to work.

Rethinking Career Plateauing

Today, people who decide to stick it out in the corporate world have to be flexible. A flexible individual is one who always plans but is willing to let events run their own course. Plans always include some room for bending, because the drive to the top often includes several "side trips." Your company may be acquired, your division may be reengineered, or your industry may be transformed or made redundant. Successful corporate climbers of the 1990s and beyond will look at these events not as tragedies, but as inevitable parts of life.

The shrewd career strategist keeps options open by networking with old friends, work peers, industry association members, and executive recruiters. For some, their entire career history may consist of advancing by changing companies every few years. Consider Jim Wilk's experience.

Since leaving college, Jim Wilk has always worked for top-rated Fortune companies like Allied Chemical, Johnson & Johnson, Bell Atlantic, Citicorp, and Health Systems International.

Working his way up from storeroom clerk, Jim quickly proved himself and made the most of new opportunities. When none were available, Jim demonstrated the uncanny ability to create his own possibilities, and it wasn't long before he was promoted to vice president at age 33.

In each position he filled, Jim provided unique contributions that not only made him invaluable to his company but also attracted the attention of industry onlookers and executive recruiters. Today, Jim is a senior vice president at

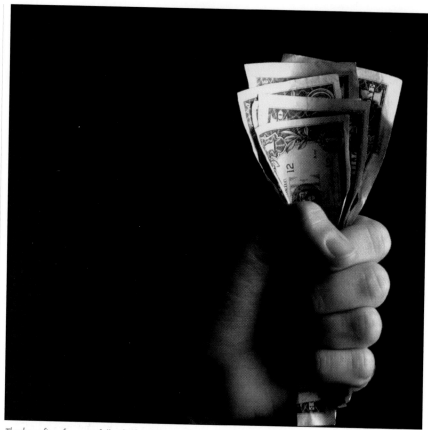

The benefits of successfully climbing the corporate ladder are many.

Health Systems International, a soon-to-be $3-billion company. Each of his career moves was well planned and orchestrated.

Since 1980, the downsizing model and its elimination of management layers have led many to conclude that their "salvation" lay in lateral moves to other positions compatible with their transferable skills. They temporarily forget about promotion and wait for new opportunities. In effect, they decided it was appropriate to be flexible.

It's an exaggeration to say that advancement opportunities are gone forever, as there are still plenty of chances for promotion. But considering the major changes in corporate structures over the past fifteen years, coupled with the anticipated changes over the next fifteen, there will be fewer and fewer openings to fill within your company's hierarchy. The people who do make it will need to possess tremendous flexi-

bility. They'll need to constantly learn new skills and keep up with the latest trends influencing their professional field. They'll need to adapt to changing environments, and always be looking for the next rung of the ladder. Corporate stalwarts possess a thirst for knowledge and bring that enthusiasm to their careers—whether they're researching on the Internet, catching up on the latest trade magazines, or checking in with old contacts.

So is being a corporate stalwart right for you? The perks of this "up-the-ladder" lifestyle are just as impressive as they've always been: prestige, high earnings, the feeling of being in control of a large enterprise. It takes someone who can add value, play the political game well, and remain flexible to acquire them. But the real question you have to ask yourself is, "Are today's corporations the best place for you to express your career?" The advantages can be considerable, but the downside includes politics, continual uncertainty, and often a feeling of powerlessness.

It's also becoming increasingly more difficult to balance a successful up-the-ladder career with family life. If you're unwilling to work long hours, travel continually, and always keep your skills a little more fine-tuned than the competition's (other people who would have your job), you probably won't advance—because someone else will be willing to do what you won't (or can't).

Creating Enterprises: The New Entrepreneurial Model

Most new economic growth over the past fifteen years has come about through small businesses. A recent survey of business experts indicates that this trend will continue beyond the turn of the century. And the information-age economy has opened up hundreds of new entrepreneurial opportunities.

Being an entrepreneur means something very different than it did a generation ago. As mentioned earlier in our general discussion of this career path, entrepreneurs in past decades were essentially middlemen or deal-makers. The key was to sell. The usual portrait was the owner of a corner grocery, hardware, or drugstore. These business owners made their living by selling products with little or no corporate planning, since they didn't need to worry about complex investments or creative ways of raising funds. They simply ran their businesses and bought the services of experts to handle more complicated matters.

In contrast, the entrepreneurs of today focus on innovation and risk taking from an informed business perspective. They create businesses to fill a perceived need, while carefully planning their strategies and managing

complex finances. What sets the "new breed" of entrepreneur apart is that they choose entrepreneurialism as a direct career path. They often study in one of the country's leading business schools, mastering topics like strategic thinking and planning, new venture analysis, financial management of growing firms, and so on. They build teams of experts and carefully guide their creations to financial success. Though not all of today's entrepreneurs can boast these credentials, most do have access to a high level of information. Many popular business books are now available to guide people through the technical aspects of creating a business plan and forming a team,

Today's entrepreneurial opportunities require a new breed of people. Like the entrepreneurs of yesterday, they're good salespeople. Yet the new economy also requires them to have four additional characteristics: a flair for innovation, an aversion to risk taking, the ability to seek help, and a sound knowledge base of entrepreneurial business. Let's examine each of these in more detail.

Building a Better Mousetrap

The first characteristic of today's entrepreneurs is that they are superbly innovative. They seek out problems and look for the most efficient ways to do things. When they find something wrong, they'll also find a way to fix it.

A recent study revealed that today's successful entrepreneurs view resources and people as tools rather than things to control. They are much more focused on results than are most corporate stalwarts. Their patterns of thinking are revolutionary; thinking "out of the box" is normal for them. Chuck Thompson is such a person.

Young and penniless, Chuck hoped for a pro-football career, but his dream was going nowhere fast. He was big and strong, and he thoroughly enjoyed beating people up. Unfortunately, he just wasn't quite good enough. Chuck needed

a "Plan B," and soon realized that his "football degree" wasn't worth much.

What Chuck did have going for him was his creativity and stubborn unwillingness to allow traditional thinking to get in his way. While walking past a construction site, he noticed a security guard on post, and this triggered his idea to start a security company. With his size and natural charisma going for him, it wasn't long before Chuck had his own patrol formed, and together they made the new security business a rousing success. But Chuck didn't stop there.

After hearing about the U.S. trade deficit on the nightly news, Chuck decided to help close the trade gap by getting into the export business. Taking note of the growing interest in a united Europe, he formed CSJ Co., and his team exported millions of dollars worth of sportswear, T-shirts, and other souvenirs to western Europe—complete with a united Europe logo.

Through his export contacts, Chuck also learned that China was in the market for scrap metal. Always the opportunist, he set his mind to figuring out how he could get his hands on some inexpensive, surplus metal. Just then, he happened to drive across some railroad tracks. "Too bad I couldn't just snatch those railroad ties," Chuck thought to himself. He screeched to a halt, got out of the car, and perused what must have been a half mile of unused track. After gaining permission from the railroad, Chuck tore up several tons of the unused track and shipped it to China. It wasn't long before Chuck's business was also exporting food packs, wheat, and rice throughout western and eastern Europe, Asia, and South America.

Entrepreneurs tend to keep their innovative sense sharp by talking with people (often whoever will listen) about their ideas. But they don't spend a lot of time in idle conversation. For them, innovation is only useful when it's applied to problems. They're eager for someone to try to express doubt, to play the "devil's advocate," so they

can think through any potential obstacles or objections. And they equally relish validation, as proof that they've come up with "a winner."

Once the seed of an innovative idea has been planted, entrepreneurs then spend the majority of their time planning, scheduling, and making deals. Always filled with energy and passion, they use every waking moment to transform their dreams into reality.

Slow to Roll the Dice

The second characteristic of today's entrepreneurs is that they are risk-averse. This runs against conventional wisdom that stereotypes the typical entrepreneur as an arrogant, bombastic, and often foolish gambler. Instead, they carefully measure the odds of success and only play the game when they're confident they'll win. As one entrepreneur said, "Entrepreneurs aren't the ones betting on the horses, they'll be the ones running the track."

The ones who succeed make informed, well thought out decisions rather than put everything behind ill planned ventures. They don't like putting money and time on the line, so they analyze a prospective business from every possible perspective, trying to minimize the possibility of failure. They don't dislike "it'll never work" advice; in fact, they seek out nay-sayers. They want to hear everything that can go wrong, so they can find a way to overcome the problems before they occur.

One of the most important tools for today's risk taker is the business plan, and a test of whether a person has the necessary traits to make it as an entrepreneur is how they write their plan. Unsuccessful entrepreneurs see the plan as a hurdle to get over; they are so sure the business will work that the planning process is nothing but mental clutter.

Successful entrepreneurs, on the other hand, treat their business plans like delicate operations. They check every figure over and over, they test

A good business plan requires extensive research and careful consideration.

their assumptions, they may even spend weeks ensuring that their cash flow projections aren't too optimistic. And they show the plan to anyone who will take the time to read it, provided it doesn't contain proprietary information.

Bob Lindberg spent years developing his business, always making sure he had one product up and running before starting work on the next. He is an example of one of today's innovative, yet risk-averse, entrepreneurs.

As engineering manager for a high-tech electronic connector company, Bob was forced to reevaluate which career path best fit his skills, values, and life-style. A victim of a corporate restructuring, Bob's engineering department was disbursed to various product groups, and Bob was given two months' notice.

While pondering his next step, he was intrigued to hear about one engineering project that wasn't faring well for the company. It seems the U.S. navy was having trouble keeping underwater plastic and rubber components bonded to ships and submarines. Within only a few months under harsh conditions, the bonding would break apart. The navy needed a solution, but nothing looked promising.

Fascinated by the challenge, Bob volunteered to dedicate his last two months with the company toward finding a solution. After several weeks of research, lab work, and interviews with engineers and scientists, Bob perfected a method for keeping these vital, though incompatible, materials bonded in harsh environments.

Rather than let him get away, the company promoted Bob and asked him to head up product development of this new technology. After a year, another corporate restructuring forced a complete change in senior management. The new leadership decided to abandon the underwater market. Once again, management asked Bob to leave the company. But this time his innovations paid off. As a reward to Bob, the company signed over all rights and patents for the new technology, and he emerged with a new business venture and impressive credentials as an industry guru. Bob named his new company RELTEC.

It wasn't long before his development efforts caught the interest of the U.S. Coast Guard, oil companies, fishery agencies, shipping lines, environmental activists, and atmospheric and

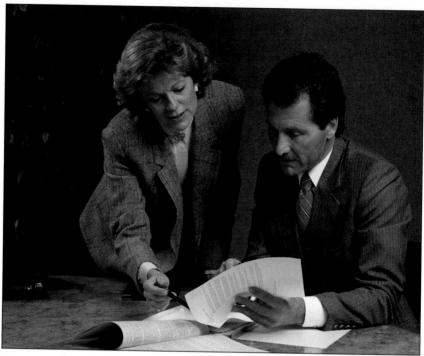

Entrepreneurs have the skills to assemble a winning team.

oceanographic scientists. Interest in his technology also spread to Canada, Europe, and Australia.

His multiuse technology is applicable to submarines, electrical cables, sonar system connectors, buoys, and permanent installations on the ocean floor. Partnering with other scientists, Bob is currently participating in state-of-the-art development for measurement of atmospheric and oceanographic conditions that will perfect scientists' efforts in measuring the global weather and ecological system. Ultimately, this will enable us to better predict global weather conditions.

With this and several other technological breakthroughs, Bob's conservative projection is for $100 million in sales by the end of the decade.

All this came about unexpectedly, yet Bob had it in him all the time. In fact, another technological breakthrough product has been sitting on his shelf for over ten years, but he's been too busy working a traditional job to market it. Do you have similar opportunities you haven't yet acted on?

After the entrepreneurs are fairly sure their plan will work, the next trait comes into play.

Building the Team

Once an entrepreneur is cautiously confident the idea is a winner, it's time to bring in the resources to make it happen. Many people think of entrepreneurs as "one-person shows," but this isn't true of the new breed. The third characteristic of today's entrepreneurs, then, is their skill at seeking out the right help.

Today's entrepreneurs have tough challenges to overcome. They need to handle financing, production, sales, management, training, quality control, and accounting—and the list goes on! To be successful, they need a team to bring the dream to reality.

Entrepreneurs may employ the help directly, in the case of bringing on an accountant; or the help may be external, in the case of consultants and investors. The key is to bring these people together to form an efficient team. Thus, the entrepreneur's unique ability to create a sense of urgency in others is just as important as his or her ability to innovate.

Getting people to align their efforts and their money is a tough but critical task for the entrepreneur. Doing it takes someone who is convincing and charismatic. The person has to seem sincere and trustworthy and must be able to point to a proven track record. Roger is such a person.

Roger was president for a subsidiary of a national nonprofit health insurance company. After a corporate merger, the new management team wanted to fire Roger, the board of directors, and his senior managers. Rather than accept this lying down, Roger filed a lawsuit in an effort to separate the subsidiary from the parent company.

After a long and bitter court battle, he and his renegade band of associates won their fight for independence. Within a few short years, their new health-care venture dominated the marketplace. In less than ten years, company earnings passed the $1 billion mark. After taking their company public, Roger and his band became instant millionaires.

Unquestionably, Roger is innovative and calculating, but the one skill that made his story successful is that he inspired trust. His associates were willing to back him—with both their time and their money.

Setting up a team becomes a different kind of challenge once the venture is successful. If you do get a start-up off and running, you will need to consider whether you're the right person to transition to a structured environment as the company grows. Several recent studies indicate that launching a company requires different skills than running an existing firm. A few people managed to do both. Ted Turner, Bill Gates, Ray Kroc, and Bill Hewlett and David Packard are among those who were successful in both situations.

Setting up and running a successful team can be the real test of entrepreneurial ability, since today's business environment is too complicated for one person to "go it alone." This process becomes much easier when the entrepreneur has the following characteristic.

Knowing the Rules of the Game

The fourth and final characteristic of effective entrepreneurs is that they have a solid and up-to-date general knowledge of entrepreneurial business. As we previously discussed, entrepreneurs of past generations often farmed out non-sales tasks to outside experts in accounting, finance, forecasting, budgeting, payroll, and marketing. Today's intense business atmosphere requires that the leader of entrepreneurial ventures play an active role in coordinating and harmonizing all of these tasks.

Entrepreneurialism is a major academic subject in many of today's business schools. This course of study now carries the same legitimacy as more "traditional" business subjects like management and finance. For the first time in history, many people are becoming experts in the study of launching, managing, and exiting from new ventures. This signals a real shift in the economy; it's no longer adequate to be a "trader" like the people who used to run corner grocery stores with the hope of someday managing a chain.

Although entrepreneurs still have to be cunning, innovative, strategic, and energetic, they also need to acquire specialized knowledge and learn creative ways of thinking.

Should you become a member of the new breed of entrepreneurs? If you're innovative, calculating of risks, able to inspire others, and willing to acquire a solid knowledge of entrepreneurialism, this career path may be right for you.

But a word of caution is in order. Be aware of the risks: Over 90 percent of new ventures fail within the first five years. The 10 percent of people who succeed are usually on their second, third, or fourth business endeavor. You can nevertheless drastically improve your odds by seeking the advice of successful entrepreneurs, taking the time and effort to construct a sound business plan, building a network of people to support you, and learning as much as possible. We will now examine the third new career path.

Achieving Results

A century ago, every small town had blacksmiths, carpenters, woodworkers, and many other craftsmen. These people made their money by doing one thing, and doing it for their entire lives. Most worked alone and didn't have to worry about payroll, expensive offices, or hiring accountants. They were paid based on results—how much they made, how much they sold.

Today the world is very different. But there are people in the economy who still stick to one skill, or task, for several years or longer. They may work for themselves or for a large company, from a downtown office or from home. But they do one thing, and they do it very well.

Achieving results is a career path, based solely on just that: results! Through most of this century, achievers tended to be commissioned salespeople, selling anything from life insurance to cosmetics. If they didn't sell, they weren't paid. If they sold well, they were paid well.

Special achievers are indeed unique individuals. They share the traits of being extremely focused, enjoying the tasks at which they excel, and deriving their primary satisfaction from a sense of competency. Today, the opportunities for achievers extend far beyond the selling arena. They include real estate agents, stockbrokers, tax advisers, movie producers, recording artists, direct mail experts, scriptwriters, and painters, as well as the more traditional

salesmen and women. These successful people place their emphasis on their greatest strengths: selling, producing, writing, or designing. They leave cash flow and business planning to someone else. They aren't interested in climbing the corporate ladder, and they don't have time for company politics.

Unlike the craftsmen of centuries past and the commissioned pitchmen and women of the 1950s and 1960s, achievers probably won't stick to doing the same thing for their entire lives. Statistics indicate that most of us will change careers at least six times throughout our working lives. But, for the moment, the achiever is content to do what he or she is best at doing. Carol Fernandez is one example.

Carol was a successful executive secretary who felt very unsuccessful. She couldn't quite put her finger on it, but she knew that something about her current career didn't suit her.

To figure out what was wrong, Carol began talking with many of her friends about what they did at work. The one skill Carol found most exciting was when some of her friends explained that they worked to help people "plan" their lives. One of her friends, a financial adviser with American Express, caught Carol's interest by saying he helped make people's dreams come true. Carol wanted to do this too.

But this concept was still too vague. Carol needed something more concrete. She enrolled in a life-planning class at her local university and, after taking a battery of personality and aptitude tests, learned that she was a natural at selling. She combined these skills with her desire to help people plan their lives and decided to become a real estate agent.

After obtaining her real estate license, Carol went to work part-time for a broker. At first, she primarily worked with her family and friends, but her name quickly spread: Carol was a great real estate agent! In less than six months, she quit her secretarial job and went into real estate full-time.

Carol's days are now filled with meeting clients, showing houses, and closing deals. She loves being out of the daily grind of an office and, for the first time in her life, is completely satisfied with her career.

Results—and Results Alone

Achievers share three characteristics. First, they are almost exclusively focused on results, which they define as "generally whatever makes them money." Recording artists focus on results by trying to create hits; commissioned salespeople, by closing as many sales as possible; investors, by producing high returns on investments; contingency fee lawyers, by successfully settling or litigating cases; novelists, by completing manuscripts publishers are willing to pay for.

This focus on results makes achievers unique. They don't have time (or usually even the interest) to build teams, plan new entrepreneurial ventures, climb the corporate ladder, have power lunches, or anything else—unless it means greater results.

This isn't to say that achievers don't have outside interests or friendships. Quite the contrary. Most are well-rounded people with families and fulfilling social lives. Yet, while at work, they are able to forget everything else and truly focus on what will make their careers successful: results. Sybil Garry is such a person.

Sybil is a contract manager with Xerox, and is paid partially on commission. She enjoys the challenge and focus of being in sales. Some years ago, after having children, she made a conscious choice not to attempt an advance up the ladder. The result of deciding to stay in sales is that she earns a good living while maintaining a flexible schedule. "My time is my own," Sybil says. "If I have to be at my daughter's pin-ning ceremony, I can." But while at work, Sybil is very focused and achieves important results.

"It takes a certain personality to succeed in sales," she notes. She recalls that she seldom procrastinated and was instead always the kind of person to get school assignments done well before the due date. Sybil attributes much of her current success to this get-it-done-early approach. She reports being able to stay focused on a project until it's completed. "Sales is based on trust and relationships. If you do it right, you build the relationship over time, and the deal closes itself because they trust you. It takes both long-term commitment to the relationship and short-term commitment to solving the customer's immediate problems."

Sybil has what she calls "a driving desire to be successful," and she thrives on the challenge and the focus of her job. By locking in on results and having the rest of her life in balance, she serves as a role model for today's achievers.

Over and Over, Faster and Faster, Better and Better

The second trait of achievers is that they have the attention span to perform repetitive tasks while seeking constant improvement in the process. Like Carol and Sybil, they find genuine enjoyment in what they do, and don't mind doing it for several years—or more. This makes them very different from corporate stalwarts and entrepreneurs, who always hope that tomorrow's challenges will be different from today's. Special achievers may have several projects going at once, but they will set up a schedule so that each one is done on time, and is done very well. Yet most achievers don't like monotony. They want to become increasingly proficient at their trade, to learn to perform their task faster and faster, better and better.

The notion of "quality speed" is the second trait of successful achievers. They have an ability to get the job done fast while doing it well. Since they're usually paid by the project or on commission, they must learn to close the deal, get a quick return on investment, or write the book faster than others can while consistently doing a job that will get them referrals or favorable evaluations.

Generally, achievers have several projects going on simultaneously: writing two books at once (outlining the first while writing the second) closing two sales the same week they list three new homes, or finishing an audit while bidding on the next two. And this means they have to be extremely organized, disciplined, and energetic.

The achiever category also includes a few talented individuals who are brought into companies to steer them out of a crisis. These turnaround specialists, like all achievers, want to do the job quickly while not sacrificing quality. Albert Dunlap is one such person.

Albert's specialty is turning companies around. Recently hired to fix Scott Paper, a large paper company, Albert wasted no time in cleaning house. In his first week, he brought in his own team, fired 90 percent of the former senior ex-ecutives, and held a "public burning" of their previous business plans. Within a year, he cast a new vision for the company, divested all noncore businesses, and returned the company to profitability.

Is being a special achiever right for you? Like all the career paths, it takes someone uniquely suited to this lifestyle. If you enjoy seeking results, have a keen sense of focus, can do one thing remarkably well and quickly, and are organized and disciplined, then this path may be ideal for you.

Most achievers, like Sybil Garry, have a deep yearning for tangible success. They want to leave work each day with a sense of results-oriented accomplishment: Because they went to work, their company generated more sales, investors had a higher return, or the world can now enjoy a new piece of art.

Achievers don't feel slighted if they're left out of office rumors, and they don't feel a sense of loss for not publishing another professional paper. They got results—and that's what important.

Becoming an Expert

Another alternative to the traditional corporate path is a career as a professional expert. As we discussed earlier in this chapter, until recently, most "experts" were doctors or lawyers. There were also a few tax experts, actuaries, and management consultants.

Today, with the rapid knowledge explosion in fields of science, technology, management theory, electronic marketing, aerospace, programming, and compensation, companies have a hard time keeping up. Many firms, now faced with increasingly fierce competition, are willing to pay large sums for expert advice. In years past, these experts would have been employed in think tanks, universities, and R&D divisions of high-tech firms and would have occasionally "loaned" themselves to other firms for an hourly rate. Today, they can work for any company or for themselves. Experts command extremely diverse fees: They may earn just enough to continue their ceaseless drive to be "on the cutting edge," or they may command $20,000 per speech on the lecture circuit.

Today's experts are motivated to always know more and to advance their field. Thus, their real loyalty is not to the person or company paying them, but to other brilliant, highly educated experts—their peers.

People who design their career around the expert path have many options. They can work in research or teaching, as consultants to media organizations, as newspaper or magazine columnists, as administrators in professional organizations, as writers or editors of professional and academic journals, or as independent consultants. Others create careers by combining several part-time jobs.

A major subcategory of the expert field is the management consultant. This field is one of the growth areas in our economy, and the U.S. Labor Department predicts the number of management consultants will continue to increase well into the 21st century. This category includes people who make their living advising companies on ways to increase profitability or effectiveness through changes in organization, management, information technology, or human resources practices. Most management consultants work for large firms, either in consulting divisions selling their services to corporations or as internal consultants advising their own companies.

Those who work as consultants for large organizations often hope to advance, either as partners supervising other consultants or as executives in a particular industry. These people are really corporate stalwarts, since they hope to rise through the layers to increasingly higher management levels. Other consultants choose to remain in their existing capacity, simply aspiring to become better and better at what they do. Their real goal is to follow the achiever career path and be recognized as people who achieve greater results.

Still others hope to leave the world of "big six" consultants and open their own boutique consulting firms, focusing on a small market segment. These people are entrepreneurs at heart, and hope to create opportunities for themselves and others through their own companies. Their real enjoyment may derive not from consulting, but rather from weighing the risks, negotiating with investors, planning the venture, designing an exit strategy, and hiring the staff.

Only a small percentage of management consultants are true "experts,"

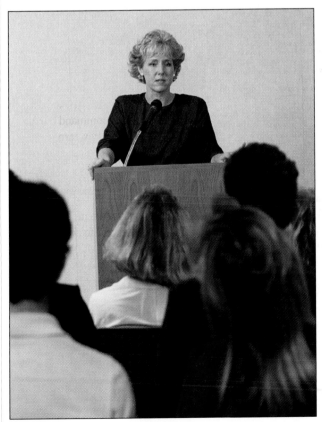

"Experts" are in demand for speaking engagements at chamber of commerce, company, or association functions.

Management consultants can work in a variety of environments.

as this book uses the term. Their goal is not up-the-ladder advancement, greater levels of achievement, or creation of a new venture. Rather, their true "customer" is the field of management science (or a related field such as information technology or organizational communication). They want to advance the field as they continually learn more. These experts often think of consulting as a way to conduct "experiments" on what really works and what doesn't. Thus, they will consult for a fee and then publish their results in professional journals read by other experts. Many of these true experts work full time as professors or researchers, and turn over the "nuts and bolts" of consulting to research assistants or graduate students.

But no matter what field the expert holds in highest regard—be it management, medicine, law, statistics, or engine design—the way to get ahead is almost always the same: learn, experiment, publish, gain esteem, and always be involved in research that other experts find interesting and exciting.

Successful experts come from various backgrounds, but most share the following three commonalties.

Doing What Others Find Interesting

The first and most important characteristic an expert requires is to have some acquired knowledge or expertise in a field for which there is a demand. Depending on the field, this knowledge or expertise may take anywhere from days to decades to develop.

For experts, perhaps more so than for people in other career paths, "perception" is as important as "reality." In fact, whether companies or other people really need what you know is often less important than how interesting they find your work. There must be something about your expertise or knowledge—a potential application of it, its utter uniqueness, or how it could influence people's beliefs or lifestyles—that creates the demand that makes other people want to know more about it.

Within some fields (philosophy and many subjects studied in graduate academic programs), knowledge for its own sake is enough. A thought or a concept is valuable because no one else has come up with it before, although "selling" that expertise may prove to be difficult. Within other fields (engineering, management, or technology), knowledge must hold the promise of changing the world in some way.

This isn't to say that all experts are academics. While many do work in universities or high-level think tanks, many others are actively designing new computer systems, booster rockets, surgical techniques, or better methods to grow crops. Barney Pell works in a field with enormous practical application.

As a scientist at NASA, Barney loves working on the cutting edge of knowledge. Holding an undergraduate degree in symbolic systems from Stanford University and a Ph.D. in artificial intelligence (AI) from Cambridge, Barney has long enjoyed helping to create the technology of the future.

He notes that the role of an expert is changing in NASA, and similar changes are occurring in other corporations. Years ago, most scientists spent more time publishing papers than contributing to the goals of the company. Now, he says, NASA is trying to roll people's expertise back into the corporation. People hired today have to be not only brilliant researchers but also able to relate well to others and to support NASA's goals.

Barney notes that experts in AI must be both corporate and academic thinkers: "You can't be totally academic, or you won't be taken seriously by people who decide which projects to fund. And you can't be totally corporate, or you won't be taken seriously in the field. Experts today have to be in both worlds at the same time."

Like many of today's experts, Barney is considering several different plans for his future career. The first is to stay at NASA, providing it remains a fertile ground for learning. But if that ever changes, he's considering launching his own company to solve more "real world" problems while continuing to be a principal player in the academic field of AI.

Being Part of a Community

The second characteristic of successful experts is their ability to add value in a community of other experts. The 1950s image of the "loner inventor" is not the model of today's experts. Esteem, recognition, collaboration, and advancing the knowledge of other people are key values for them today. In short, having an esteemed place in the community of colleagues is of primary importance.

In long-established, highly professional and academic communities (such as law, medicine, and the pure sciences), establishing oneself can take decades. In these fields, it's important—and often crucial—to be sponsored by someone who is already established.

The key factor to ensure success in these privileged circles is to do good work. In most fields, no amount of smoke and mirrors will make shoddy effort seem worth anyone's attention. In fact, in the most prestigious groups, it's frowned on to publicize any work unless it's considered ground-breaking. Deborah Dunn is in such a field.

As the latest addition to the faculty in the department of communication at California State University at Fullerton, Deborah is trying to become established in the academic community through her studies in organizational communication. While earning her Ph.D. at the University of Southern California, Deborah was quickly recognized by professors and researchers as being bright and motivated.

At USC, she began presenting her academic work at professional conferences. She soon earned a reputation as an up-and-coming scholar. While her academic work was progressing, Deborah opened her own consulting firm with the hope of sharing what she was learning with businesses. Several large companies in Southern California quickly hired her.

Yet Deborah's real passion is for advancing the field. She is currently working on a book and enjoys discussing the latest research with her graduate students. Deborah also relishes her role as expert and looks forward to sponsoring her best students in the field, just as people sponsored her when she was getting started.

What really separates experts from people in other career paths is their motivation. They desire more than anything else—more than earning money, building a company, or rising through the ranks of management—to devote themselves to study, research, experimentation, and to their community of expert colleagues. Some, like Warren Bennis, Peter Drucker, and Michael Hammer, earn substantial fees. Others, like Carl Sagan and Stephen Hawking, receive tremendous fame for their abilities. Yet most experts are like Barney Pell and Deborah, devoted to their field and to their tightly knit community.

Is this path of the expert right for you? If you feel a strong calling toward advancing your expertise and knowedge, and if you believe you can find people willing to help you stay on the cutting edge, it just may be. Such a career path unquestionably requires patience, attention to detail, a true love of learning, and a desire to push the boundaries of what people in your field know. We will now focus on the final career path.

Facilitating Others

In reading about the first four career paths, you may have been amazed by the diversity and complexity of the new economy. The world has so many new career options—some overlapping, some parallel with one another, others completely independent—that people need a way to "come together" to obtain information. Even different groups within the same corporation don't realize how much valuable knowledge they could interchange with others in the same enterprise. Often these groups compete rather than cooperate, and the flow of information comes to a screeching halt. And if this situation happens within a single company, it happens much more often—and with far greater consequences—*between* organizations.

Doing business in today's world is challenging, but it's made easier because of a few uniquely talented and trusted people. Simply put, these people know lots of other people—some with specific needs and some with special skills. Known as facilitators, these people make their living introducing, so to speak, the "left hand" to the "right."

Facilitators may work as bankers, recruiters, or corporate executives. They exist in almost every industry, from aeronautics to finance to logistics to semiconductors.

Small-talk Wizards

Generally, facilitators have three personal characteristics that set them apart from people in other career paths. First, they're masters of conversation. While corporate stalwarts, entrepreneurs, and consultants rely more on the results of sociability, facilitators need to master specific social skills. They must put everyone at ease, gather the required information, communicate the seriousness of their intent, and produce an enjoyable and productive experience for all involved—and all at the same time.

Facilitators need to exude confidence and outgoingness yet always remain in control, a balance partly learned and partly inherited. Still, most facilitators' initial careers began by doing something else. They may have been executives, consultants, or salespeople. But in the course of their business, they met a lot of influential people and earned their respect.

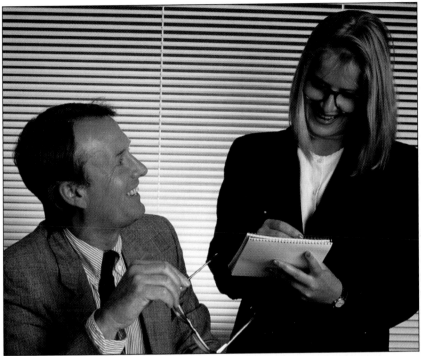

Gifted facilitators maintain an extensive network.

Earning a Living out of Your Rolodex

The second characteristic of facilitators is that they've acquired a well-developed network. If a potential client asks a facilitator for the name of someone with specific skills and is disappointed with the referral, the client probably won't call again. The facilitator has to know someone (or know someone who knows someone) who can do just about anything. Many facilitators often develop their networks by acting as consultants or coaches.

A Reason to Be Taken Seriously

In addition to having exceptional social skills and a well-developed network, most facilitators have acquired a reputation for something specific. Michael Ovitz, for example, is known primarily as a Hollywood deal maker.

Most facilitators concentrate their efforts on one or two areas. An executive recruiter, having once worked himself as a human resources vice president, will focus on that segment of the economy, and an investment banker will focus on finance. Roger Chartrand used his knowledge of acting and producing to develop a strong focus as a facilitator.

Roger was a national account executive for a value-added computer reseller, earning over $250,000 a year. Although he was satisfied with his career, his real passion was acting. So Roger developed corporate clients in the entertainment industry, hoping to leverage his contacts into acting opportunities. As it turned out, he did meet many influential entertainment executives while automating their offices.

One of these encounters was with Mel Brooks. When Roger shared his aspirations of becoming an actor, Brooks eyed him with that perplexed look only he can deliver and said, "That makes perfect sense. Just keep selling computers and some day you'll be a successful actor!"

Remembering Brooks' advice to pursue his passions, Roger discovered other ways to capitalize on his interests.

An avid health, fitness and martial arts enthusiast, he completed the necessary training to become a certified personal fitness trainer and also began selling a line of health and weight-loss nutritional supplements.

As often happens, Roger's efforts soon turned full circle, as his personal training clients from the entertainment industry began to present opportunities for Roger's acting career. One of these included an infomercial where he's featured as a personal fitness trainer.

Today, Roger is a partner in a highly successful agency specializing in commercial print, commercials, and nonunion television shows. This affords him the opportunity to assist other actors. Knowing so many people has catapulted his acting career as well as his role as a facilitator.

Is being a facilitator right for you? If you have significant contacts, are generally thought to be trustworthy, and if you think people would be willing to pay for your referrals, then facilitating may be the appropriate career path for you.

But just how does someone get to be a facilitator? Most people gradually move into the job, as their networks and reputations expand. And since most facilitators started by doing something else, they first used their contacts for their own advancement and then for the development of other people.

Even if facilitating isn't right for you, it's a sure bet that you'll come into contact with people in this line of work. For that reason alone, it's a good idea to know as much as possible about this career path.

The Fork in the Road

Since you're taking the time to read this book, you're probably asking yourself some deep questions about where to take your career. You probably have a number of successes, but now something has changed. You're growing tired of your job, or you've been outsourced. Perhaps you've been working as a consultant but would now like to lay down some roots.

Whatever your situation, like millions of other people you now find yourself standing at the fork in the road. You probably have some idea about which of these five career paths is right for you. But don't make up your mind just yet. The rest of this book will take you through a series of exercises to make sure your choice is right. And additional exercises will help you design and execute your own unique career plan.

The road lies before you. It's time to take the next step.

Chapter 2

Considering Ourselves

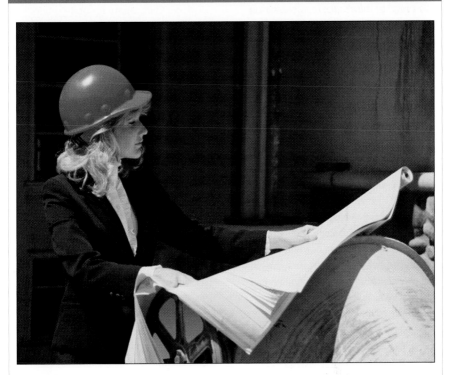

The rules of the new economy let us exercise more self-determination than ever before. With surprisingly few limitations, people today are creating their own uniquely crafted careers.

A career today is not the result of a single choice made in college but, rather, a lifelong series of choices. Careers are paths, not places. For some people, this means working at home as special achievers. Others enjoy being a facilitator with a prestigious career as a corporate stalwart. Some are with their families almost the entire working day, while others exclusively choose a career over a family life.

And though the landscape of work is swirling faster and faster, it's nevertheless providing increasing opportunities for us to consider our own career options. Yet, as individuals, we don't change like the labor department's list of growing and shrinking industries. For us there will always be things we do well and don't do well, like and dislike.

For work to be the joyous expression of our self-identities, we have to know ourselves. Only by acknowledging our strengths and limitations can we make the choices involved in creating a successful career. This chapter will help you learn to "look inside yourself" and, through this self-examination, perhaps begin a wise consideration of which of the five career paths is appropriate for you.

Beyond Plateauing

In the late 1980s, many executives and would-be executives felt both their hearts and their careers deflate in what job experts called "career plateauing." Victims of this career bust often sought understanding and solace through professional counseling.

While trying to come to terms with the usual end result of this plateauing—job displacement—many of these people came to the surprising conclusion that the cause of their sorrow was not their lack of career success but, rather, the sense that they had somehow betrayed themselves. Carl Willis is one of those people.

Carl was a rising star in a West-Coast media firm. Having recently completed a midcareer MBA, he felt that his personal life and his career were finally coming together. He told himself—and anyone else who would listen—that he wouldn't rest until he was a senior executive in the $500-million company.

And Carl had reason to be optimistic. In his six years with the corporation, he'd been promoted three times, most recently to financial manager of a major division. His next promotion would be to director, then senior director, and finally chief financial officer. Carl truly felt he was living the life of a successful corporate stalwart.

After three years as financial manager, however, Carl realized something was wrong. His performance evaluations were always top-notch, but the company's growth was slow. The industry was shedding excess employees, and the people above him weren't leaving. In a word, Carl felt stuck.

Most troubling was the continual questioning from his friends. "When's the next big promotion coming?" they asked, not realizing how this made him feel. Carl didn't blame them, after all, his ambitious "ladder climbing" was all he had talked about for years. But now it felt like the whole world was out to get him!

After another year and no promotion, Carl left the company and began hunting for a job with more opportunity. In six months, he was finally offered a position: as a financial manager in a media company smaller than the one he'd left. He considered declining the offer but decided it would be better to forget his dreams—and "eat crow" with his friends—and resign himself to the security of simply having a place to go on Monday mornings.

Like Carl, many up-and-comers in the corporate world felt the most pain when they had to confront the expectations of others. The "career plateauing" phenomenon triggered many self-doubts: Why hadn't they been promoted? Weren't they good enough? When would their turn come? Many simply got tired of inventing answers.

For others, the glut of talent became a reason to reassess their values. By focusing on themselves—and learning what made them happy—they used the time constructively to refocus, regroup, and make fresh start. This was Peter Dunham's experience.

Peter bitterly remembers the day he was called into his boss's office. Instead of news of an eagerly anticipated and long overdue promotion, Peter got a speech about the company's financial instability and the soon-to-come phasing out of his job.

He had worked as an accountant in the company for over a decade and had always planned on eventually moving into general management. While in a company-sponsored outplacement program, his counselor suggested that Peter reflect on what he had liked about his old job. In mulling it over, Peter was amazed by his conclusion: He really didn't want to be a manager at all. He had enjoyed his position as an accountant; although he'd wished for more variety on the job, accounting was "his thing."

Upon further self-reflection, Peter also came to realize that the only reason he had sought a management career was that he had been basing his satisfaction on the preconceived notion that only corporate stalwarts could consider themselves successful. And he did want to be successful.

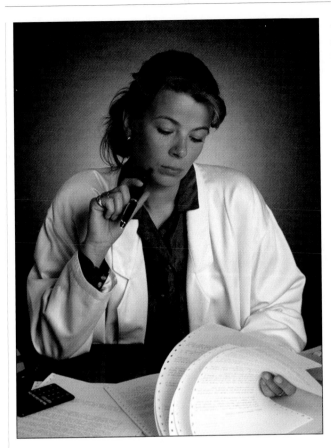

Analyzing your current position is an important step in choosing the right career.

After receiving advice from a member of the Service Core of Retired Executives at the local SBA (Small Business Administration) office, Peter opened his own accounting business. Through his persistant networking efforts, he managed to obtain eight businesses as clients, and the list quickly doubled. After only a year, Peter was earning more money—and having more fun—than he ever would have had as a manager in a large company.

In time, Peter had to return to school to learn more about the particularities of entrepreneurilism. But the key for him is that he had finally discovered what truly made him happy: a career as a new entrepreneur. But he had reached this realization only by a very thorough examination of his own values.

Many a man and woman displaced in recent shifts in the job market were undoubtedly told by a friend, spouse, or ex-boss that "some day you'll look back at being terminated as the best thing that ever happened to you." Most of them probably resented those words but, ironically, later found them to be true.

Reviewing Your Personal Contracts

One of the central themes of this book is that your best career will allow you to do what you most enjoy. Yet if Aladdin's genie offered to conjure up your perfect career, would you even know what to wish for? We will begin the discovery process in this chapter, which includes a systematic analysis to aid you in assessing your current career. Later chapters will then help you crystallize your ideal career into one of the five paths discussed in chapter 1: corporate stalwart, new entrepreneur, achiever, expert, or facilitator.

Like many things worth doing, analyzing your present career situation may come with some mental discomfort. Through this process, you may decide you've taken a wrong turn here or there. You may find that your career isn't quite on the perfect track after all. If your career has taken a wrong turn, you'll eventually have to face that reality, although ultimately many people deny the truth until it's too late. Some even wait until they're about to retire. Others are on the right career track but are afraid to examine their lives, fearing they'll uncover unpleasant issues they're not ready to confront.

Whichever group describes you, this process will be helpful. If you need to make a course correction, you still have time, if no change seem necessary, this process will nevertheless give you additional assurance that everything is going according to plan. Consider Sheila Brown's career track.

Ever since Sheila was five years old, she wanted to be a writer. When she learned what a book was, she dreamed of writing one, when she watched TV shows, she fantasized about creating her own script.

But while growing up, Sheila's parents discouraged her dreams of a writing career. "Get a job that will earn good money," they told her. When she enrolled in college she chose to study education, but deep down she wanted to attend writing classes.

After college, Sheila launched a successful career in the publishing industry. She managed desktop publishers, editors, and writers but always felt she was in the wrong place. Soon after her thirtieth birthday, Sheila realized she hated going to work every morning. Despite a likely promotion in the near future, she often wished her company would close—just so she could stay home.

While browsing at the bookstore one day, Sheila picked up a volume on self-analysis. While working through the exercises, she realized that all along she had been denying her dreams of writing. Like many people in our soci-ety, she had assumed the role of a corporate stalwart. But, in her heart, she had always wanted to be an achiever.

Sheila enrolled in an evening masters' program in professional writing. After a year in the program, she sold a short story. Sheila remembers that as the happiest day of her life. The next year, she sold a screenplay for a TV show. Her novel followed not long after.

By age thirty-five, Sheila felt she had finally answered the call of her childhood and was doing what she wanted to do—on her terms.

Recently, psychologists have written about what happens when people decide to do something important in their lives but fail to do it. They call this "expectancy violation." It's as if we've defaulted on a contract with ourselves. Though we may not be full aware of these contracts, our unconscious minds keep track of them. If significant contracts remain unfulfilled, we may experience symptoms that indicate a serious problem (and we're usually equally unaware of the causes). These symptoms can include deep depression, restlessness, feelings of inferiority, and constant questioning of the relevance of our lives.

Such free-floating anxiety is often perceived by some people as an indication of the onset of a nervous breakdown or, as previous generations referred to it, a "midlife crisis." But these crises can occur throughout life, often beginning in our twenties.

Some psychologists believe that our minds review contracts—whether career or personally related—about seven years after we set them. The "seven-year itch" in marriage may be our minds reviewing our expectations about marriage. If things haven't gone as planned—that is, according to "the contract"—we may feel restless about the relationship and begin searching for alternatives. Many people experience "seven-year career itches" (a sense of career anxiety) around their late twenties, about seven years after they graduate from college, and then again in their mid-thirties, in their early forties, and sometimes beyond this point.

While many books have been written on expectancy violation and methods for coping with these problems, the best treatment is to recognize the contracts for what they are: expectations we set with ourselves. They may be realistic or unrealistic, wise or unwise, but, as in Ron Hamilton's case they are unquestionably important.

Ron didn't know what was wrong: He couldn't sleep through the night unless he took a pill, he could barely eat, and his coworkers complained that he seemed angry at the whole world with no apparent provocation.

Even Ron was surprised by how quick-tempered he had become. Not only was his marriage in trouble, but his children actually seemed fearful of him. He used to think of himself as an even-tempered, easygoing person, but now he seemed to be 'going crazy.'

Ron began to think back over his life. "I'm thirty-nine," he said to himself in a discouraged tone. He had what he considered to be a good career as an account executive with a major advertising firm in New York. He didn't always like his clients, but he made good money. So what was wrong?

Ron recounted his early career days. After graduating from NYU, he had dreams of changing the world. He wanted to use his talent at persuasion to encourage companies to become more environmentally and socially responsible. He started off working for a non-profit environmental group, but then he met Jan and they became serious. He wanted to get married, but the money just wasn't good enough to settle down and begin a family.

So when a large advertising company approached him, Ron resigned from his job and "went corporate." All went well until his early thirties, when he began to feel empty inside. He shrugged it off. Soon the feeling, like an unwelcome stranger, left him. But now the stranger was back, he thought.

Ron's boss, afraid of losing one of the company's most lucrative employees, convinced him to seek psychiatric help. During therapy, Ron realized that he felt he had betrayed himself by going to work "for the enemy."

After this realization and some more soul-searching, Ron talked to his boss and asked to work with a select list of clients devoted to social issues. His boss was skeptical but finally agreed.

After some time passed, Ron's "unwelcome stranger" came by less and less. His energy level increased, and he actually began looking forward to work. His home life became better than it had ever been. And now he's earning more money and is doing exactly what he wants to do.

Most truly successful people—those who can't wait to begin work in the morning—are living in harmony with their important contracts. The rewards they get for fulfilling their expectations are happiness, contentment, and optimism. Harvey Mackay is such a person. *In Swim with the Sharks without Being Eaten Alive*, he writes that he always knew he'd run a company some day. When he finally took steps to fulfill his dream, he became energized and alive.

Career success comes down to living in line with our expectations. We first have to identify what type of career would make us the most fulfilled and then design a way to bring that career to life.

Most people don't think about their contracts. The lucky ones end up in the right career and are happy. But many are off target, and they pay the price.

Where Did You Think You Would Be Now?

The best way to prevent these contracts from expiring is to catalog your expectations. This process involves mentally reviewing your first memories about work and then moving systematically from your most distant enemies to your most recent. In the process, you will create a "career log" or journal that will also help you understand your impressions of work and let you come to terms with your expectations.

This works best when you set aside a specific time and place for quiet reflection. Though this sounds simple, most people don't do it properly, and, thus don't reap the full benefits of this helpful exercise.

You'll also need a careful way to make notes. It's essential that you have the confidence that no one else will read your work unless, of course, you want them to.

Your Career-Log Entries

Start off by letting your mind wander around the word *work*. What does it mean to you? What early memories do you associate with work? Do you remember your mother or father coming home from "work"? Do you remember them saying they'll return after "work"? Do you remember conversations among adults about what kind of "work" they did? This should be your first entry in your career log. Just what did "work" mean to you when you first learned about its meaning? What were your expectations about it—and about what your relationship with work would be?

"Carol" started her career log at a troubling point in her life. She worked as a sales representative for a large manufacturing company. She enjoyed the interaction with her customers, but something was missing. "Whatever that something is," Carol thought, "it's holding me hostage."

Carol created a new file on her laptop computer and titled it "Career Log." She closed the door to her home office so that her family would give her some space. She closed her eyes and began to think about work. A collage of images formed before her. She remem-

bered her father coming home from work (he always seemed relieved to get away from the office). She could see the look on his face, and this image saddened her.

And she remembered her mother, a successful attorney. "Work," she recalled, is what took her mother away so much. Carol's eyes popped open, and she began to type into her word processor: "My earliest memories about the word 'work' are negative. It made my father sad. And it took my mom away a lot." Carol was surprised by the association. She continued to think.

For your second entry, envision a milestone in your thoughts about work—perhaps another early experience with a parent or some business involvement of your own. What was positive and negative about the experience, and what impressions did it leave? What expectations do you now have as a result?

Next, for your third career-log entry, move ahead into your early teens. Think back about what "work" meant. Did you fear it or look forward to it? What experiences did you have with "work," and what expectations came from them? What expectations were forming about the outcomes of your future jobs? Did you envision a certain standard of living? A certain amount of authority? Make the result of these reflections your third entry.

For your fourth entry, move to high school. You were probably crystallizing a belief about your future line of work. What expectations did you have? Were they time-bound or loose? What did you think you would be doing now? What were your emotional feelings about work? Dread, optimism, or some feeling in between?

As Carol began her fourth entry, she was thinking of high school. She remembered being unpopular in her class, and she recalled seldom attending any of the dances. In fact, work was her social life. Her mother had arranged a part-time internship for

How have your career expectations changed since Graduation Day?

Carol with one of her clients—a real estate brokerage firm. Carol had spent her afternoons filing, sorting, making phone calls, and cleaning out the coffee machine. "It wasn't much," she typed into her computer, "but it gave me what I never had in school—a sense of belonging."

For your fifth entry, move to the end of college. Were your expectations different from those in your fourth entry? If so, in what way? What work experiences did you have? How did these influence your thinking about the future? What standard of living did you anticipate for your early career? And, most important, where did you think you would be now?

For your sixth entry, move ahead to your early career. What was your first job after college? How did you get it? What were you promised? What did you promise yourself? What path did you expect your career to take?

Carol reflected on her first job after earning her B.S. in marketing. She had worked as a marketing analyst for a clothing manufacturer in Massachusetts. She remembers feeling very hopeful about the future—and very free. A smile crossed her face as she envisioned the cubicle in which she used to work.

But then Carol remembers how her mother convinced her that she was being underpaid. "You are being exploited, Carol. Keep your job but look for something that will at least allow you to pay back your student loans." Carol can't recall with certainty if these words actually came from her mother or herself.

For your seventh entry, select a time between the start of your postcollege career and the present. Think about a milestone—either positive or negative—in your career. Perhaps a big promotion or a promotion that didn't happen.

Perhaps a career change or a shift to another company. Whatever the event, it should be a notable one. Using this time as your focus, let your mind drift back again toward "work." Where was it taking you, and where were you taking it? Where did you envision you would be in the future?

For your eighth entry, move to the present. Without recording your current work activities, think about what contracts you've made with yourself. Where do you expect to be in the future? When is your target date to have accomplished the main provisions of these contracts?

Carol typed "Entry Eight—the Present" into her laptop and began to think once again. She remembered taking the job because the company promised her a large salary increase compared to her last job. And they did keep their word: She had earned 30 percent more last year than the year

before when she had worked for a competitor.

But Carol realized that she had promised herself more than the company had. She had accepted a job as a sales rep, and yet she expected to be part of a team. "Why did I think that?" she asked herself.

Carol came to the conclusion that what was very important to her—having social contact at work and sharing the experience of work with others—wasn't being fulfilled. She had fulfilled her contract about money, but not her contract about people. She typed her conclusion into the word processor and then continued to think.

Your ninth entry will be different from the others. Go over your career log—from the start to the end of your last entry—and pick out any contracts you made with yourself. Make a list of them, including when you set them, how important they were to you, what

Review your personal contracts in your career log or journal.

the contract demanded you to do or become, and when the contract would be completed. Most contracts don't have a clear end point; rather, you may just have a vague picture of yourself at a future time engaged in a certain kind of work. Record the end date as accurately as you can without adding information.

Before you end your ninth entry, record your reactions to these contracts. Did any of them expire? If they did, what effects did they have on your life? For contracts still "open," do they empower or imprison you? How important are these "open" contracts?

Carol began to put it all together. In high school, when she worked as an intern, she saw "work" as place to belong and show her competence. The school setting had not provided this. She had set a contract with herself that she would work in an environment where she would feel like "part of a family." And this was the case when she had worked as a marketing analyst.

But when she took her mother's advice and went for a better paying job, she began to feel unfulfilled and unhappy. She was in violation of her own contract because she put pay over work environment.

Carol realized that by working as a sales rep—at least at her current company—she would always be an outsider. She wasn't family with her customers, and the sales department didn't have a team environment. She began to understand how she was in violation of an important contract, and it was making her miserable.

Before moving on, it's critical to realize that everyone has contracts that they won't complete. It's just part of being human. But successful people understand and manage their contracts instead of letting their contracts manage them. Jim Givens's career path, while not linear, is a good example.

Even before he graduated with a degree in chemical engineering, Jim set some clear and compelling career goals, the most important of which was to advance quickly in his line of work and to eventually become a senior executive in a Fortune 500 company.

Jim's career didn't unfold as he planned in the first few years. He worked for several biotechnology firms that seemed unappreciative of his talent or ambition. As a result, he jumped quickly from company to company, always looking for "greener pastures." Ten years after graduating college, he had been employed by eight different companies.

Yet during this difficult period, he never felt down or depressed. And he never felt that he wasn't making progress. Instead, he kept telling himself that by working in so many different companies, he was learning the ins and outs of the industry very quickly.

And, eventually, it paid off. Jim was offered a job as a manager in a small but growing biotechnology company. He accepted, and within six months he became an associate director. Within three years, he was a senior director with over five hundred people reporting to him.

Looking back, Jim attributes his success to having a high goal, not backing down from it, and giving himself time to make mistakes. He admits things went slower than he planned and that at times he doubted whether he would make it at all. But he says that he wasn't a slave to his goal, and his goal wasn't a slave to him. "My goal and I were partners," he comments.

Where Is Your Career— Right Now?

So far, your career log is a record of where you thought you'd be at certain points in your life. And, most important, it's a record of your personal contracts about how you anticipated your career would be at this time.

We now move to the last, very crucial phase of this introspection: where your career is right now. When people ask us about our careers, it's only human to exaggerate. But like a wanderer trying to find his way, we need to know exactly where we are before we know how to get where we're going.

The tenth entry in your career log is your chance to take an unblinking look at your career and chronicle exactly what you like, what you don't, and what specific aspects need fixing.

Return to your place of reflection and let your mind float around the idea of your career. Take note of your first reaction when you bring up the thought. Is your reaction positive, negative, or neutral? Does it fill you with hope and optimism, or dread and pessimism? Record these thoughts and feelings.

Next, think about your job duties. Are they what you planned? Do they fulfill your personal contracts? Do they offer enough variety and fulfillment? Why or why not?

Also consider your work relationships. What kinds of people do you interact with? What amount of authority do you have? Is this enough for you? Record these thoughts.

Finally, ask yourself what needs to change. Specifically, what aspects of your career need fixing to be in line with your personal expectations? Often, people cite only one thing—such as money—that they need to repair. But almost always this single "deficiency" is just one of a larger cluster of issues. Let your mind wander around the problem until you have uncovered all of the interrelated elements. Now record them.

Assessing the State of Your Industry

Although understanding the state of your personal contracts is a vital part of understanding your career, these contracts make up only one hue in the overall picture.

In this age of career volatility, you also have to know how your industry is evolving. Changes in technology, employment, and consumer preferences are destroying old industries and creating new ones in record speed. Chapter 8 will look at the future of the five career paths. But, for now, think about your particular industry.

Even if your career is on track, you need to know where your overall industry is today. This will give you clues about where it may be tomorrow.

The first step is to define your industry. Like most Americans, you are probably part of several industries. Consider the example of Ruth Brazelton, a manager of corporate purchasing in a large HMO. Ruth is part of at least three industries: purchasing, health care, and general management. To do her job, she must have knowledge about many other industries, including computers, medical research and development, and management consulting. If the purchasing industry were to disappear, Ruth would have the advantage of her additional expertise in management and her working knowledge of these other industries.

The same is probably true for you. In your career log, begin your eleventh entry. In it, write down all the industries that you contribute to or that affect you. Brainstorm a little. If your log is in longhand, leave plenty of room between each industry.

Once your list is complete, look it over. Now write down your connection to each industry—this might include membership in a professional association, your actual job title, your supervisory authority, your consulting experiences, a college degree, or just a passive interest.

Before concluding your eleventh entry, go over your list one more time. Now write down your thoughts about the state of each industry. Your thoughts should include your "gut feeling," stories from coworkers, what you've read in the newspapers, and

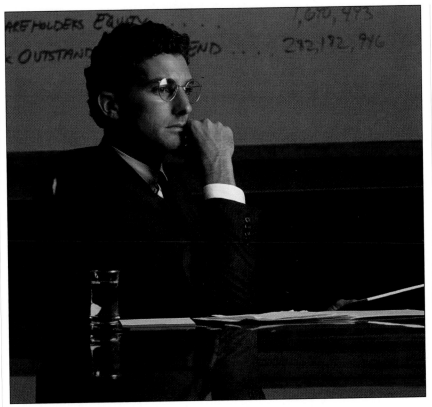

Where do you fit in?

any other sources of information. You've probably heard something recently in the financial news—layoffs or new hiring, plant openings or closings. Write all that down.

Don't conclude this entry just yet. Spend a few days thinking about it, keeping your eyes open to news stories, bringing it up in conversation with colleagues and consultants, and so on. As you acquire more information, be sure to write it down.

Finally, look over the information, thoughts, and feelings you have written for this entry. After you've reviewed it all, summarize it in one or two sentences. We'll return now to Carol's case to help you with this process.

Carol realized that her main industry was in trouble. Manufacturing was declining in the United States, and especially in the East. The more she listened to the news, read business magazines, and talked with her customers, she came to the conclusion that her

company and her industry were in jeopardy of moving overseas.

Yet Carol's other main industry—selling—was quite lucrative. In fact, many salespeople with abilities less developed than her own were doing very well. She summarized her feelings in her career log.

Toward Boom or Bust?

Once you understand where your industries are today, the real work and the real fun begin. Where will your industries be tomorrow? In poll after poll, successful senior executives identify vision as one of the requirements for growing a company and growing a career. "Vision" is seeing something before it happens, and taking action while most people are still uninformed.

It's important to understand the distinction between visionaries and prophets. Prophets see something that will happen, something they have no control over. Prophets are often pessimistic about the future, thinking that circumstances can and will only get worse. Alan Blair was an example of just such a prophet.

Alan's coworkers called him "the sage," because he had a reputation for giving advice that always seemed dead-on. As senior staff to the CFO, people often sought his recommendations.

But Alan's advice was usually negative. "Prepare for corporate disaster," "Just hang on as long as you can, then have your parachute ready," were among his words of wisdom.

Alan's bleakest prophecies for his own career came true when a new chief information officer joined the executive team. He quickly labeled the sage "Dr. No," and pointed out to coworkers that Alan's advice was nothing more than a self-fulfilling prophecy.

The new executive agreed that the future for the firm looked bleak, but he saw new possibilities by moving into new markets and developing key new products. As time progressed, the CIO saw his influence increase—as did the company's profits and market share. Eventually Alan found himself de-

moted to a regional office. His prophecies for the company had failed when a visionary came on board. But his prophecies for his own career were entirely accurate.

Visionaries, in contrast, see what is possible and actively create the future. Reinventing your career requires you to become a visionary. You can begin to see what is possible and then take steps toward creating it. Bill Owens is an uplifting example of visionary optimism.

Two years out of college, Bill started his own business producing and selling promotional material. Within five years, he sold the business and retired as a multimillionaire.

Bill continued to network with the contacts he made while in business. One of his old creditors—and now one of Bill's golfing buddies—told him about a small manufacturing company that had just filed Chapter 11 bankruptcy. His friend said that if Bill would come in as CEO, he would offer the firm an additional $500,000 in credit, enough to keep things operating for another two months.

Bill accepted the challenge. Having only this short time frame to turn things around, he acted quickly. At the

One of the new trends is a shift toward a global economy.

end of the first week, Bill had fired three of the top five executives and implemented what he called "emergency strategic planning." The planning process revealed that the company's major product line would probably sell very well in South America. Bill used more of his contacts to arrange shipment and distribution in Brazil, and the first shipment of products was off in less than three weeks.

At the end of the second month, Bill's new firm was in the black and the creditors were satisfied. Bill's vision of a successful company and his "can-do" attitude produced a business turnaround.

Many notable executives have attributed most of their success to vision. Walt Disney, who died before the completion of Disneyland, commented that he had already seen it finished—in his mind. Two young college students, Bill Gates and Paul Allen, predicted that personal computers would revolutionize the world. Then they brought their future to reality by creating Microsoft. And the list of today's successful visionaries goes on and on.

In looking toward boom and bust cycles for your industry, balance conventional wisdom with what the mavericks say. And don't forget your own visionary voice.

John Naisbitt, author of *Megatrends* and *Megatrends 2000*, has proven his ability to predict overarching trends. People have used his advice to make their careers more rewarding and successful. Recently, Naisbitt has focused his attention on two key trends he believes will shape almost every industry—including yours.

The first trend is the move toward a global economy. This trend includes shifting patterns of employment to the "lowest-bidding" countries. At the same time, international markets will expand. Globalization is good news for innovative companies and bad news for companies incapable of implementing rapid changes.

The second trend is the move toward smaller, leaner, and more responsive business units. Even large companies, like GE and AT&T, are creating more autonomy within their businesses to let small parts of the conglomerates "turn on a dime."

Several other key trends may impact your career. One is the move of large companies to shed their layers of bureaucracy, while hiring people to help with these innovative businesses. Bureaucrats are watching their jobs disappear, while people trained as generalists are seeing increasing opportunities. "Paper pushers" are rapidly being displaced by customer service representatives with high-tech computer knowledge, superior communication skills, and an eagerness to learn.

Other business writers have predicted that jobs which don't appear to add value will be phased out. Chief on the list are real estate agents and car dealers. With increasingly sophisticated computer technology linking the country together, it's possible to preview a house from your computer screen or test-drive a car with your mouse. And though people will still want to see houses before they buy, and test-drive cars before they lease, these industries may be on the decline.

So is your chief industry heading toward boom or bust? Consider these trends and what effect they will have in your line of work.

Even if you decide your industry is about to bust, don't despair. Successful people can use vision and backbone to carve out their own small pockets of growth. Susan Ellington, for instance, bet on one trend—and won.

Late in 1988, Susan headed the human resources division for a large Texas savings and loan organization. She added significant value to her company by finding, retaining, and developing the best financial analysts and bankers, along with excellent general managers and savvy salespeople.

As far back as the early 1980s, she predicted that S&Ls would increase market share at the expense of banks, since S&Ls could offer higher rates of return for most investments.

But in 1988, the same keen insight warned Susan that she was in an industry about to bust. She saw warning signs when land developers gained increasing power over S&Ls in her state, and she saw more and more bad debt. She feared the entire S&L system might simply collapse.

By predicting the trend, Susan became a true visionary by seeing opportunity and building a job around it. Since she had strong contacts in all the major S&Ls in Houston, Austin, and Dallas, she decided she would open her own firm that would specialize in outplacement counseling for former S&L employees.

Susan quit her job and opened her business in early 1989. Most people thought she was crazy, since the S&L industry was still booming. But later that year the now infamous S&L scandal hit the front page of every major American newspaper.

Most human resources consulting firms tried to take advantage of the trend but were too slow. But Susan's business was already established, and she was perfectly positioned.

While Susan hated to see many old friends and colleagues out of work, her new business helped her help them. Not only had she made their transitions less painful but she also made herself a lot of money.

Even if you decide your industry is about to bust, you can find many ways to add value. Visionaries, for example, helped defense contractors downsize after the Cold War, and others worked with homeowners who lost money in the Southern California real-estate meltdown that followed.

Reviewing your contracts gives you insights into yourself. Examining

your industry helps you see opportunity before it happens. But there is one more piece of the puzzle you need to fit in: analyzing where you work right now.

Analyzing Your Company's Profile

The final piece you have to examine is your place of employment. Some computer professionals have a hard time believing they're in a booming industry because they haven't seen big promotions—or even raises—in years. The problem may not be with them or with the industry but with their specific company.

Many people make a string of good career choices: They select the right career path, review the proper education, and work for the right firm. But then they make an unwise jump to a new company—perhaps overly tempted by a higher salary or promises of promotion. Others see their "perfect job" downsized away. Feeling the need to quickly seek out another job, they decide to take a lesser position, and use that as a base to look for something better.

If any of these scenarios sound familiar, you need to assess your current job. Two elements are especially important. The first is politics. Ken Buchanan's story is a case in point.

Ken's philosophy was simple: Do a good job and don't get involved in corporate politics. He came into work at nine o'clock every morning and left a little before five. He knew that some people tried to make an impression by working longer hours, but he felt good about his decision not to play that game.

While driving into work one morning, Ken was listening to his usual "golden-oldies" radio station. In the thirty seconds of news (the only news Ken ever heard!), the anchor stated

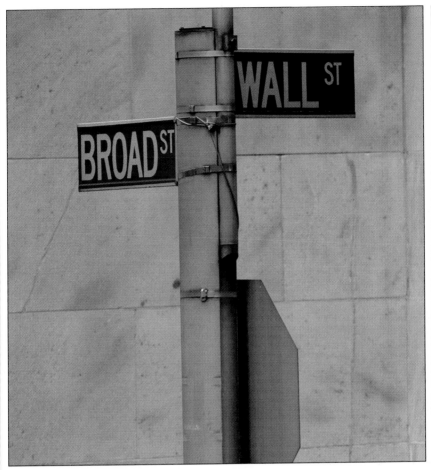

How is your company faring in the marketplace?

that Ken's company was soon to merge with its largest competitor.

Ken's heart jumped. "Mergers mean fewer jobs," he told himself. "But, oh well, I've done a good job and that's all they'll look at. Right?!" He was scared.

When Ken got to work, his boss held an immediate meeting. "Most of you have known for some time that this merger was inevitable," she began. Ken thought that he must have been the only one not to know. His boss promised to keep everyone up to date.

For the next two months, Ken simply did his job and tried to tune out his colleagues' speculations about who would survive and who wouldn't. Finally Ken was called into his boss's office. "Ken, I'm very sorry. . ." In the next five minutes, Ken's manager announced that she could only retain 20 percent of the employees in the department, and several other people had proven that they could add value after the merger. Her speech to Ken concluded with "I'm sure you'll find something soon." And that was that!

As Ken drove home that day, he began to rethink his career strategy. Maybe if he had been more politically aware, he wouldn't have been the last to know about the merger and he would have found a way to keep his job. But that thought quickly passed. Ken switched on his "golden-oldies" radio station and tried to think more pleasant thoughts.

Many people like Ken try to be above politics but end up being swallowed by them—and then spit out.

"Politics" just means dealing with people. So, by being human, we're automatically playing the game. Some people just do it better than others. If you don't do it well, your career may fall victim to people who play better than you.

The faster things change, the more important politics become. Rapid change puts a premium on information. And times of rapid change can advance the careers of people who are politically astute.

Ask yourself how well you play the game. A revealing exercise for people at all levels is to write down the names of all the people at work *(See the chart below)*. If you're employed with a very large company, write down only the names of people in your department and your immediate peers in other departments. Make sure you note the names of the people in positions above yours. Also write down the names of all the top executives and decision makers.

Now find two people who share information on a regular basis and draw a line between them. If they share information daily or even more frequently, make the line thick. Now find two other people who communicate often, and draw the line accordingly. Repeat this process until you have lines between all the people who communicate often.

Now look the chart over. Who are the "players"? Who are the political "dimwits" like Ken? Most important, how politically connected are you?

If something big were to happen— a merger, a change in corporate strategy—would you know about it before it became common knowledge? Who should you involve in your political network to make sure you're among the first to know?

Now look at your list of names from a different perspective. Who is gaining power? Who is losing power? Usually, if several people communicate very often (people who have thick lines on your chart) and one of them gains power, the others will also gain power. Are you connected to people who are increasing or losing power? Are you increasing or losing power? Here is what happened to Bob Montgomery.

Bob had just been promoted to CFO of his company, a controversial move, since he had a reputation for being a maverick. His new job would require him to reign in corporate spending—raises, new equipment purchases, and executive perks. Many of the company's executives would lose tremendous power if he succeeded, and thus Bob considered them his enemies.

The decision to promote Bob came directly from the chairman of the board, overruling the objections even of the CEO. Before accepting,

Information-Sharing "Players"

Bob stipulated that he would only accept the job if the chairman would back him wholeheartedly were his enemies to attempt a "sabotage." The chairman agreed, and the two men shook hands.

Bob proceeded to assume his new job duties, thinking he was immune from political backstabbing. He dropped his old habits of keeping tabs on his enemies and focused solely on balance sheets, expenditures, and the findings of the internal auditors.

Six months after his promotion, the chairman called from the corporate jet. In between the crackles and static of a bad connection, Bob began to understand the message: He was fired!

The chairman explained that "new information had arisen" about the way Bob operated his own departmental budget. When Bob asked what information had surfaced and the sources, the chairman became vague. "It's probably not true," the high altitude voice admitted. "But we have to have a CFO above reproach, you know. We don't want the stockholders to become nervous."

As Bob cleaned out his office that afternoon, he thought about the handshake that initiated this job. He remembered having felt a Supermanlike elation. "I guess even Superman had to keep an eye on Lex Luther," he realized. "But I won't be this gullible again."

Two years later, Bob was rehired as CFO, after the three executives who had framed him resigned in an embezzlement scandal. And, true to his promise, he never again succumbed to such gullibility. It took three more years, but he managed to cut expenditures and increase earnings per share by 20 percent. This time, he kept one step ahead of his "enemies" and their potentially underminings.

Can you see parallels in your situation? Are you being squeezed out, or are your opportunities expanding? What can you do to increase your political leverage?

The second element in assessing your job is what value you add to the corporation. Nonprofit organizations are filled with people who play the political game very well but offer little to the bottom line. But in for-profit companies in the 1990s, your future is only as secure as the people's perception of your value.

Traditionally, most CEOs of large corporations rise through the ranks of marketing or engineering. A few others rise through finance. Very few top executives come from administration. Conventional wisdom says marketing and engineering add significant value, while such administrative services as legal, hum-an resources, purchasing, and accounting are often largely expensive overhead.

Like most conventional wisdom, this perception is often wrong. But when companies downsize, administration and middle management are often the first to go. Payroll is outsourced, human resources are cut by about 30 percent, and accounting systems are reengineered. Often, the same companies will hire more technical staff, marketing wizards, and customer service personnel simultaneously. Although the perception may be flawed, when your job is on the line the perception may be all that matters.

The key in the 1990s is to continually increase value. Then, when downsizing comes, you'll be in a much safer position. Even if your job is cut, you'll be an industry leader with good prospects for other jobs. And if times in your company are good, you'll be on the fast track for more opportunity. Consider Irving Blake's case.

Irving was director of purchasing for a large biotechnology firm. The company's profits and cash reserves were in good shape, so good that the company became a target for a hostile takeover by a larger firm in the same industry.

During the long process of stockholder approval, Irving sprang into action. He realized that purchasing

Staying on top of corporate trends can help you turn obstacles into new career opportunities.

would be decimated unless he could add significant value to the company and create the perception that his area was worth saving.

To do so, Irving began intensively networking with innovative purchasing managers. In the process, he discovered that the trend was to reengineer the purchasing function and drastically reduce staff.

Yet Irving saw this not as an obstacle, but rather as an opportunity. He brought in business process reengineering consultants to shave time and personnel. And instead of trimming his department's size, he hired several highly respected MBAs and realigned the vision of his department.

The new theme was reducing corporate expenditures. Instead of being known as just a purchasing department, Irving changed the name to "Corporate Purchasing and Business Solutions." Irving sought out corporate waste and recommended dramatic solutions to the interim CEO, who would be influential in deciding which functions to scrap and which to keep.

In time, Irving gained a reputation for being indispensable. When the buyout finally occurred, purchasing was outsourced, but Irving became purchasing director for the new parent company. He now had four times the staff and a new mandate: "Do for us what you did for them." Immediately Irving went to work.

Like Irving, you can reinvent your career. The first step, which has been the theme of this chapter, is to know yourself and your current job. Chapter 3 introduces the next step, which is to look deep inside yourself and begin to see which of the five career paths is right for you.

Chapter 3

Living the Life You Love

Everyone wants to be happy, to live a life they love. Yet not everyone chooses to be happy—that is, to do the things that evoke this feeling. Most people fail to consider their own internal makeup. Few ask themselves what would bring them the greatest joy.

This is ironic, since studies have shown that people perform optimally in activities they find stimulating and enjoyable. The ideal situation would allow you to intersect your true interests with your profession. In reinventing your career, an essential step is to consider what you really love to do. This insight then becomes the basis for selecting which of the five career paths (or any combination of them) is right for you.

Using a series of case studies, discussions, and self-evaluation tools, this chapter will help you to identify the areas you enjoy the most that might serve as a career foundation and consider which career path best suits and meets your personal objectives.

We will focus on five areas to help you analyze your internal makeup. The first section discusses "doing what you enjoy most." Many professionals have chosen their career because their parents pushed them in a specific direction or because society values a particular profession as honorable (doctors, managers, lawyers, and so forth). The result of this is that many end up in an unenjoyable and, thus, unfulfilling career.

This chapter will help you honestly examine not only yourself but also the realities of your present career path—and the possibilities for change. Like chapter 2, this process may be painful, but it's necessary to bring about many self-revelations. The first evaluation will involve analyzing what you were most interested in during your formative years. Are you currently working in a profession that complements these interests, or did you get sidetracked? Hopefully the insights gained here can help you get back on track—that is, *your* track, the path that would make you happy. Otherwise, you might be headed for major frustration, boredom, and burnout—or are you experiencing these already?

The next section will help you focus on your strengths. What do you do best? Where do you shine? Which of your skills and activities elicit the most approval and praise from others?

Next, we'll examine different work environments and how they affect performance and satisfaction. These environments, or work cultures, include diverse management approaches, structure, dress codes, values, beliefs, and behavioral norms. Are you working in the most ideal culture for you? Are you at ease in your environment? Do you feel successful working in your current environment? The culture in which you work may have more to do with your success than the quality of the plan you develop, since your plan can only be successfully implemented if you're comfortable in your surroundings. Indeed, a particular work culture can both support and hinder your efforts, so selecting the right one is vital and can provide you with a significant advantage over your counterparts.

Another key aspect we'll explore is your life goals. In this section you'll identify your personal, relationship, career, and financial goals. Many people limit themselves by pursuing goals that are too easily attainable. This keeps them from achieving their full potential. Instead, we'll discuss methods for setting and achieving "monster goals,"

Find a career path that complements your interests.

goals that require you to push yourself to new levels you never thought you could attain.

To assist you in this process, we'll discuss the importance of developing a sense of contentment. Without that feeling of inner satisfaction that comes from being at peace with yourself, you'll be unhappy no matter what you achieve in life. You'll simply trudge forward, toiling in vain.

We'll talk about that mysterious inner voice that leads—or misleads—us through life. You'll work through a self-analysis of your values, which are fundamental parameters that govern your commitment to your life goals. If, for example, you desire personal wealth, a career in education would no doubt be in conflict with your values. Or a career in international marketing might interfere with your desire for a large, close-knit family.

By the end of this chapter you'll understand what makes you special—what makes you unique. Your life experiences, personality, and skills and values differentiate you from your peers. You possess special knowledge and ability that others don't have. *You are special in your own right.*

This realization is very important as it relates to your career. When prospective employers, job partners, or clients evaluate you with other candidates, they need a reason to select you. Being comfortable in your own skin—that is, understanding and embracing your strengths and weaknesses, skills and values—will greatly enhance your interpersonal communications. This, in turn, will favorably distinguish yourself from other job candidates and help get you where you want to go.

In this age of niche markets, mass customization, and a growing interest in diversity, you need a firm grasp of who you are, where you fit in the world, and what you're capable of achieving. To help you capture this snapshot of who you are, a self-analysis is provided to examine your unique educational background, experience, and work accomplishments to help you plan your future career path.

Doing What You Enjoy Most

Just who are you? What makes you happy? How do you like to spend your time? If you could do it "your way," what would that entail?

A large part of our personal happiness will depend on how and where we spend the forty-plus years of our working lives. Day in and day out, we spend a majority of our time on work-related tasks. Either we're at work, getting ready for work or traveling to and from work (about 12 hours each day). And that's a low-ball figure—most corporate stalwarts spend much more time. Most experts "eat, breathe, and drink" their work; they always seem to be reading, experimenting, writing, or meeting with their colleagues. The vast majority of entrepreneurs work long hours as well. Thus, it's important that you choose the right career path for you.

Choosing isn't an easy task. Most surveys indicate that two out of three people are discontented with their jobs. This dilemma, however, can and should be resolved, since everyone has the right and opportunity to pursue the activities they enjoy the most. But this is a discovery that you—and you alone—can make.

To begin your self-evaluation, get out a blank sheet of paper and answer the following questions:

1. What were my favorite subjects in school?

2. What are my favorite hobbies?

3. How does my current profession relate to my favorite subjects and hobbies?

4. What would I consider my "ideal" job?

5. In what ways does my current profession relate to my ideal job?

Now let's evaluate your answer to the last question. How close are you now to your ideal job? Are you already doing what you thoroughly enjoy, or, like most people, are you only partway there? The rest of this chapter—and the rest of this book—will help you on your quest to get closer.

Focusing on Your Strengths

Life is most satisfying when you're involved in activities you enjoy, and people usually enjoy doing what they do well. Good writers write. Speakers speak. Actors act. In the business environment, planners plan, organizers organize, negotiators negotiate and deal makers make deals. Naturally, you seldom get much enjoyment out of things you do poorly. So you're way ahead of the game if you know what you do well, and you focus your effort on those areas of your life.

Such concepts may seem simplistic, but many otherwise intelligent people waste their time worrying about their weaknesses. Although it's true that certain shortcomings can limit your progress, it can be helpful to remember that your weaknesses are actually the same as your strengths when viewed from a different perspective. For example, people with a lot of compassion often get their feelings hurt easily; the executive who sees the "big picture" may be weak at implementing day-to-day activities; a good motivator may be viewed as pushy, naive, or opinionated by his critics; and excellent teachers are often seen as obnoxious know-it-alls by others.

At this point in your self-evaluation process, take a few moments and make a list of your work-related strengths. You probably already know them well, but it's nevertheless valuable to review them from time to time. On a separate

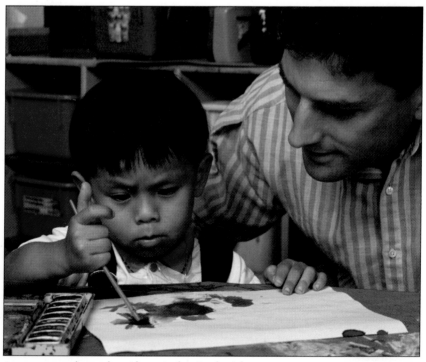

Let your personal strengths guide you in choosing the right career.

sheet of paper, make a list of your strong points—your "selling" points. These are what you have going for you—your winning formula, your bag of tricks. They're what make you victorious in every area of your life.

To facilitate your effort, consider the list of descriptive action words or phrases below—along with any others you can think of—to describe yourself.

Now that you have your list of strengths, consider whether you're using these qualities in your current job. If you are, you're probably quite content. But, if not, then you might want to consider a change to a new job or a different career path.

Take a moment and reflect on the five career paths: corporate stalwart, entrepreneur, special achiever, expert, and facilitator. Which path are you on right now? Would another path allow you to better express your strengths?

Generally, the corporate stalwart excels at analyzing, budgeting, controlling, deciding, collaborating, delegating, encouraging, managing change, organizing, motivating, negotiating, planning, resolving conflict, speaking, supervising, team building, and vision casting. The corporate stalwart is an innovative leader who commands respect while encouraging openness.

The entrepreneur takes pride in achieving, analyzing, collaborating, coordinating, creating, deciding, following up, inventing, leading, organizing, planning, promoting, researching, and vision casting. The entrepreneur is usually a genuine self-starter.

The special achiever needs to be skillful at achieving, collaborating, creating, designing, editing, following up, innovating, implementing, scheduling, selling, and writing. His or her strength is in doing one thing very well, while always looking for ways to improve the process; this involves a long attention span and a real desire to bring about results.

The expert tends to be good at achieving, analyzing, collaborating, designing, innovating, inventing, pioneering, planning, researching, strategizing, systematizing, teaching, and writing. The expert's strengths include genuine innovation and a sound and reliable knowledge of important topics.

The facilitator needs to master the skills of coordinating, counseling, empathizing, encouraging, facilitating, following up, inspiring, interviewing, leading, mentoring, negotiating, persuading, promoting, selling, and supporting. The facilitator's strength is in human relations, and in his or her ability to balance

Descriptive Action Words and Phrases

Achieving	Designing	Managing change	Serving
Administrating	Editing	Mentoring	Speaking
Analyzing	Empathizing	Motivating	Strategizing
Budgeting	Encouraging	Negotiating	Supervising
Coaching	Expediting	Organizing	Supporting
Collaborating	Facilitating	Persuading	Synthesizing
Commanding	Following up	Pioneering	Systematizing
Controlling	Implementing	Planning	Teaching
Coordinating	Innovating	Promoting	Team building
Creating	Inspiring	Researching	Vision casting
Counseling	Interviewing	Resolving conflict	Writing
Deciding	Inventing	Scheduling	
Delegating	Leading	Selling	

sensitivity toward others with goal-driven motivation.

Only when you're on the career path that lets you utilize your strengths, can you reach your fullest potential. Your performance is maximized; your decisions are on target; and your credibility increases. New opportunities may seem to "rain down," making work much more fulfilling and increasing the joy and overall sense of well being you will experience in every aspect of your life.

Identifying Your Preferred Business Environment

Each career path encompasses many specific work environments. Some will suit you; others will not. But most people haven't a clue about how to find the appropriate one. A good way to start is to analyze your current company's culture.

A company's environment, or culture (we'll use these terms interchangeably), reflects the shared values of the organization. Culture is the organization's personality. It provides meaning and direction.

Answer the following true/false questions (mark "T" or "F" in the space provided) to help you better identify your organization's culture. You'll soon begin to see whether your current work environment is a "fit" or a "misfit." The answers to these questions will also help reveal why you're either very successful or struggling in your current position.

1. Your culture encourages innovation, risk taking, and personal initiative. ____

2. You would describe your organization as nonbureaucratic (very few rules and regulations to follow). ____

3. The approach of your company's managers is more coaching than dictating. ____

4. Company management rewards results rather than perceived importance. ____

5. Your company's "in-crowd" has its own jargon. ____

6. It's easy to tell who's important because they're the best dressers in the company. ____

7. Executives compete for corner offices, expense furnishings, reserved parking, and other power trappings. ____

8. Management places personal loyalty over the achievement of results. ____

9. It's very common for departments to work together rather than compete against one another. ____

10. Employees at all levels are generally proud to be part of your organization. ____

11. Long workdays are discouraged in favor of a healthy, balanced lifestyle.____

12. Office layout encourages cooperation between departments. ____

13. Your company loves to process paper, paper, and more paper. ____

14. The organization's leader is more of a king than a president. ____

It's very important to understand the impact of culture on morale, productivity, competence, and organizational health. Culture patterns affect everyone's feelings, behavior, and social interactions. Your performance is influenced much more by the environment in which you work than by your work habits and the job strategies you implement.

Working in the culture that appropriately "fits" you can lead to better performance, while a "misfit" will significantly hinder your effectiveness.

Now review your answers to the fourteen questions above. If you had it your way, how would your preferred culture "look"? What environment would allow you the most opportunity to succeed? To define your preferred working environment, use a separate sheet of paper to rank the following work culture components to describe what your *ideal* business culture would be like.

1. Acceptance of innovation, risk taking, and personal initiative
2. Level of bureaucratic procedures
3. Management style of company managers
4. Reward system
5. Company cliches
6. Dress code
7. Management's orientation toward results
8. Collaboration versus competition
9. Company pride
10. Work ethic
11. Layout of facilities
12. Support of total quality programs, reengineering, or other process-improvement programs
13. Perception of upper management

You should now have more clarity about your current organization's environment and your preferred working environment. Surprisingly, many people "beat their heads against the wall" in frustration over their company's culture, yet they stick around, naively hoping that it's going to change.

Instead of change, what often results is a form of corporate codependency, an unhealthy experience for those better off in a different environment. But if you hope to succeed, to get the most out of your career, to live out

your career satisfied and content, you have to work in a compatible culture.

Reflect once again on the five career paths. Would one of them likely connect you with more compatible work cultures? For example, if you value flexible work rules and lots of freedom and independence on the job, the expert career path might present you with better cultures than would the corporate stalwart. *Write your answer down* (it will be important later).

Steps to Help You Attain Your Life Goals

You can't simply do it overnight, but you can make systematic progress toward achieving your life goals. The first—and most challanging—step is to create an emotionally balanced, satisfying personal life.

Seek Out Contentment

The overall goal of this chapter is to learn how to live a life you love. You've spent time outlining your interests and strengths, and you've evaluated your present and ideal work environment. So you know what you do best and enjoy doing most, and you also have an idea of which work culture will bring you success.

Success is a relative, subjective term that means something different to everyone. Are you a successful person? If you've ever achieved one of your goals, you were successful at least in that regard. Yet many people who match the dictionary definition of success don't feel very successful.

The real prize is in achieving contentment. Or, as psychologist Abraham Maslow described it, a need for self-actualization. People who are self-actualized fulfill their life potential by learning to live the lives they love. Another way of stating this is that content people are typically emotionally healthy.

Maslow attributes the following seven characteristics to a self-actualized person: (1) an accurate picture of reality, (2) the ability to remove oneself from daily turmoil, (3) a personal mission to make a difference in life, (4) a sense of satisfaction from one's own personal development, (5) a capacity to experience and greatly appreciate life, (6) a passion for both the goals pursued and the journey toward those goals, and (7) sufficient opportunities for creativity in one's work.

This level of appreciation for your life is possible if you are willing to expend the effort. Most of us would like to experience tremendous personal growth and live in a manner that expresses our values. We all want self-actualization in our lives and careers. We all want to find contentment. But are *you* content with your life? Let's find out.

For years, human behavior experts and educators relied on the IQ test to evaluate a person's chances of succeeding in a profession or the classroom. Now experts are relying on another indicator, a person's emotional health, to determine their chances for success.

According to Menninger and Levinson in their insightful book *Human Understanding in Industry*, our emotional health can be measured by using several factors to evaluate our personal contentment. (While this test has been around for years, it's still widely used.) These factors include:

- Ourselves

- Our personal lives

- Family, friends, and acquaintances

- Life's difficulties

- Career progress

- Our ability to control circumstances

- Our ability to focus on various tasks

- Our ability to make decisions

- Openness in communication

- A willingness to take risks

Complete the following questions to evaluate your emotional health. On a separate sheet of paper, answer "yes" or "no" to the following questions.

1. I am generally happy with myself. yes__ no__

2. I am reasonably able to handle daily problems; either I overcome them or I make successful compromises. yes__ no__

3. I am emotionally stable and have few mood swings. yes__ no__

4. My memory is fairly good. Although I forget things occasionally, it's rare for me to draw a complete blank. yes__ no__

5. My energy level is too low. yes__ no__

6. I have a need for order that is excessive and counterproductive. yes__ no__

7. I have trouble applying myself to productive activity. yes__ no__

8. I am usually not afraid of such things as open places, dogs, or heights. yes__ no__

9. I have a need to dominate that is harmful in my interpersonal relationships. yes__ no__

10. I rarely waste time in arguing, complaining, envying, or resenting others. yes__ no__

11. I readily take responsibility for my life. yes__ no__

12. Pressures are getting me down. yes__ no__

13. Making choices upsets me. yes__ no__

14. I am realistic in my evaluation of other people. I see them as they are, as opposed to seeing them in

overly negative or overly positive terms. yes__ no__

15. I profit from experiences, as opposed to repeating the same mistakes. yes__ no__

16. I hear voices, see visions, or smell odors that others do not. yes__ no__

17. I am reliable. If I say I'll do something, people can depend on me. yes__ no__

18. I often talk to myself, even when others are present. yes__ no__

19. I find myself thinking that people are plotting against me, talking about me, or watching me. yes__ no__

20. I have trouble understanding myself. yes__ no__

21. I rarely have headaches, stomach pains, or other physical symptoms of excessive stress. yes__ no__

22. I am able to accept frustrations. When things go wrong or someone doesn't do what I want, I take things calmly and try to find a better way. yes__ no__

23. I often do dangerous or foolish things. yes__ no__

24. I am usually able to adjust to the people with whom I live and work. yes__ no__

25. I have bodily ailments that seem impossible to heal. yes__ no__

26. I don't seem to care about anything or anybody. yes__ no__

27. My job is generally satisfying. yes__ no__

28. In addition to my work, I have other interests that provide satisfaction such as family, home, hobby, sports, pets, and community activities. yes__ no__

29. I feel in control of my life. yes__ no__

30. I am not overly obsessed about anything—such as money, sex, or work. yes__ no__

31. I am not overly compulsive in my behavior—such as having to wash my hands constantly. yes__ no__

32. I do not displace emotions onto innocent parties (such as releasing my hostility on coworkers because of home problems, or vice versa). yes__ no__

33. I have a positive attitude toward myself and toward life. yes__ no__

34. I am not overly critical of the shortcomings of others. yes__ no__

35. I am too submissive and rarely exert my own ideas own wishes. yes__ no__

36. I can easily give recognition and credit to somebody else, as opposed to requiring all of the attention and praise myself. yes__ no__

37. I am relatively free of tension and anxiety. yes__ no__

38. I have trouble sharing with others. yes__ no__

39. I am too security conscious; I am afraid to take risks. yes__ no__

40. I have an excessive need for approval from others. yes__ no__

To grade yourself, give yourself one point for each of the following questions if you answered "yes": Questions 1, 2, 3, 4, 8, 10, 11, 14, 15, 17, 21, 22, 24, 27, 28, 29, 30, 31, 32, 33, 34, 36, 37.

Give yourself one additional point for the following questions if you answered "no": Questions 5, 6, 7, 9,

Strong emotional health can be a factor in determining your emotional success.

12, 13, 16, 18, 19, 20, 23, 25, 26, 35, 38, 39, 40.

Now add up your score. A perfect score is 40. While this test is only an indication, a score of between 35 and 40 generally suggests that you have strong emotional health. A score of 30 to 35 indicates reasonably good emotional health, yet you might want to focus on improving your environment (just slight improvement may give you a few more points). A score of 25 to 30 suggests relatively serious issues with regard to your mental health. A score of below 25, and you may want to evaluate the many ways in which you can improve your emotional health.

Whatever your score, you should review those questions for which you didn't receive points. Try to understand the reason for your responses. In general, an answer that would have given you points represents a healthy emotional mind-set. By making your behavior more in line with these answers, your emotional health will likely improve.

It's just as important to maintain good emotional health as it is good physical health. Since this aspect of your life is so critical, you have to be willing to modify or change your behavior as needed. If you're vulnerable in a certain area, figure out why and try to resolve these issues.

If your unhappiness is due to a stressful personal relationship or an unhappy job situation, you don't necessarily want to get a divorce or resign your position, but you do need to clean up the personal habits that are limiting your ability to cope. This may mean exercising regularly, allowing yourself time to reflect, cutting back on excessive eating and drinking, or making changes from negative to positive attitudes.

A lack of emotional health may also signal a need for a more drastic change to a new career path. Look critically at the answers on the test that didn't earn you any points. Which of them would (or might) change if you shifted to one of the other five paths? Which path would help you become more emotionally healthy?

Live by Your Values

This step is to help us better understand our values. We all uphold certain values that dictate our preferred lifestyle, career, and family life. Our values are our filter for how we process information and make important decisions. When we're clear about our values, we make our decisions consistently, proactively, and with confidence. Thus, our values affect our destiny, and we can't really be happy unless our decisions and goals are consistent with our values.

Our values change throughout our lives, making it important that we re-evaluate ourselves every few years to make sure we're clear about them. Many factors go into determining our

personal values: parental influences, other family members, social and economic status, peers, heroes, television, movies, music, government, teachers, romantic relationships, coworkers, bosses, religion, and nearly every other life experience. When our goals are compatible with our values, we experience the satisfaction that can only come from achieving those things that mean the most to us. Thus, value assessment is a critical step in reinventing your career.

Take a moment now to "check in" with your values. On a separate sheet of paper, make a note of those statements listed on the next page that you agree with. If you don't agree with a statement, rewrite it to reflect your current beliefs.

You should notice some consistency between your analysis of your preferred working environment and your work values. Is your current work situation compatible with your values? If not, you should plan to make some changes.

It's also important that your work values be compatible with other areas of your life. Now review the following list that likely reflects many of your other life values. Make a note of those statements you agree with, and rewrite those statements that reflect your actual values. You may want to add to this list to better clarify your foundational values. Naturally, both your life goals and career path should reflect your values.

For example, you won't want to work in a culture that creates a conflict with your family life. If you desire community involvement, you may put off going back to school. A pacifist might pass up a high-paying job with a defense contractor. If you're still in the Dark Ages and think wives should stay at home, you might feel uncomfortable in a company composed of 75 percent women. (That's not to say that all values are good and constructive. Some, like racism, can actually be quite damaging.)

Value Analysis

Work Values
▼

Being a team member is rewarding.

I avoid taking risks.

Ideas are my bread and butter.

I want to rise as far as possible in my organization.

It's important to me that I have people
working for me.

Security is very important to me.

Variety is the spice of work life.

I get status by telling people where I work.

I need autonomy.

What I do is important to society.

Counseling others makes me feel needed.

I make the decisions.

Having my own business is a dream of mine.

Traveling for my company validates my importance.

I live for recognition from my boss for
my accomplishments.

I enjoy change.

I dress for success.

I will never work for a woman (or man).

Success to me is rising to the top of my profession.

I prefer to be around people.

Schedules limit me.

I compete with my coworkers.

Family and Other Relationships
▼

I spend considerable time with my spouse, children,
and immediate family.

My spouse is the most important person in my life.

I would sexually harass the other sex if I could get
away with it.

Wives belong at home with their children.

Monogamy would not be my first choice.

I want as many children as I can afford.

My children will respect their elders.

Living in mild climate is more important to me than
my career progress.

I feel sexually inhibited.

My parents greatly influence my decisions.

I have a problem controlling my temper.

Close personal relationships are worth more to me
than career success.

Money
▼

I work for the money.

I spend money in ways that show others how
successful I am.

Financial security is a priority.

I have money put aside for a rainy day.

My car(s) reflects the image I'm trying to portray.

I want to provide my family with everything
I lacked as a child.

I live or plan to live in one of the nicest neighbohoods
in town.

Government
▼

Most people on welfare could be working if they
weren't so lazy.

Politicians can never be trusted.

Too much was made of the Watergate scandal.

I'm offended when I hear of protesters burning
the flag.

Victory in Vietnam would have made it okay.

The government needs to get tough with Japan.

Too many of my tax dollars are spent on
social programs.

Religion and Social Issues
▼

I take my spiritual life seriously.

I look forward to an afterlife.

I keep a positive attitude.

There are no heroes today.

Abortion is up to the individual.

I serve in my community.

The Bible/Koran/Torah reflects my
foundational beliefs.

Music is getting out of hand these days.

The meaning of life affects how I spend my time.

Television and movie content should be regulated
by the government.

I'm a good neighbor.

My faith should be spread to the "unbelievers"
in other countries.

I support my local church and other charitable causes.

Health and Leisure
▼

Looking healthy is more important than eating
what I want.

Having a long, healthy life is worth denying myself junk food.

Exercise is part of my regular routine.

I can't wait until the workday ends so I can do what I really enjoy.

My favorite tool is the remote control.

I prefer theater over bowling.

Taking drugs on a social level is acceptable.

I would live a life of leisure if I didn't have to work.

Drinking at business lunches is acceptable if I don't overdo it.

Education
▼

I'm a lifelong learner.

My children will attend the best schools money can buy.

I look down on those who haven't completed college.

Schools are failing to educate our children.

I read at least one book a month.

You won't be content with your life if you make decisions contrary to your values. Your values provide you guidance to live a life of contentment, or as Maslow calls it, a life of self-actualization. Take the case of Laura Campobasso.

Coopers and Lybrand recruited Laura out of the MBA program at the University of Texas at Austin. Even though she performed exceptionally well and was awarded a partner track position, Laura felt a calling to take on worthy causes by serving organizations that often can't afford to pay expensive consulting fees.

Laura decided to open her own firm, Progressive Strategies, and focused her energies and organization-development skills on serving wildlife preservation, local communities, the environment, and other nonprofit organizations. Her reputation spread internationally, and she began working with groups in Canada, South America, Slovakia, and the Caribbean.

It wasn't long before governments of developing nations started calling on her to help them with their management issues. A natural team builder with a passion for making the world a better place, Laura let her values dictate her career path, and she's much better off because she did.

Now that you're clearer about your values, we're ready to discuss the goal-setting process. But before you

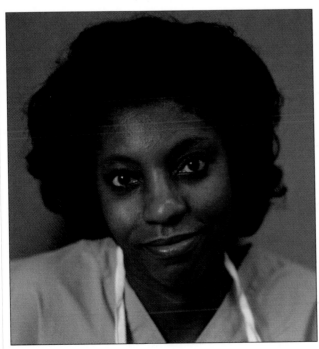

Break down your old mental barriers and clear the way for positive thinking.

Allow yourself to set "monster goals." The possibilities are endless.

prepare your goals, it's important that you remove any mental barriers that may be standing in your way. Unfortunately, those barriers are invisible, so you can't see them. You *can* hear them, however. These barriers come from within yourself, from within your mind, and you need to remove them before we proceed further. You'll recognize them as those feelings of doubt you experience when you listen to that "inner voice" inside you—not the positive but the negative one. Let's examine this in more detail.

Listen to Your Inner Voice

You know the one. It's the voice that doesn't believe in you; it tries to talk you out of even trying; it thinks everything is too hard—*and it won't let you have what you want!*

Too often, we listen to this little voice inside us; the voice that tells us we can't actualize our dreams. It makes students think they'll fail their exams, and it tells downsized executives that they're failures.

It's best not to listen to this negative inner voice. Instead, focus on the positive inner voice that says everything is going to be okay; the voice that tells you that you can get financing for your new venture; that the company *will* hire your consulting services because it needs you; that your paper *will* be a favorite at the next conference. When this self-affirming voice reminds you of what you'd like to do with your life, you should listen to it.

As you become clear about what you'd like to do with your life, you need to acknowledge yourself. Are your dreams too big? Ignore that negative inner voice. Believe the one that tells you that you can accomplish your dreams.

Such advice is certainly easier to give than to follow, especially if you had no experience from your role models. Your parents may have had their dreams shattered. It was very common for those growing up during the depression to accept any job they could get, and they often carried that burden with them for the rest of their lives. Many people were grateful simply to be employed—at anything—as long as it allowed them to feed their families. Studies have shown that even in today's modern world, over 80 percent of the workforce stumble aimlessly into a profession.

People often endure unpleasant career choices because they feel trapped. It's almost as if their lives are predestined to mediocrity by a power outside their control. Thus they take no responsibility for their career path and instead trudge through many years of boredom, frustration, and, finally, burnout. They are the proverbial "victims." But you don't have to be one. You can dream any dream and set any goals you want.

Set "Monster" Goals

Setting goals is definitely a good thing, but the problem is that many of us tend to set goals that aren't big enough.

We set safe goals, goals that are easily attained. After all, we wouldn't want to take a chance on failure, would we? Although it is conventional wisdom, this concept is limiting. It does us little good to set small goals that don't really challenge or drive us, but rather keep us in our comfort zones. Too often, we set goals that only *improve* our lives instead of transforming them.

Instead, we need to set "monster" goals! Goals that put something at stake. Goals that require shedding of blood, sweat, and tears. Goals that require courage and guts to pursue. We need to think big—bigger than we've ever thought before. What are your dreams? The next section will help you figure out *exactly* what they are.

Brainstorm for Goals

Just as groups within organizations use brainstorming techniques to create innovative solutions to solve their companies' problems, individual brainstorming is often an effective technique for creating life-changing goals.

The same rules that apply to group brainstorming also apply to individual brainstorming. The purpose is to produce ideas without imposing limits on your creativity. While brainstorming, be outrageous in your thinking. If your goals include becoming president of the United States, or founding a firm that does billions in sales, or performing ground-breaking research, or meeting the "rich and famous" in some industry, write it down. This doesn't mean that you have to commit to each and every idea, but you shouldn't be afraid to explore your innermost desires.

Take the time to generate as many exciting ideas for your life that you can. Use the broad categories of Personal, Relationships, Career, and Financial. You may want to take a few days to do this. Write down some goals until you seem to have exhausted the supply of them. Then come back a few hours later. You may need to repeat this cycle three or four times until you really feel that you've hit on the major issues.

During this process, make sure you come up with short-, medium-, and long-term goals. A good way to do this is to ask yourself, "Where would I like to be in a year?" For medium-term goals, ask the same question about three years from now; and for long-term goals, ask yourself where you would like to be in five years.

First, *measure your ideas against your lifelong interests for compatibility.* Do your ideas match those areas in which you enjoy spending your time? If your idea is to invest in futures and options but you've never enjoyed learning about finance or you never read the financial section of the newspaper, this would probably not work for you. And so on.

Next, *measure your ideas against your strengths.* Have you shown an aptitude in this area? Or is this something that you feel you could develop? Do you imagine yourself succeeding at this? Don't let that negative inner voice talk you out of it. Be positive but objective. If you've been exceptional in these areas, chances are that you should go for it.

At this point, you should try to determine how your current work culture would affect your ideas. Is this the right culture for you? Will it allow you to accomplish your objectives? If not, what type of culture do you need to be successful with your goals?

You've already examined your level of contentment and your current emotional health. How will this affect your ability to accomplish your goals? What changes do you need to implement to avoid self-limitation?

Now, what about your values? Are your goals in line with how you view life? Are they in harmony? This is very important, as you can't successfully pursue goals that are contrary to your values. This just wouldn't work. You would compromise your integrity and fail to achieve contentment.

But when your values are in harmony with your goals, the synergy will propel you farther and faster than you may have thought possible. You'll be happier than you've ever been. You'll feel content with your life. You'll be living a life that you love.

Later on in this book, you'll take these ideas and develop action plans that will catapult you into productive life changes. It takes many people twenty to thirty years before they determine what they're going to do with their lives. But once you establish an action plan, your life will fall into place more easily and quickly—and for the better.

Many people have experienced the sad realization that they're terribly unhappy with their work or their life, yet they feel powerless to do anything about it. Some don't admit it for ten, twenty or thirty years, but one day they just "break down." Feeling beaten,

hopeless, and miserable, they wished they had only been courageous enough to pursue their dream earlier. Some compensate through excessive eating or becoming couch potatoes. Others abuse drugs or alcohol. None of this is healthy, and none of it is necessary. It's much better to just deal with the problem head-on. This is exactly what happened to Kevin Palmer.

After fifteen years in the purchasing department, Kevin had worked his way up to a purchasing director's position with an international magazine publisher. Despite his success and reputation for competence and professionalism, he started to dread coming to work each day. He was terribly bored and soon began to wonder if he was cut out for a purchasing career. After much introspection and some counsel from his career coach, Kevin realized that he really longed for an opportunity to express his creativity—so much so that he was willing to give up his lucrative director position to start over in an entirely different field if necessary. He had always thought of himself as a corporate stalwart, but now he was filled with uncertainty.

Kevin did a lot of soul searching—and value searching, and goal setting. He asked his best friends for advice. Although he finally reached the conclusion that he was indeed a corporate stalwart at heart, he needed a way to maintain this career path and be creative at the same time.

Despite facing a substantial cut in pay, Kevin transferred to the marketing division of his company, which had a reputation for encouraging creativity. As it turned out, Kevin quickly stood out as a natural marketer with superior instincts. It wasn't long before he earned management's support to completely overhaul their international marketing strategy. In the process, he developed several new products that became instant successes and provided a financial boon.

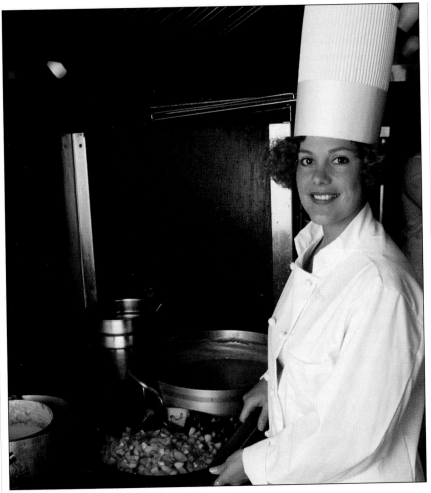

Learn how your special skills set you apart from others.

After reviewing the company's advertising strategy and ad campaign, Kevin proposed an entirely new and innovative focus that increased sales and heightened the company's visibility. He also won approval for new company mission and vision statements, and he authored their new marketing plan. It wasn't long before he also became the main company spokesman for explaining the new strategy to other company directors and to executives and shareholders. Within a year, Kevin was earning one and a half times his previous salary and was loving the daily challenges that came with his new role. He had taken a big chance by starting over so late in his career, but he never regretted it.

Kevin refused to be a victim to "the system" and took control of his life. He threw himself enthusiastically into his new role and within a year surpassed several twenty-year veterans within his department. He's happier and more productive, and has a bright future. Bottom line: there's no reason to remain in a job or stay with a company if it's going to adversely affect your long-term happiness.

Knowing What Makes You Special

Part of being happy is figuring out where you best fit. How do your unique interests, skills, and values set you apart? The combination of these are good indicators of the most appropriate career path for you.

As we've emphasized throughout this chapter, all of us are unique and special. Behaviorists have identified numerous personality types, talents, and skill sets. We all possess distinct intelligence, temperament, and emotional health. These natural traits—along with our personal experiences, environment, culture, and social status—are what make us unique individuals.

Now that you've completed the many self-analyses in this chapter, it will be helpful to pull it all together and "put a ribbon on it." Go back through your notes now and prepare a self-profile. This vivid description and analysis of your interests, strengths, preferred work environment, emotional health, values, and life goals will serve as your "passport" for the rest of your life's journey.

And now take one more look at the five paths described in detail in chapter 1: corporate stalwart, entrepreneur, achiever, expert, and facilitator. If you're like most people, one of these will be emerging as the preferred path to explore. It may be different than the one you've been on, or, like Kevin, you may simply need a slight career readjustment while staying on the same path.

Which of these paths seems right for you? Write it down on a sheet of paper. You aren't completely committing to it yet, but you need a good idea of where you're going.

In chapter 4, we'll cover a variety of skills and resources needed for success in any career, and how you can master them.

Chapter 4

Sharpening Your Career Skills

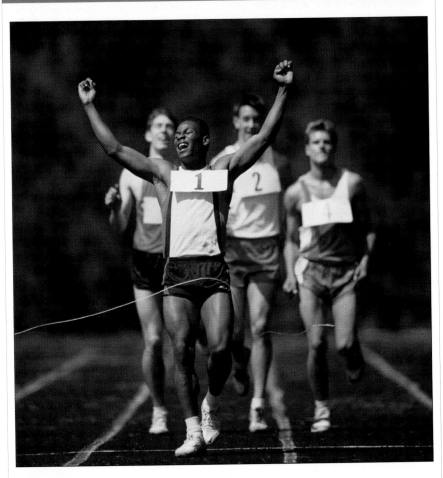

einventing your career is a difficult but exciting task that requires vision, determination, and guts. So far you've examined your own career goals, assessed where you are in your plans, looked at what makes you unique, and started to put all this information together. And at the end of chapter 3, you made a preliminary decision about what career path is most suited to you.

Michael Hammer, coauthor of the book *Reengineering the Corporation*, recently admitted that most corporate reengineerings fail. The reasons are varied and complicated: Some companies lack the commitment to breakthrough thinking; others don't seek qualified consultants; and some simply tire of the process.

Many people fail to successfully reengineer their careers for the same reasons. They lack both the stamina and the vision. In short, their skills aren't up to the job. Are your skills sharp enough to take on the challenge of reinventing your career?

This chapter focuses on determining which skills are most important for you, and it will help you make plans to sharpen them. In order to succeed in your new career path, you need to identify your degree of proficiency in each skill and determine any areas that need sharpening. This process of skill identification follows what you've done in previous chapters. Assessing your skills, much like the self-assessment processes you've already tackled, may be one of the most rewarding things you will ever do.

Think for a moment about how many people you know who really understand themselves and actively sharpen their skills. You probably know some, maybe quite a few. Your list probably includes several up-and-coming corporate types, an entrepreneur or two, a few special achievers, and perhaps a facilitator. And if you think back to college, you probably know some experts.

If you made a second list of the most successful people you know—and in it included people you think are destined for career greatness—the two lists would probably be very similar.

The point is that people who are in touch with themselves, who practice career reinvention on a regular basis, are initially more successful. And yet few people take these steps. Why is that?

Public speaking runs parallel to career reinvention and gives us clues as to why some people don't assess their skills and keep them sharp.

A recent survey showed that public speaking was one of the top fears of most Americans. Yet many other polls of successful executives, career counselors, and employment officers show that people who can speak well in public get more job offers, are promoted faster and further, and earn more money. The few people who break through the fear reap big rewards.

As with public speaking, most people are afraid of what they might see if they look in the "career mirror." Perhaps they'll have to view their own mistakes or acknowledge that they haven't measured up to their own image of success. To avoid these sometimes painful revelations, people often follow the "safe" route by not looking at all.

But those people who break out of this "safe zone" do better. They confront their mistakes, affirm their successes, plan for the future, and earn big rewards.

This chapter details six skills that everyone needs—whether your ideal career path is that of a corporate stalwart, an entrepreneur, an expert, a special achiever, or a facilitator. It also discusses additional skills that are important to your specific career, and helps you learn to assess the suitability of your proposed career path.

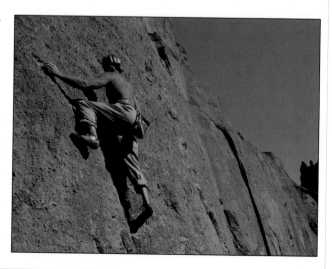

Nothing ventured, nothing gained—exploring new boundaries.

The concluding section of this chapter addresses the mix of skills you'll need to succeed in today's business economy. Some skills are absolutely vital for you, others are important, a few may be a little helpful, and some won't matter at all, but you need to determine which ones to develop right away and which ones can wait until later.

An Overview of Today's Critical Skills

Only a few decades ago, employers often advertised jobs that required loyalty to the company and the ability to get along with employees at all levels. Essentially, companies were looking for people who would fit into the social mix of their cultures. People who could prove their ability to do the job while being collegial were hired. These same skills propelled people to supervisory, management, and even executive jobs.

A theme of this book is that people today should be loyal to their careers, and not to a single company. Even being dedicated to a single industry can sometimes be dangerous.

Robert Waterman, who (along with coauthor Thomas Peters) shook corporate America in the 1980s with the insightful book *In Search of Excellence. . .*, has recently taken up the banner of the "new contract" between employees and employers. The old model, he asserts, was child-parent, with the employees completely dependent on the goodwill of their superiors. A termination was like Dad moving away (or, more accurately, Dad ordering one of the kids to leave the house). Even senior executives quivered at the whims of their boards of directors.

The new model, Waterman proclaims, is adult-adult. People today form alliances with companies for clearly stated reasons which may include full-time regular employment, part-time or temporary consulting, long-term data collection and analysis paid on a project-by-project basis, or many other kinds of relationships. When a win-win relationship is no longer possible, people have the right *and* the obligation to move on.

The skills of the old model were centered around survival: fitting in, not taking major risks, maintaining stability. Companies rewarded these behaviors.

So what are the critical skills for today's careers? They have to equip you, in Waterman's model, to be an adult. There are five such skills, applicable to any of the career paths you might choose. Let's examine each skill in detail.

Skill #1: Keeping Fit

The first is maintaining good health. This skill, which is often overlooked, is absolutely key for everyone in every career path. Under the child-adult model, a person who became sick was comforted and put on disability by the company, while other employees covered for the one who had fallen ill. But today there isn't enough "fat" in the economy to treat people this way. Like soldiers in a war, if one falls, there simply isn't enough time to pick him up, get him help, and continue the fight.

The costs of a health crisis, even a temporary one, can be extreme. Whether your reinvented career path takes you up the corporate ladder out into the world of experts, into the lives of the powerful through facilitation, into a strong focus on results as an achiever, or into the new world of entrepreneurialism, your career is only as strong as your health.

Today's successful people make more contacts, work more deals, plus take the time to envision what is possible and bring that future about. Today's patterns of work require more energy, a greater sense of focus, and more stamina than ever before.

A Health Checkup

American health is improving in many areas but getting worse in others. For instance, heart disease rates are declining due to lower fat intake and better drugs for high blood pressure; yet physicians warn that as the population is aging, it is also getting fatter, thus leading to higher diabetes rates. Cancer is also on the rise. While the causes of this disease are less clear, recent research has linked certain types of cancer to high fat intake, insufficient exercise, and environmental pollutants.

Most of us know how to achieve good health, but in the quest to live successful lives we sometimes take shortcuts around healthy habits. The result can be short-term achievement at the expense of the long term. How is *your* health? Here are some specifics you should consider.

Weight. Recent research indicates that the average American is too heavy. However, weight standards have changed dramatically from the life insurance charts of the 1950s. Consult your physician to determine the current health standards for the appropriate weight and percentage of body fat for your height and frame size. If you are more than 10 percent over or under your ideal weight range, it's time for action. You're probably already feeling the consequences—reduced energy, lowered stamina, and diminished self-confidence. If you need to reduce your weight, cut fat and calories from your diet, and increase aerobic exercise. For more serious weight problems, consult a physician. On a separate sheet of paper, write down which action steps you will take to improve your weight.

Diet. The U.S. government recommends a "pyramid" diet, emphasizing grains, vegetables, and fruits.

Every day, you should consume at least six servings of grains (bread, cereal, rice, and pasta), three servings of vegetables, two fruits, two servings of dairy (milk, yogurt, and cheese), and two servings of meat, poultry, fish, dry beans, eggs, and nuts. Eat fats, oils, and sweets sparingly. How do *you* fare?

If you're not eating enough of the healthiest servings (those at the wide part of the pyramid), then it's time to start. Cereal for breakfast instead of eggs, vegetables as a side dish at dinner and lunch, fruit for dessert instead of cake. Just a few simple corrections, and you'll be well on your way to better health.

Evaluate your current eating habits, and jot them down. Note what you are currently doing well (e.g., eating enough grains), and what areas of your diet are weak (e.g., too much fat, too many sweets). Then commit yourself to the specific actions you will take to improve (e.g., adding a midday snack of a piece of fruit or switching to a low-fat, high-fiber breakfast). Be sure to put in writing all of your commitments to improve.

Exercise. Many Americans claim that they are simply too exhausted to exercise. This is ironic, since exercise improves energy, focus, concentration, productivity at work and overall health. In most cases, you should exercise aerobically for at least 20 minutes a day, three days a week. Use caution as you get your pulse in the health-building range. And since exercise can make certain conditions worse, seek qualified medical advice before starting an exercise program.

Even if you're not exercising at the recommended level, carve out a small portion of time in your schedule for a short aerobic workout. Many busy people work out either the first thing in the morning or during lunch, and soon discover that the extra energy they gain more than makes up for the time the exercise consumes. Write down which steps you will take, if changes are necessary.

Sleep. Several recent medical studies report that America is a sleep-deprived nation. In an effort to balance a successful career with a satisfying family life, many people take time away from their sleep. The results of sleep deprivation can be serious: irritability, inability to concentrate, lack of energy, and, ultimately, loss of the will to work. Ironically, as people try to become more effective by working longer hours, they become dramatically less effective by compromising on sleep. Rather than viewing sleep as an impediment to achievement, think of it as a valuable investment in the next day's work. So, how are *you* doing in this important area?

Ask yourself the following questions to determine if you're getting enough sleep. Do people often tell you that you look or sound tired? Do you "crash" on the weekends, perhaps getting ten or more hours of sleep on Friday or Saturday night? Do you find that you feel exceptionally sleepy after lunch? Do you suddenly "come alive" just before it's time for sleep? If you answered "yes" to any of these questions, it's probably time to change your sleep habits.

The average person under age 50 needs eight hours of sleep, and a small percentage can satisfactorily function with five or six hours. But many more pretend they can—and pay the price of reduced effectiveness. Most of us get by reasonably well with only seven hours. In general, we suggest that you set a goal to get a "solid eight" for optimal performance at work and to avoid feeling irritable.

In today's fast-paced world, some people find they have to slow down to sleep. And, even if they try, many people find they *can't* sleep. If your sleep follows this pattern of insomnia, there are several remedial steps you can try. First, don't use your bed for anything other than sleep and sex;

otherwise, you will begin to associate being in bed with not sleeping. Second, if you can't fall asleep in 45 minutes, get up and do something else until you feel sleepy. Third, don't exercise within two hours of the time you need to fall asleep. Fourth, reduce or eliminate your caffeine intake. Finally, if these simple solutions don't work, consult your physician to see if other underlying problems exist.

Once again, evaluate yourself on paper. Jot down what healthy things you are doing with regard to sleep (e.g., getting your work done early enough to relax for sleep), what things you can improve (e.g., occasionally staying up past your normal bedtime), and what new, healthy habits you can begin to acquire (e.g., making sure you get to bed at least eight and half hours before you have to get up).

Drugs. Drugs, even legal ones, can undermine your performance. We all know this is true. But it's so easy to drink an extra cup of coffee (or two or three or four!) in the morning. And it's so easy to drink an extra glass of wine before going to bed. Or to smoke an extra cigarette. Or to pop an over-the-counter sedative. Most drugs, legal or otherwise, can diminish our long-term effectiveness.

Serious addictions—including alcohol and tobacco abuse—often require more than "self-control" techniques to successfully overcome. People often become substance abusers because of a psychological issue, such as dissatisfaction with one's career or personal life, in an attempt to numb the pain of the unresolved issue. But when they attempt to quit, the pain of the issue returns, often with greater intensity, causing them to fall back into the addictive pattern. Thus, because it's often necessary to simultaneously address the psychological issue and the physical addiction, seeking professional help is advisable.

Other people avoid taking drugs that can help them, perhaps even

Serious addictions require more than "self-control" to overcome.

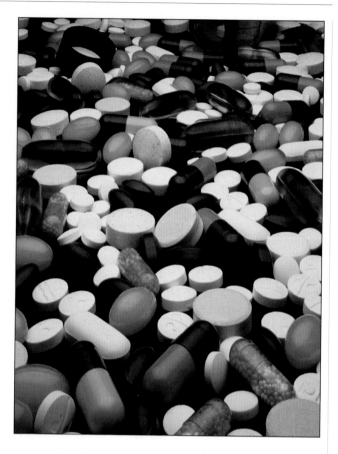

medically beneficial drugs, such as high blood pressure medication. Overall, the best rule of thumb for a well-balanced life is to exercise *moderation:* seek medical help for legitimate problems and avoid or minimize drugs that serve no legitimate need. If you require some behavioral change with regard to drugs, now is the time to list on paper what steps you will take. Consider Tom Webster's story.

Tom was a management consultant with excellent organization development skills. He was widely recognized as a man who could come into a company, talk with a few people, and get a good feel for what was working well and what needed changing. More im-portant, he was known as a man who could bring about quick and dramatic organizational change. A blend between an expert and a special achiever, Tom was also a leader in the professional field, holding a doctorate

and authoring several books widely read in universities.

Tom often joked that he spent the first two decades of his career on airplanes, flying from New York to Los Angeles to Beirut to Johannesburg. His diet was just as hectic—cheeseburgers and fries when he was at home, first-class airplane food when he traveled. And since his clients usually bought dinner, he became fond of just about every type of dessert.

By the time he turned 40, he was almost fifty pounds overweight. At first it didn't bother him; he always had enough money to buy the latest clothes, so he just bought each year's hot wardrobe in a size larger than the previous year.

Around age 45, while 30,000 feet over Denver, he felt as if someone had just dropped a bank vault on his chest. Two hours later, he was in an emergency room in a Los Angeles hospital, suffering from a minor heart attack.

After this health crisis, Tom focused all his energy on getting well. He enrolled in a stress reduction workshop, took up jogging (under a doctor's careful watch), and joined a weight-loss center. Just nine months after Tom's heart attack, he was in the best shape of his life: He was just ten pounds over his ideal weight, could jog five miles a day while keeping his pulse in the safe zone, and had more energy than ever.

After his heart attack, Tom added a new element to his consulting services: He emphasized that a competitive organization must have skilled and healthy managers. By adding this element, Tom was able to expand his consulting business even as his health improved.

Thus far, this chapter has required you that you evaluate yourself in a number of different ways. Take a moment and review your strengths and weaknesses for each of the major categories in this section; record these in the first blank chart column below.

Next, write down the specific areas that need improvement in the second blank column, and specific steps you will take to achieve these improvements in the third column.

Finally, in the last column, commit yourself to dates by which you will have completed the steps.

Now, copy these "due dates" for your action steps into your schedule for the next week, month, and (if necessary) year.

Improving your health is essential for all of today's careers. These steps will help you do a better job in your current career and will aid you in transitioning to your ideal career.

Skill #2: Good Communication

Second in importance to good health, without which we can't have a career at all, is communication with other people. The ability to communicate has consistently been proven one of the most important skills for today's successful people. It's not an exaggeration to say that good communication makes good careers, and poor communication spells disaster.

As time goes on, an increasing number of jobs and employers are demanding good communication skills. Like good health, being able to communicate is a broad skill and is

Health Evaluation

Health component ▼	Current self-evaluation ▼	Areas that need improvement ▼	Steps you will take to improve ▼	Date by which you will have taken steps ▼
Weight				
Diet				
Exercise				
Sleep				
Drugs				

important for everyone working in today's economy. It includes speaking to people over the phone, making formal presentations to large groups, typing E-mail messages, writing reports, even practicing good listening.

Communication skills are especially important for corporate stalwarts, facilitators, and entrepreneurs. People in these paths need to communicate on a regular basis, and must be understood by many different types of people (direct reports, investors, top decision makers, clients, and so forth). Experts and achievers who regularly interface with such people as brokers, salespeople, and top consultants will also need effective communication skills.

Over the past 20 years, the American Assembly of Collegiate Schools of Business has sponsored numerous studies on the importance of communication skills. Each study ranked written and oral communication skills as number one in importance for success in business.

Other studies conducted by top researchers indicate that communication skills are: (1) the top criterion in determining managerial success, (2) the performance factors most likely to affect upward mobility within an organization, and (3) the tools most likely to prepare one for general management.

In addition, courses in business communication are ranked highest in the entire business curricula, according to several surveys of business graduates and employers.

Evaluating Yourself

The test of whether you are a good communicator is simple. Basically, you are a good communicator if people do what you want them to do. If you ask them to buy something, they buy it; if you want a promotion, your superiors give it to you; if you want to arrange a meeting between two business contacts, they both agree. The formula is deceptively simple: good

communicators are good persuaders. Because this formula is so simple, we need ways of evaluating ourselves in the four most important communication contexts.

We will examine communication within the following different contexts—interpersonal, groups, public speaking, and writing—and then provide specific self-assessment exercises. Be sure to keep a piece of paper handy to record thoughts, reactions, and action steps.

Interpersonal. The interpersonal context of communication is most important to business success for most people. It includes all the one-on-one meetings you have with other people, as well as work done over the phone and through E-mail. Through interpersonal communication, people learn about us and our personalities, form opinions of us, and decide whether they can trust us.

A good way to evaluate your interpersonal communication is to determine if people tend to do what you ask. Think about the activities of your present job that take you into contact with other people. Ask yourself whether people tend to follow through on your requests, or instead delay or ignore them. Include the following questions in analyzing your interpersonal skills:

- Are your telephone calls promptly returned?

- Do people attentively respond when you request information?

- Do people buy from you (assuming you're in a sales position)?

- Do people frequently initiate conversations with you?

- Are you often invited to outside office parties, socials, or other activities?

Based on these questions, write down (on a separate sheet of paper) your strengths as you perceive them.

Evaluate how well people respond to your invitations and requests.

Also include what you believe to be your weaknesses—your areas of potential improvement. Finally, based on on these questions, write down what actions you will take to improve.

The next step in analyzing your interpersonal communication is to ask other people for feedback and advice. This step requires you to find people who will be both honest and helpful. (Many people will not tell you anything negative—even when they can think of something—to avoid hurting your feelings. Others will tell you *only* negative things! You need people who will balance honesty with an effort to be helpful.) Elicit their advice in three areas: your current strengths as an interpersonal communicator, what aspects of your communication style require improvement, and what you can do to improve.

We all know people who have no trouble pointing out our weaknesses but are not as astute when it comes to offering helpful suggestions. If you feel that the improvement steps offered by others won't be sufficient to provide truly helpful feedback, here are several suggestions that might help. First, many colleges and universities offer classes in interpersonal communication, usually as part of larger courses of study in psychology, business, sociology, or communication. Many of these classes can be very beneficial, both in providing you with more knowledge about interpersonal communication and in giving you practice and exercises for improvement.

Second, several private consulting and training organizations offer classes specially designed to help professionals improve their interpersonal communication ability. One of the most famous is the Dale Carnegie group, which offers classes in most major cities. The phone book may list other organizations in your area.

Third, several nonprofit groups offer training programs designed to better people's communication patterns. Generally, these groups offer the classes as some sort of community improvement efforts; the list includes religious groups, community centers, community college extensions, high schools, and adult training centers. For the most part, these classes are neither as knowledge-based as those offered by colleges nor as skills-based as those offered by private companies, but they still can be effective.

Fourth, some psychologists, social workers, counselors, and communication consultants offer individual sessions and facilitate small groups to help people improve their communication patterns. This type of help is most beneficial when the interpersonal patterns spring from a deeper psychological issue or when they are too complicated to be addressed in less expensive treatments.

If you decide that you need some help with your interpersonal communication, it's important to do so without hesitation. Most problems of this nature don't go away by themselves, and the vast majority will eventually inhibit your success. By taking proactive steps now, you will greatly increase your ability to transition to your reinvented career.

Group. Communication in groups is crucial to some careers, including the corporate stalwart path, where people must often work in team-based companies. Entrepreneurs frequently have to meet in groups of staff members, investors, customers, suppliers, or other stakeholders. Group work may also be important for people on the achiever, expert, or facilitator career paths.

To assess your current skill level in small groups, reflect back on your time spent in business-related groups. Most people naturally fall into a particular role: "experts" bring an informed perspective to meetings; "socioemotional leaders" care for the feelings and emotions of other people; "task leaders" guide discussion about the substantive issues; "jesters" help break up tension through the use of humor; and "inquisitors" ask questions to clarify other people's positions.

By reflecting on your past group work, try to determine which role you assume most frequently. It's important to note that groups need all these roles, yet some are more accepted in certain types of groups. (Inquisitors, for example, tend not to be favored by groups working on projects under time pressure, as the constant questioning delays the group from finishing its work.)

Now ask yourself whether the role you tend to fall into is the most appropriate one for the types of groups in which you most frequently interact. Are there other roles that might serve your groups—and your career—better? For example, a power broker (part of the facilitator career path) needs to be able to lead the discussion of others; a socioemotional leader may be the most appropriate. Write down your analysis of your group role.

Next, ask yourself if people tend to invite you to join groups. If you seem to be invited regularly, that's good, because it shows that people think you have something to offer. If not, ask yourself why this might be. Is it because your current job doesn't naturally bring you into group work, or is there another reason? Write down your analysis.

Finally, ask for advice from those who've seen you at work in groups. Get their feedback and criticism. If they point out areas of weakness, ask them for specific steps you can take to improve. Ask them if your comments in groups are valuable and if you help or hinder the group process. Again, write down your analysis based on this feedback.

Now combine all this accumulated feedback into (1) a list of things you currently do well, (2) a list of areas in which you need improvement, and (3) a set of steps you should take to improve. Many people, when they reach this point in their self-evaluation, find that they understand what they *don't* do well, but they don't have a tangible, workable understanding of how to improve. If this is your situation, here are steps you can take to improve.

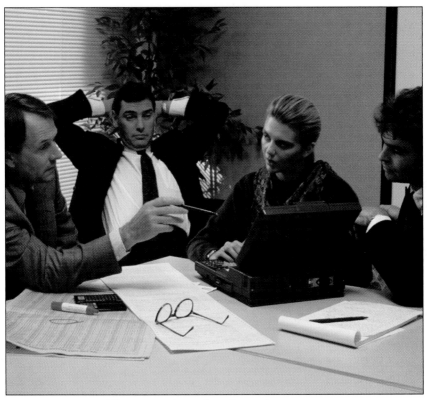

Group communication skills are essential regardless of your role.

First, turn again to colleges and universities and sign up for a class in small-group communication. Largely catering to working professionals in their thirties and forties who are looking for ways to add value to team-based companies, many of these classes are offered at night.

Second, there are several good books on the market that can help. They include: *Building Team Power: How to Unleash the Collaborative Genius of Work Teams* by Thomas Kayser; *Leading Business Teams: How Teams Can Use Technology and Group Process Tools to Enhance Performance* by Robert Johansen; and *Groups: Leadership and Group Development* by Hedley Dimock. You may also find numerous insightful articles in professional journals written about group communication as related to your particular field.

Third, some people find that they don't do well in groups because of a deeper personality issue. If this is your situation, you may need to consult a psychologist. A good rule is to consult a professional if you've tried to overcome a problem without success or if the problem seems too complex to fully understand on your own. Psychologists, psychiatrists, and therapists can often be helpful in these cases.

Finally, if you work consistently with the same people in a group, it may be worth bringing in an outside consultant to perform a "small group diagnosis and intervention." Such a process often requires the consultant spending time observing the group interactions and then creatinging a program designed to improve the group's specific weak points. This may involve personality assessment (such as administering the Myers-Briggs personality test to everyone in the group), team-building exercises, or facilitating a series of meetings until people learn new communication strategies.

Don't underestimate the importance of strong written communication.

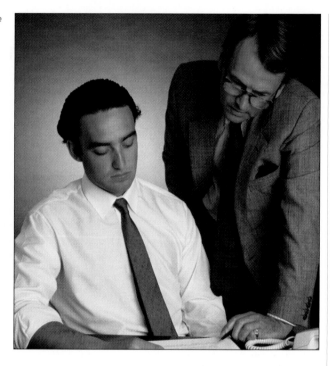

With an increasing number of companies becoming team-based and with more and more people outside the corporate stalwart career path also spending time in groups, resolving any issues in this area is a good investment of your time. The more value you can add to groups, the faster you can achieve your career goals.

Public speaking. As we mentioned in an earlier section of this chapter, public speaking is often considered to be the number-one public fear in America. Most people dread giving a formal speech, and the vast majority of Americans get some kind of stage fright. Yet you need to be able to address a crowd and accomplish your purpose in speaking—whether *to inform* (giving status updates, presenting various options, or providing background knowledge); *to persuade* (getting a board of directors to endorse your idea, swaying a team of engineers to include your product in their designs, etc.); or *to entertain* (being the master of ceremonies for an awards banquet, being an after-dinner speaker, etc.). Think of what purposes your career

path includes—or will include. Now ask yourself (honestly) whether you have the ability to accomplish these purposes.

If you need to take some action steps, there are many options. One of the best is to join Toastmasters International, a group of local speaking clubs that has helped thousands of people to overcome stage fright and increase their ability to inform, persuade, or entertain large groups. You might also consider taking speech classes through universities, colleges, or community centers. A number of private courses, including those through the Dale Carnegie organization, can also help.

Writing. Writing is quite different from communicating orally. Many good writers are not good speakers, and vice versa. But today's world of work demands that you do both effectively. Measure your ability as a writer in the same way you graded yourself for public speaking: are you able to accomplish your purposes? Are your letters read? Do people do what you request? When you send E-mail, do people give you the information you desire or take the action you suggest? What feedback have you received on your writing? Is it friendly or corrective? Warm or cold? Consider the written communication skills demanded not only in your current job but also what your new career path will require.

Many writing improvement courses are offered by colleges or private companies. In addition, a number of good workbooks are available at most large bookstores.

In working through the self-evaluation questions in this section, you have probably compiled several different kinds of notes. Take a moment and record the most important points in the chart below (or copy this on a separate sheet of paper).

Now, copy these "due dates" for your action steps into your daily schedule. This way you will be working through them in your natural course of business.

Taking this step of improving your communication skills is vital for almost all of today's careers. By focusing on your ability to communicate—and by taking the necessary steps to improve— you will be better able to transition to a more ideal career.

Skill #3: Networking

Simply put, networking is the skill that gets you in touch with other people in a mutually beneficial way. Third in importance to good health and communication, your networking skill is directly tied to your ability to succeed.

As John Naisbitt explains in his classic *Megatrends*, "Networks exist to foster self-help, to exchange information, to change society, to improve productivity and work life, and to share resources." As the economy continues to grow and to change, networking becomes more and more important for people in every career path.

For people in the corporate stalwart career path, networking with other people is key to bringing innovative ideas and new operating methods to their own firms. And it is through networking that "up-the-ladder" people get ready for their next career step.

Entrepreneurs also need to network. They need to know investors, bankers, suppliers, potential employees, inventors, and customers. Always looking to better their own team, entrepreneurs

Communication Evaluation

Communication context ▼	What you currently do well ▼	Areas that need improvement ▼	Steps you will take to improve ▼	Date by which you will have taken steps ▼
Interpersonal				
Group				
Public speaking				
Writing				

network with other people to learn new ideas, meet powerful people, and establish useful relationships.

Achievers use networking to spot new ways of producing results, find new customers for what they produce, and keep an eye out for new opportunities. For commissioned salespeople, networking may literally be how they make their living. Brokers find new customers and develop existing customers. And for people who produce things from novels to new polymers, networking is the key to remaining at the top of their fields.

Networking with other informed people is the ultimate objective for experts. The expert community is always looking for new advances and new approaches, and networking is the way for experts to know about both. In addition, experts need to network to find new sources of income, through employment or consulting, so that they can remain at the top of their fields.

The facilitator is almost synonymous with "one who networks." People in this career path seem to know everyone, and they have to be masters of networking to be able to make introductions that benefit everyone involved, including themselves.

So how is networking "done"? How good are you at networking? This section will help you evaluate yourself.

Steps Toward Effective Networking

There are three main steps to networking effectively, and once you master them you can better position yourself for your ideal career.

Making contacts. The first step to networking—and the first way to evaluate yourself—is to reflect on how many new people you meet in an average week, not random individuals you encounter on a plane or in the grocery store, but people who can potentially benefit you, and who you can benefit in return. Generally, you find such people

in conferences, in professional association meetings, and in universities (especially at the graduate level). You might also meet them during non-business-related activities: playing golf; meeting in a place of worship; at a charity drive meeting, or at a health club. The most important question to ask is, how many people am I meeting with whom I could set up a potentially beneficial relationship?

Determining *how many people* represents a sufficient number with whom to network is largely relative to your particular career path and your overall industry. For example, a cardiologist working in private practice may think she is networking very well to meet one or two experts in the field each year; but for an achiever working as a real estate broker, meeting one or two potential customers each day may not be sufficient.

So ask yourself the subjective question, in relation to your proposed career path, "Am I meeting enough people?" Think of successful people you know in your proposed career and career path. How many people are you meeting compared with them? Don't yet plan action steps, just write down the results of your introspection.

Finding mutual benefit. The real key to networking is not just in meeting people (a skill almost anyone can learn, even the most introverted among us), but in finding a reason to continue the relationship with the person you just met. Most people who meet for the first time will never see each other again, but the successful networker manages to pull a large number of these people into their ever-growing Rolodex. And they do this by finding mutual benefit.

There are two keys to this step. First, discover what the person is doing and the nature of his or her needs— perhaps finding a new secretary or a new job, being hired by another client, learning about the latest research in a certain area, or meeting a specific

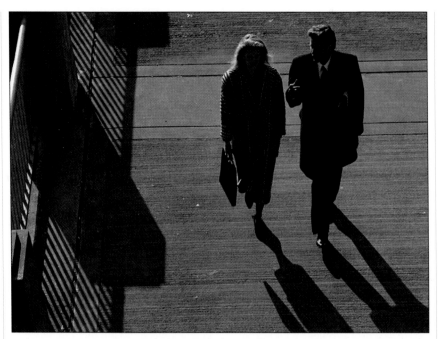

Making new contacts and sustaining them are the keys to effective networking.

person. The problem is that most people aren't comfortable talking about what they need; instead they're generally more confident when they talk about what they already have. One effective method to uncover people's needs is to highlight the importance of their previous successes—and to do so without seeming patronizing. Debbie Fineberg provides a perfect example of a savvy networker.

Debbie is a "master" at working a room. As the agent who represents screenwriters in Hollywood, she has to meet many people and keep current on "who's in." It's her job to make what she has—lots of screenplays written by her clients—fill the needs of the people she meets.

As a successful person working in the facilitator career path, it's imperative for her not to seem overly pushy or abrasive. She does this by highlighting the successes of the people she meets.

At a recent Hollywood screening of a fairly low-budget movie, Debbie took time to congratulate the producer, director, and all of the actors, none of whom she had previously met before

(she had been invited by the movie's scriptwriter). She inquired with interest as to their secrets to producing a quality movie. At first they responded with a vague reply ("working with a great group of people"), but several of them more specifically elaborated that it took an accommodating screenplay writer. She then asked a key question: "What's the secret to working with a writer successfully?"

"The key is to find a good one— and it's a hell of a lot of work," replied the director. At this point, Debbie introduced herself as a friend of the scriptwriter and as an agent, representing many scripts written by reputable writers.

By highlighting the accomplishments of her newfound acquaintances, Debbie showed—without abrasive or overly intrusive behavior—how she could add value to their careers. Her networking skills paid off by providing mutual benefit.

Most people, now feeling that you're "on their side," will open up about what they don't have, about what they need. Another way to do it is to first establish rapport with the person and then ask something like: "Things seem to be going very well. What do you see as the big challenge in the next year?" People will often respond in a confident way, but at the same time reveal one or several key pieces of information that could serve as effective networking catalysts.

The second step is to show that you have value to add. This is tricky: do it wrong and you either seem like the proverbial "slick salesman" or come across as simply arrogant. If you fall into either of these pitfalls, your potential relationship with the person will end even before it begins. The impression you want to leave instead is that you are competent, friendly, and have the means to help this person. Although the exact means to accomplish this will depend to a degree upon your particular industry and your career path, a general rule can almost be successfully applied: indicate as objectively and as humbly as possible that your experience, background, education, abilities, or contacts *in some way intersect with the person's needs*. This is the foundation on which all successful networking is built.

Take a moment now to evaluate yourself on how well you create mutual benefit in your professional relationships. You might even consider how many people you know in your potential career and career path, as a general indication of your ability to network.

Most people in the process of reinventing their careers find that creating mutual benefit is one of their biggest hurdles. If you decide that you need to improve in this area, the end of this section includes some suggestions.

Following up. After you meet someone and find mutual benefit, the third key to networking is in following up. Again, the best methods may be specific to your industry and career path. But take a moment and evaluate how well you keep in touch with people you meet. If almost all of your new contacts never go beyond a handshake and a "let's keep in touch," you probably need to improve. If, on the other hand, most of your initial interactions lead to phone calls, follow-up letters, and a true relationship, you're in excellent shape. Following up is a very transferable skill; people in the corporate stalwart career path transitioning to the facilitator path, for example, will find that their habits of following up also transfer.

If the chart indicates that you need to improve in this area, a good way to begin is to locate someone in your industry and career path who seems to be a natural networker (which probably means that they've invested lots of time learning how to do this right) and ask them for advice. Most of us will need to find a mentor in this area, someone who will "take us under their wing" for an extended period and show us how this is done.

Many professional associations offer free mentoring programs, as do some university alumni associations. Yet the best mentor will probably be someone you already know. Take a look at the story of Brian Wong, a corporate stalwart who not only seeks out mentors for himself but also serves as a mentor to others.

Brian is a manager at a company that provides computer services in the Midwest. While in college, one of Brian's business professors took the time to mentor him about corporate politics. Through the professor's help, Brian landed a job as a management trainee in the company where he still works. Reflecting back today, Brian isn't exactly sure why the professor took the time. "It wasn't ability—there were smarter people than me in the class," he says. "I guess it was that he saw potential and desire. And he wanted someone he could help, someone he felt could grow, and someday perhaps be able to help him."

One of the professor's lessons is that a group of people have a better chance of succeeding than one individual alone. As a result, Brian formed a group of entry-level people he believed had both the ability and the desire to climb the corporate ladder. Brian arranged informal (and, at first, off-the-record) lunch meetings with this group and his old professor. For the first five or six meetings, the professor discussed politics, communication, and proving yourself through superior performance. When the professor stopped attending, Brian would show self-help business videotapes. The group would then discuss them, and brainstorm ways to apply their lessons within their work culture. Although Brian was at the same level as his new friends, he quickly became a mentor to them.

When Brian was promoted, he brought along several coworkers from his group, and the self-development meetings turned into regular staff meetings. Although he now had more business issues to discuss, he continued to discuss professional development techniques and ways to implement them.

Brian also obtained new mentors in his immediate boss and the CEO of his company. He did this by once again displaying his potential and desire, but this time he had to show that he could help them. He waited for a business

problem to arise that neither his boss nor the CEO could solve alone. Brian then arranged a meeting with them and his old professor, who provided expert advice and some potential solutions to the problem. In the process, Brian positioned himself as a valuable corporate resource, someone who should be "kept in the loop" and developed. By becoming a mentor to others, and by being mentored, Brian set up his career for rapid promotion.

Record your evaluation of your networking ability in the chart below, just as you have done in other sections. Now, copy these "due dates" for your action steps into your daily schedule. By using this method, you will be well on your way to increasing your ability to network.

Skill #4: The Creative Edge

The fourth major skill is creativity. While some modern career paths—such as special achievers working as novelists—are based on creativity, *every* successful career requires a degree of creative thinking. Corporate stalwarts need new approaches to

Networking Evaluation

Networking component ▼	What you currently do well ▼	Areas that need improvement ▼	Steps you will take to improve ▼	Date by which you will have taken steps ▼
Meeting people				
Finding mutual benefit				
Following up				

complex problems; entrepreneurs make their living by engaging in innovative businesses; experts need to answer old questions in new ways that will lead to breakthroughs; and facilitators must manage their relationships to ensure the presence of added value. The creative mind is involved in accomplishments in all of these career paths.

Creativity has been defined as "creating what previously did not exist" or "coming up with something new." Being creative can mean originating new ideas or implementing old ideas in a new way. It can mean finding new alternatives to old problems, or defining an old problem in a groundbreaking way.

We can *all* learn to be more creative. Many psychologists believe that we are all born as creative creatures but that most of us, as we mature, lose the ability to "come up with something new." They contend that when we enter adolescence we want to emulate other people. A strong desire for conformity, unfortunately, often stifles our creative potential. To learn to be creative means recapturing that childlike instinct we had when we were very young. But there are several specific techniques we can use to enhance—and increase—creativity.

Stepping Stones to Creativity

It's not unreasonable to "practice" being creative. By consciously addressing the steps to creativity, you've already unearthed a bright, inquisitive side of your brain. The following steps will help you figure out what to do next.

Develop a questioning nature. The question "Why?" is a cornerstone in the creativity development process. Before formulating the theory of relativity, Albert Einstein asked himself why light travels as it does. Before painting his masterpieces, Picasso asked himself why life is the way it is. To question "why" forces us to think

in new ways, to invent new answers to the question.

Why did you not receive the promotion you sought? *Why* are you so good at selling? *Why* did your last project turn out as it did? The more you question, the more creative you'll become.

Think about how often you ask "why?" Many people don't ask it very often. Some see the question as a sign of weakness; smart people wouldn't need to ask, they think. But remember: There are *many* ways to look at every situation. Each perspective carries with it different methods of dealing with the issues. Do you ask "why?" often enough? This is a subjective question, but try to evaluate yourself. On a separate sheet of paper, write down your answer to this question. In particular, think of situations when a creative person would have asked "why?"—when a situation turned out differently than expected. Note both when you asked "why?" and when you didn't. Evaluating yourself in this way is the first step toward self-improvement.

Brainstorming with others. Many studies have shown that people working in groups come up with more and better solutions than if the same people worked independently. Brainstorming actually utilizes conformity to bring out our creativity; since everyone else in the meeting is being creative, we *also* become more creative.

The rules of a brainstorming meeting are simple, and they were partially discussed in chapter 3. Conduct a meeting exclusively for the purpose of coming up with new ideas. Before starting the meeting, state that every comment contributed by group members will be valuable. Begin by presenting the focus question to generate the new ideas. Allow no one to contradict, put down, or attempt to edit any idea presented, but inform group members that they can always originate new ideas that include portions of other ideas. Designate one person the

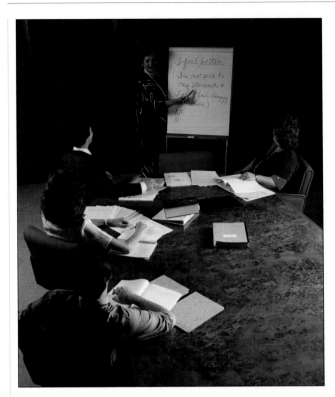

Harness your creativity through a team brainstorming session.

task of writing down every idea proposed in the meeting.

Although brainstorming is simple, most people either don't do it or don't adhere to the rules. Some see brainstorming as a waste of time. Others view creativity as something soft and weak, as "mumbo jumbo." A few people even think it's better *not* to be creative, reasoning that creativity means taking risks which, in turn, get people into trouble.

But in study after study, brainstorming has been shown to produce excellent business results. While it's true that some of the ideas people think of are off-the-wall and a few are just plain stupid, the "brainstorming mix" almost always includes a few gems that can sell more products, generate higher revenue, turn companies around, or serve more people. The winning ideas—though perhaps few in number—are often well worth the time, the trouble, and the risks. Monte Abrams is someone who has used brainstorming to create a new and exciting career.

A design director for a publishing company, Monte supervises a staff of sixteen people, including painters, designers, computer graphics specialists, and other artists. As part of a strategic planning process, he analyzed the strengths, weaknesses, opportunities, and threats facing his area and determined that outsourcing was likely to replace most of his department.

Monte decided to become proactive and try to add different types of value to the company, chiefly by distributing a memo to every manager in the company offering the services of his creative people in brainstorming solutions to different problems. At first, only one manager accepted his offer.

The problem the manager brought to Monte and his staff was the need to invent a new product that could be marketed to a yet-untapped market segment. The manager met with the group, explained the problem, and then Monte and his staff went to work. At the end of a three-hour meeting, they had brainstormed over 100 new ideas. Monte admits most of them were less then stellar, but five proved worthy of further study.

The manager then performed some market research on the five potential winners, and one of them seemed to have great potential. And when the company finally launched the new product, it did indeed prove successful. The company newsletter carried the story, and soon dozens of requests came in for Monte and his people's brainstorming talent. While Monte knew that outsourcing was still a potential threat to his department, he had proved how much value they could add—which made him and his employees much more indispensable.

How would you rate your brainstorming skills? In brainstorming meetings at your workplace, do you usually view the process as helpful or as a waste of time? Are you good at combining, refining, or sharpening other people's ideas? Take a moment to write down your strengths and your weaknesses in this area. If you feel that changes are required, list specific steps you will take to improve.

"Thinking outside the box." Creative people have the ability to think in new and different ways, often ways that are radically novel. But being in a profession or a career path can sometimes be constraining. Simply stated, it's easy to start thinking like everyone else in your career path. Thinking in new ways is difficult, and as we've already mentioned, some people feel threatened by creativity. We all have our own unique reasons for sometimes avoiding creativity.

But the rewards of venturing outside the dominant thinking patterns can be far-reaching, and has been proven so in many modern-day examples. Bill Gates and Paul Allen thought of computer science not as it was, but as it *could be*, and they created a new industry. Lee Iacocca thought about what the leading car maker in the world would be like, and

though his new thinking patterns made him some enemies, his nonconventional thinking also turned Chrysler Corporation around.

Good creative thinkers are able to pull solutions from other fields. Being creative means that we can draw on experiences from other situations and other fields for helpful insights and ideas. When you're faced with a problem you haven't previously encountered, try asking yourself the following questions:

- What experiences do I have from completely different situations that can help me now?

- Who can I ask for help who is an expert in a completely different field?

- What would another person (one you admire, perhaps from a different field) do if he or she were in my present situation?

Consider the case of Robert McNally.

Robert is good at thinking outside the box. Several years ago he wrote computer games under subcontract from various software companies. Several of these companies also had full-time programmers, and most were poorly paid or worked without benefits. Robert felt a desire to form a company that could operate within a more nurturing culture and still create truly innovative computer games.

As a history buff, Robert was familiar with the medieval concept of trade guilds—groups of artisans who came together for mutual support. Speculating that this concept might work well in the gaming industry, Robert formed a company called The Dreamers Guild, which he incorporated and modeled in this very democratic trade guild-type style. This open, consensus-driven organization was a success, and The Dreamers Guild is now a competitive force in the world of computer games. By drawing from a concept outside his specific field, Robert solved a difficult business problem, creating a better life for himself and the other company members.

Are you able to "think outside of the box"? Do you make this part of your daily routine? If so, give yourself a good grade. But be honest and evaluate yourself accurately, and at the same time, try to assess your ability in this area as compared to others in your new career path.

If you need to improve your creative ability, start by reading magazines and newspapers from outside your field. Seek out "off-the-wall" thinkers and make them your friends. Read books on creativity, such as Alex Osborn's *Applied Imagination*, Tony Buzan's *Use Both Sides of Your Brain*, and Roger Von Oech's *A Whack on the Side of the Head: How to Unlock Your Mind for Innovation*. Most universities offer classes in creative thinking that may also help you.

Now record your self-evaluation and your improvement steps in the chart below.

Finally, commit yourself to following through on the action steps by copying them to your daily schedule or by posting them in a way that will be visible to you every day. If you take these action steps, you will be well on your way to becoming a more creative person.

Skill #5: Changing with a Changing World

In decades past, stability was a key skill for corporate advancement. People who showed up for work and consistently demonstrated one key ability for eight or ten hours a day did well. The ability may have been engineering, sales, general management, or clerical work. But the rewards were usually the same: raises, promotion, bonuses, greater recognition.

A central theme of this book is that the world today is fundamentally different. It didn't just become different; the ground began to shift. Slowly at first, then more quickly. The landscape today is different, but the changes continue.

What will tomorrow be like? Futurists, visionaries, and prophets are not in agreement (although chapter 8 highlights how the likely trends will affect each of the five career paths).

	Creativity Evaluation			
Creativity component ▼	What you currently do well ▼	Areas that need improvement ▼	Steps you will take to improve ▼	Date by which you will have taken steps ▼
Asking "why"				
Brainstorming with others				
Thinking outside the box				

How adaptable are you to dramatic changes in the workplace?

But they *do* agree on one point: The people who will fare well will have to possess the ability to change. To change quickly and dramatically. And then to keep changing. Adaptability is the fifth skill that everyone needs.

This skill is especially critical for special achievers, experts, and entrepreneurs. These paths are the ones closest to the market, and include such diverse occupations as sales and scientific positions. People in these paths must be willing to reinvent the service they offer—often requiring change "on a dime." Facilitators and corporate stalwarts tend to have a larger buffer between them and the market (such as lots of people they know or corporate infrastructures), so they may have slightly more time to adjust. But change will eventually affect everyone, and responding to it in the most effective way is essential to "staying afloat."

The new economy is filled with successful people who are performing tasks for which they weren't formally trained: attorneys work as agents; professors serve companies as consultants; English teachers write novels. Their backgrounds help them, but their backgrounds aren't sufficient to explain their success.

The people who are doing well today use their background—overall experience, education, training and natural ability—as a springboard to a career that satisfies them. At the same time, they recognize that, as the world continues to shift, their niche may disappear. If it does, they'll just find another one.

Key Factors in Acquiring Adaptability

Although some people are naturally more flexible than others, adaptability in a work environment is a skill that can be learned or improved upon.

Stepping out of the safety zone. Most people love being in a job that feels safe and comfortable. The job may be challenging, but it's something that provides stability and routine. This is what psychologists refer to as our "safety zone." It includes using only the habits that have become comfortable—and not pushing ourselves to learn new skills. It also includes staying within environments that seem non-threatening—such as corporate cultures or industries that we feel we completely understand and can easily thrive in.

The problem is, a place that seems secure may not be secure at all. Many defense contractors thought their world was safe in the mid-1980s, but they learned otherwise.

What is your safety zone? What types of jobs do you feel safe doing? What types of skills do you feel safe using? Do you need to have a nine-to-five job with a salary and benefits to feel safe?

How comfortable are you stepping out of your safety zone? When was the last time you ventured out into a new social gathering or job setting? How did it feel?

As you look into the future, imagine that you have to make a total career change (even beyond the change you're considering right now). You must leave behind everything that seems comfortable—your office, your income, everything that seems familiar—and make it alone. How does this image strike you? Is it thrilling or frightening? Is it a combination of both?

Stepping out of our safety zone is difficult. We wouldn't be human if it didn't provoke at least a bit of anxiety, frustration, or disappointment. But living in the new economy requires that we be prepared to walk beyond what we know. We may not have to entirely abandon our safety zones, but if we're not comfortable—and potentially prepared for this possibility—we may trap ourselves through negative thinking.

On a separate sheet of paper, evaluate your own safety zone. First, ask yourself how wide it is—that is, how many types of skills you're comfortable using, how many different types of business cultures can you be in without feeling overwhelmed, and how many different types of people you're able to talk to with ease. Write down your answers to these self-probing questions.

Next, evaluate how comfortable you are in leaving your safety zone. Think of how often it happens. Do you feel free to explore new ideas, learn new skills, and meet people who are different from you? Write down your answer. Then recall the last time you left your safety zone. Did it happen because you felt the need to take risks, or did circumstances force you? Write down the reason, as this may provide insights into the parameters of your comfort level when leaving your safety zone becomes necessary.

If you believe you need to expand your safety zone and increase your ability to leave it, there are several steps you can take. First, make it a habit to probe unfamiliar ideas and concepts. Read books outside your field, listen to a wide variety of music, meet people outside your field and social circle, vacation to exotic and mysterious places. Second, force yourself out of your safety zone when the need arises. This means taking the steps that you know will enhance your career but that (for whatever reason) you haven't taken—getting your MBA, going for another professional certification, running for office in a professional association, writing an article in a trade journal. As simple as it sounds, one of the best ways to expand your safety zone is simply to force yourself out of it. Now write down the specific steps you will commit to.

Anticipating change. Author John Naisbitt has helped many people to learn to anticipate the types of changes that will occur throughout their lifes. Smaller-scale trends that will affect industry, company, business, or personal life are also important.

Part of being adaptable is knowing what changes are likely to occur, and which will be most important to you. During the corporate downsizings of the early 1990s, for instance, the small minority of insightful people who had anticipated this trend set up

Expand your horizons by reading a daily news or financial publication.

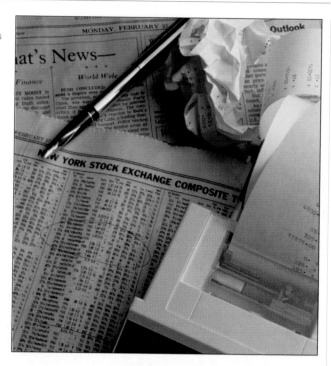

businesses to help companies streamline. Others in faltering organizations saw the changes coming and made plans to get out before most people even realized the potential problem.

Do you know what changes are likely to affect you? Here are some questions to help you self-evaluate. On a separate sheet of paper, answer the questions below that seem most relevant to you and your future career:

1. Think about the overall economy. Are you up on the latest trends in employment, durable goods, consumer prices, inflation, and consumer confidence? What do most analysts expect the stock market to do in the next year?

2. Consider your specific industry. Do you know what the current trends are? Do you read industry papers? Do you attend professional conferences? Do you know what most businesses in your industry are doing?

3. Now move to your specific business (or your own business, if you're self-employed). What is happening to it? Is it growing or shrinking? What divisions are increasing, and which are getting smaller? According to expert

forecasters, where will the business probably be five years from now?

Summarize the answers you've written. First, what are your strengths in this area? What areas need improvement? And what steps will you take to improve? Write down answers to each of these questions.

If you're not sure how to increase your ability to anticipate change, here are some suggestions. First, find people in your industry (or in the industry and career path you're considering) who seem to be well-informed, and ask them for their sources. If your reading time is limited, stick to sources that speak of trends, not just events. Second, spend more time reading general business sources. Turn off the local news and open *BusinessWeek* and *The Wall Street Journal*. The Internet probably has some great sources of information for you as well.

Creating change. By reinventing your career, you can feel more in control of your life. There are people in every career path who know the world is changing, and they respect the trends that affect us all. Yet they also feel that they can affect their world in profound ways.

The expert can create ripples through the field. The superachiever can establish trends in sales or the arts; the corporate stalwart can shape the company in dramatic ways; the facilitator can influence many businesses and individuals by creating waves through many social circles; and the entrepreneur can invent new businesses and influence people's patterns of investing, working, buying, and even living.

To put it broadly, do you feel like the world is yours, or do you feel that you belong to the world? This is what psychologists call "locus of control." It refers to whether people feel that they can change events, or that events change them. People with an internal locus of control trust in their capabilities to change their environments, and thus they generally earn more money, are happier, tend to be more charitable to others, and are much more satisfied with their own lives. While locus of control is difficult to change, we can *act* "as if," even if we don't feel much initial self-determination.

To see if you need to change your actions, take this evaluation test. On the fill-in rule provided after each of the following statements, indicate "A" if you "agree," "N" if you are "neutral," or "D" if you "disagree" with each:

1. I feel that the world is largely within my control. ____

2. I take every opportunity to shape my field of business. ____

3. I am more of a participant than a player in my profession. ____

4. I believe that circumstances are more powerful than individual actions. ____

5. I am a visionary in my field, seeing potential that others can't. ____

6. Planning my life would be just a waste of time; situations I can't foresee always take over. ____

7. I believe that leaders in their field are just people with better luck. ____

8. People look at me as a role model in my field. ____

9. People seek out my advice, because they know that others follow my lead. ____

10. I believe that getting what I want mainly comes down to luck. ____

For questions 1, 2, 5, 8, and 9, give yourself two points for every "agree" and one point for every "neutral." For questions 3, 4, 6, 7, and 10, give yourself two points for every "disagree," and one point for every "neutral." Twenty points are possible. If you scored 16 or higher, you are very capable of creating change in your field and are well on your way to becoming a leader. If you scored between 12 and 15, you are capable of creating change more than the majority of people, but you're still held back by some degree of negative thinking. If you score 11 or less, you are strongly controlled by others, and you don't feel empowered to create change in your field.

If you believe that you need to increase your ability to change your field, you need to "act like" a leader—if you don't feel like one right now. Examples of such behavior include networking with "movers and shakers" in your field, finishing an advanced degree, applying for jobs with more prominent companies, or presenting a paper at a professional conference. If you need to take action, use the chart on the next page to write down specific ways in which you will become an agent of change.

Just as you've done before, copy your due dates for the action steps into your career journal. By following through on your improvement steps, you will be on the road to mastering this skill, and better equipped to face your new career's challenges.

Flexibility Evaluation				
Flexibility component ▼	What you currently do well ▼	Areas that need improvement ▼	Steps you will take to improve ▼	Date by which you will have taken steps ▼
Your safety zone				
Anticipating change				
Creating change				

Skill #6: Using Computers Effectively

The sixth and final skill that most people need involves computers. No matter what career path is right for you, technology will almost certainly be part of it. Today, artists draw with computers; bookkeepers calculate with electronic spreadsheets; novelists "write" into word processors. Experts employ (and invent) electronic tools of all types. Entrepreneurs create business plans in specialized software. Facilitators use communication tools, like E-mail, and many use electronic organizers. And corporate stalwarts in almost every functional area use local and wide area networks, E-mail, and several software packages.

It's not important that you become a minicomputer scientist, unless doing so will enhance your career (as in the case of experts or special achievers who primarily focus in technology). Most of us will always be users of technology, not implementers or analysts of it. In most cases, you may not require special expertise in the use of the most current microprocessors, microcode, or communication protocols—unless, of course, these are special tools of your career path. On the other hand, you shouldn't be the last one on your "career block" to learn the latest electronic tools of your trade. A good compromise is to aim to be in the second 25 percent of your industry to become familiar with the latest equipment. People in the first 25 percent often spend more time and money getting the technology to work. Those in the last 50 percent are generally not considered leaders in their fields, since their technological know-how lags behind.

Keeping up with Computer Basics

There are a few basics with which you should become familiar—regardless of your specific career path. Let's examine each one in detail and then assess your strengths and weaknesses.

Word processing. Two decades ago, "Do you type?" was a favorite question of employment officers trying to fill entry-level jobs. Today, this inquiry is replaced with "which word processors can you use?" It's now become difficult to even make it through college without knowing the basics of a good word processor.

Computer word-processing skills are essential to most career paths.

There are a number of ways to learn word processing. The most common is to buy a book, sit down at a computer, and work through the book's exercises. Many companies conduct in-house training sessions, and these classes should get you up and running very quickly. Community colleges and vocational centers also have classes. And some computer stores even teach introductory classes for a small fee if you purchase their software.

Spreadsheets. Modern spreadsheet packages are complex enough to run a middle-sized company's finances, but most users of spreadsheet software don't need this much complexity for their purposes. The important elements include storing and retrieving files, inputting data, and using simple formulas. These steps will suffice for tasks such as keeping a computer checkbook, running a departmental budget, and even keeping a small company's books. If you feel that you need to increase your skills using spreadsheet software, you can turn to books, videos, or classes as further resources.

Graphic user interface. Today's computer software—whether on the Macintosh or PC—is essentially similar. Whether you're using a spreadsheet, statistical program, or computer-aided design package, the software will probably include pull-down menus, tool bars, and a common "feel." This common "look" to software is called a graphic user interface (GUI), and becoming familiar with it is extremely important because it enables you to quickly learn new software packages. Even if you've never used Microsoft Word or Excel, for example, you can still utilize these basic commands.

Being familiar with a GUI is more important than knowing specific software. Yet we learn how to use a GUI through induction; that is, we start with one software program, then move to the next, and only then begin to see the commonalties.

Learning a GUI is easy, but it does take time. If you're not already familiar with how one works, just begin "poking around" several different software packages that run on PC compatible systems or on the Macintosh.

Now consider all your knowledge of computers. Are you up to date in relation to most people in your proposed career path? How does your knowledge of word processors, spreadsheets, and GUIs measure up to others in your field? Even if you rate yourself poorly, learning computers is becoming a much simpler process.

Yet it's important to plan action *now*, since being computer literate is increasingly critical for success in most careers. Summarize your self-evaluation, as well as what steps you will take, in the chart below.

By making these due dates important parts of your schedule, you will follow through on your goals for improving your computer ability.

Skills Specific to Your Career Path and Industry

We believe the six skills outlined in this chapter are important for every person in the 1990s, no matter which career path you are—or will be—on.

Yet your specific career will require its own unique and specialized skills. These skills might pertain to advanced mathematics or computer expertise, teaching, bilingualism, creative writing, leadership, selling, solving technical problems, designing, researching, organizing, and countless others.

This section will help you determine which specific skills you may need to develop. To do this, start off by imagining your future career (later chapters will help you sharpen your mental image, but just let your mind wander for the moment). You might want to review your exercises from chapter 3. Write down—on a separate sheet of paper—how you imagine your future career.

Now picture a typical day in your new career as vividly as you can. What types of activities fill your time? Be specific. And assume your health, communication skills, networking ability, creativity, adaptability, and computer expertise skills are all adequate. On the same paper, describe what a typical day might be like.

What other skills will you need for this career? You might require a strong system of personal organization, if your future lies in the facilitator career path. Or a strong ability to manage people in a multicultural environment, if your ideal career includes international

Computer Skills Evaluation				
Computer skill component ▼	What you currently do well ▼	Areas that need improvement ▼	Steps you will take to improve ▼	Date by which you will have taken steps ▼
Using a word Processor				
Using a spreadsheet				
Using a GUI				

management as part of the corporate stalwart path. Perhaps you'll need advanced computer expertise, if, for example, you're planning to work as a computer scientist in the expert path. Now make a list of the first five or six skills that come to mind.

Review your list again, this time consciously becoming more analytical. Which skills—of those you just listed—will be *critical* to your success? Which will be *important?* Which are *not significant* to your career? Write down the top two or three skills that seem vital to your success.

Finally, fill out the chart below—just as you've done in previous sections—to evaluate these top two or three skills.

Just as you've done before, copy your due dates into your schedule so that you will give them the same attention you will give to the first six skills.

Your Unique Mix of Skills

While you will need all six of the common skills, as well as some additional ones, some, of course, will be more pertinent to your specific career

path than others. An investment advisor, for example, has to be sharp on all six basic skills, but computer expertise will rank higher on his or her priority list than it would for a special achiever working as a screenwriter. For the screenwriter, creativity would be the key skill.

Write down all eight of your skills (including the two additional skills you brainstormed), along with your overall evaluation of yourself for each. Ignoring the evaluations for a moment, which of these skills is most important for your career? Which is second? Prioritize them from first to eighth. Write them, in order, on the page below:

Prioritized Skills

1.
2.
3.
4.
5.
6.
7.
8.

Critical Skills Evaluation

Critical skill ▼	What you currently do well ▼	Areas that need improvement ▼	Steps you will take to improve ▼	Date by which you will have taken steps ▼

And now review your "due dates" for each of your goals. You might need to adjust them, now that you have finished prioritizing. Make sure you work on the most important skill first, the second second, and so on. Consider the case of Ben Gordon as he analyzed and prioritized his skills.

Ben had worked most of his life as a sales representative for a large manufacturer of high-end musical equipment. He did well at his job, consistently earning a middle six-figure income when he added in his commissions.

Yet Ben felt his career had hit a speed bump. He enjoyed selling, but he felt that his real interest and ability was in working as an agent. As a sales rep, he had met many of the influential people in the music industry, and he felt he had a knack for helping unknown musicians with talent by introducing them to people who could help them. Ben had always worked in the facilitator career path, and he decided to make a career change that would allow him to stay within that path.

In evaluating his skills, Ben decided that communication was most important. He had always been good at closing a sale, but small talk had never come easily to him. In this area, he gave himself only an average evaluation; however, most of his other skills were very well-developed.

Ben decided that his first priority was to improve his skill at making small talk. He purchased a videotape and workbook package on "establishing casual conversation," and enrolled in a Dale Carnegie course. He made quick

progress, and used his new techniques to launch what turned into a successful second job as an agent. Within nine months, Ben was able to quit his job as a sales rep to work exclusively as an agent. He had successfully transitioned to his new career.

Toward a Personal Plan

Chapter 1 presented you with the five new career options. Chapter 2 helped you see which aspects of your current career were working well and which needed some change. Chapter 3 gave you insights into your ideal career and helped you decide which of the five paths is right for you. And now you have a better idea about how to develop your key skills.

This is a good time to revisit your career path decision. Now that you've had the chance to evaluate your skills in relation to other people in this path, perform a "reality check." You might decide that the career change is not feasible, or that it will take more time than you can give. Don't be pessimistic (remember, the average American will change careers several times—it *can* be done), but be realistic. Most likely you will decide that it is possible, but that you have some work ahead of you. The next chapter will help you put it all together by guiding you in the process of creating a life plan for yourself if you decide to make the jump to your new career path.

Chapter 5

Putting Together the Action Plan for Your Life

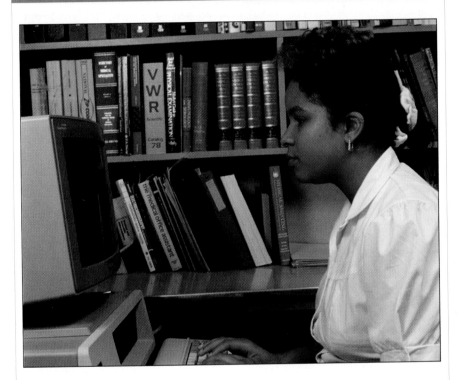

We've covered a lot of ground in the first four chapters. By now you should have gained some new insights about your ideal career, and you should be focusing on what career path you're most suited for.

This chapter will help you plan how to get to your new career. It will assist you in assimilating the information you've documented about yourself, and help you produce a written document, much like most organizations do to prepare for their futures. This document will help you to ultimately reach your ideal career path by pulling all of that information together.

This plan will also help you work out the details of transitioning to your new career path (if a large change is required) or of fine-tuning your current career (if you don't need to make a major shift). As a written document, this plan will help make your new career a reality by laying out a definite course of action.

Your Overall Life Plan

Individuals and organizations alike have found that planning enhances performance and success. The planning process will help you focus on your life purpose, delineate your strengths and weaknesses, settle on specific life goals, and prepare a strategy for moving forward. Tough decisions will become a little easier to make. You'll feel more in control of your life—and less like life is controlling you.

As you move forward with your plan, you can monitor your progress and make adjustments where necessary. You'll be encouraged to dream, to use your imagination. You'll think of new possibilities, new opportunities for growth and accomplishment. Rather than muddling through the rest of your life, you can now set an effective, strategic course.

You have already prepared yourself by analyzing your interests, strengths, and values. You've identified the culture you prefer to work in, and you've determined your personal goals. You are now ready to put it all to-gether. *The first step in this chapter is to check in with your life purpose.*

Your Life Purpose

Your individual purpose propels you in the direction of your life goals by providing focus and clarity. While your goals provide direction and your values act as "rules for the road," your purpose provides the means for getting where you want to go.

Just what *is* your purpose? What difference do you hope to bring to the world? What do you want written on your statue or gravestone? Without solid answers to these questions, it's easy to fall short of ambition or to become immersed in meaningless activity that seems to be leading nowhere.

A clear life purpose is what drives great men and women to succeed against formidable odds. Purpose made the founding of the United States possible. It drove social reformers—Martin Luther King, Jr., Indira Gandhi, Nelson Mandela, and Mother Teresa, to name a few—to great heights. It's led entire countries and peoples to recover after terrible disasters. And it has led many

leaders in industry, in entrepreneurialism, and in the arts to accomplish great and important feats.

Defining your life purpose can't be done in one sitting. It takes time, reflection, and effort. You may need to write and revise it twenty times over a few days or weeks before you finally reach the point where it rings true. But the results are well worth the effort.

You are ready to start writing this purpose. Start by examining the results of your previous self-analyses. Look for a common theme that seems to predominate. And then just write down, in one or two sentences, what you think your life's purpose may be. Let's follow Scott Malone as he begins his journey toward defining his.

Scott reflected on how he had spent the last fifteen years of his life— the years since graduating from the University of Michigan with an MBA in marketing. He had moved immediately into a corporate job, always believing that up the ladder was synonymous with success.

While reviewing his contracts and analyzing his values, preferred culture, and emotional health, he came to the conclusion that a dramatic change was needed. "It's time to follow my heart and do what I've always wanted to do," he thought. "I want to work for myself, and open my own company specializing in market research for midsized companies."

Reflecting on what really excites him, Scott realizes that providing employment for others while giving the world a key service is how he would like to spend the rest of his life—or at least the next few years.

Backing up from his preferred career path, Scott drafts the following: "My purpose in life is to create positive opportunities for myself and others through technical expertise, innovation, and participation."

He looks at what he has just written. "It does seem to capture what I want my career to represent," he thinks.

It encompasses market research and entrepreneurialism but isn't bound by them. Scott decides to put what he has written away for a few days and revisit it, just to make sure.

Your Present Situation

In chapter 2, you examined your present situation, compared your current status with your previous goals from years past, and analyzed your progress and future direction with your current goals. You then reviewed changes that your profession has made and will make—over the next five to ten years. You restated your successes and shortcomings. Now is a good time to review your findings, especially in light of your life's purpose. Let's continue with Scott's example.

After revisiting his life purpose and feeling very comfortable with it, Scott wrote the following:

"My present situation is that I've been promoted to a position that's compatible with my interests, strengths, and values. It provides me with an opportunity to grow within the company. Yet my dream of using my broad base of business knowledge to create my own opportunities seems impossible as long as I remain a corporate stalwart."

The next step is to explain how your present situation relates, or fails to relate, to your life's purpose. In this step, see what the overlap, or lack thereof—is between the first two steps in this chapter.

"My present situation allows me to fulfill my life's purpose only in part," Scott wrote. *"I'm actively involved in creating change for my staff, but I'm overly constrained by things that just seem to get in the way, like bureaucracy, politics, and so many approval layers."*

Your life purpose statement, in a manner of speaking, justifies your existence. It becomes the most important contract you set with yourself to ensure that your life has meaning, that

you'll make a difference in this world. Most people who burn out in their fifties or sixties find that they aren't living in line with their purpose; most had never really considered what their purpose was! To avoid this major life "oversight"—and to make your working years as enjoyable and meaningful as possible—you must consider if your present situation is in line with your purpose.

The next step is to clearly state in writing exactly how your present situation is falling short of completing your life's purpose (strategic planners and corporate reengineering experts call this a "gap analysis"). In this step, ask yourself if your career is on the right path for you. If not, which path should you be pursuing?

Scott sat back in his chair. He had a clear sense of what was missing in his life but was having trouble putting it into words. Deciding he needed some advice, Scott had a long talk with his wife, whom he truly felt was also his soul mate.

After the conversation, he felt motivated to write. "I need autonomy, freedom of expression, and the ability to act quickly without having to sell all my ideas to people who should be on my side already. I need to run my own team—a team I can share management authority with. Otherwise, I'll continue to feel like a cog in the corporate wheel. My life purpose demands otherwise."

This gap analysis will become the basis of your strategies. Take the time now to fully reflect upon your findings. By examining your needs and goals at this stage, you'll be able to better determine what will work for you, what won't, and why.

It's smart idea to review this analysis with your family, mentors, and close friends. Get their input and advice. But, in the final analysis, make the final determination regarding this step. *Don't* let others talk you out of a change that you truly believe would benefit you.

Overcoming personal stumbling blocks can open up a variety of new career paths.

Opportunities and Threats to Your Career

No person is an island. Outside influences affect all of us. Our family and friends, our society and economy, changing technologies, government legislation, political platforms, co-workers, adversaries, and the ever-present media—all these affect our outlook and either provide opportunities or create threats to our careers.

For the next step, think about what external forces are creating opportunities for you in your new career or career path. (You might want to review your answers to some of the questions at the end of chapter 2.) When you're ready, list these opportunities.

Scott knew that being an entrepreneur would be a challenge, yet he felt the economy would support what he had in mind. He listed out the following:

"Proposed changes in government legislation will make starting a small business easier.

"Companies downsizing often need to hire small firms to take up the slack that they lose. This could lead to opportunities for me.

"So many out-of-work professionals will provide my business with a rich labor pool."

Also, as a part of this step, list those influences that you think may hinder your work in your new career or career path. (Review your career log in chapter 2 for assistance.)

Scott quickly typed his "list of threats" into his word processor. As a careful risk evaluator (as are most new entrepreneurs), Scott seemed to focus more on the downside than on the opportunities. His list of threats included:

"Large businesses cutting costs will be better able to compete with small, entrepreneurial firms.

"Starting a new venture is risky— over 90 percent of them fail.

"If the economy slips into recession again, small businesses will be the first to feel the squeeze."

By working through your threats, you may think of additional opportunities. If so, you may want to go back and revise what you've already written.

We now turn to you personal strengths and weaknesses.

Your Strengths and Weaknesses

Chapter 3 briefly discussed strengths and weaknesses and how they affect success in your new career. Faced with the prospect of new opportunities or potential threats, your strengths and weaknesses can greatly influence your ability to respond.

For the next step, list out your personal strengths that will help you achieve success in your new career. You may need to review your notes from chapters 2 and 3. And if you find it difficult to acknowledge your own strengths, it's often helpful to gather the opinions and feedback of your family, friends, coworkers, and other close contacts.

Scott's strengths included a sound business education, expertise on the subject of entrepreneurialism gleaned from research gathered while attending business school, a rational approach to decision making, a natural ability to evaluate risks, a wide network of potential employees and customers, and a supportive spouse with a well-paying job (a "plus" in the event that his business isn't profitable immediately).

Now, as a part of the same step, list those weaknesses that might limit your chances of achieving your new career. These might include gaps in education, personal qualities that could hinder progress, or a lack of personal or financial resources.

Scott looked over his notes and began to write: "I have a low tolerance for routine. I'm often impatient with people who don't see the vision right away. I'm also a perfectionist, and delegating important projects is often hard for me."

Keep in mind that *everyone* has weaknesses. Making a smooth transition into a new career or career path requires that you know your weaknesses—and make plans to address them and/or find ways to minimize their impact.

Your Future Issues

You should now have a clear understanding of your life purpose, the relationship of that purpose with your current situation, exactly what has to change in your present situation, your opportunities and threats, and your strengths and weaknesses.

The next step is to look forward in time and anticipate what outside influences will affect you. It's important to plan for these influences now, before they create an obstacle to your success.

Scott had a good read on the anticipated trends in the economy that could affect entrepreneurs, but he still didn't feel he had quite enough information. He spent several days talking with his business colleagues, performing research on several on-line systems, reading back issues of business journals, and trying to put it all together in his mind.

Scott came to the conclusion that the biggest three trends that could affect him were: (1) the increasing adaptability of companies will result in entrepreneurial firms having to become even more adaptable, (2) the amount of information in the business world continues to increase, making it even more important to "know the right people," and (3) personal changes will continue, thus necessitating contact with with several people in each company purchasing the entrepreneur's services or products.

Now answer the following questions related to these issues. Are there any that could limit your ability to fulfill your purpose? If so, how?

Scott noted that all three trends could potentially limit him as an entrepreneur. The first might limit the life cycle of good products and services. The second could limit the effectiveness of traditional marketing methods. The third might limit the effectiveness of a small network of people.

Next, write out what changes you'll need to implement to meet these new challenges, should they

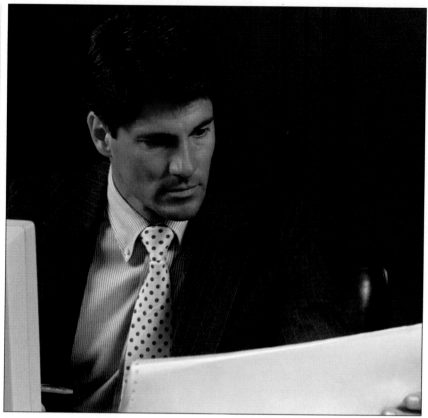

Devise your own career strategy.

occur. Use as much detail and precision as possible.

Scott focused this step on his increased need to network. He resolved to become active in the Michigan alumni association and the American Marketing Association, and he decided to join several entrepreneurial groups. In addition, he renewed contact with several old friends who work as economists and outplacement counselors. He believed that, by expanding and revitalizing his network, his chances at entrepreneurial success would be greatly enhanced.

So far, this analysis may have led you toward a reconsideration of your life purpose or proposed career shift. At this point, revisit your life-purpose statement and revise it as necessary to improve its clarity and focus.

In addition, take as much time as you need to revisit your planned career shift. Most people will become nervous about such serious decisions, but it's important that the decision feel right. If it doesn't, ask yourself why not. You might need to review your notes in chapters 2, 3, and 4, and to seriously investigate any conflicting feelings you may be experiencing.

Scott reviewed his life-purpose statement and found that it still satisfied him. In fact, after working through the exercises so far in this chapter, it seemed more on-target than before. He decided not to change it. His proposed career plans also seemed to be in place.

Formulating Strategies

Now that you've identified and evaluated your life purpose, future opportunities, potential threats, strengths and weaknesses, and future key issues, you're ready to move into the strategic stage of this process. It's time to define exactly what action steps you will take to position yourself for your new career.

Start by reviewing your gap analysis. Then ask yourself what specific steps you would have to take to "fix" the problems you identified. Keep these steps—which will become your strategies—fairly broad and general. Judy Ward and Don Hartley set two solid strategies for their lives. We'll follow them throughout the rest of this chapter as they formulate their life action plan.

Judy and Don were employed by Lockheed in Southern California. Judy worked as a financial analyst but had made the decision not to try to advance up the ladder; she described herself as being in the special achiever career path. Don worked in management, and described his job as being in the corporate stalwart path. As time went on, they both became increasingly dissatisfied with their lives, which included a two-hour commute from their residence in Huntington Beach. Traffic jams, corporate politics, and defense industry downsizing were major influencing factors in their mutual decision. When Judy and Don became engaged, they decided to make a dramatic career transition together.

In performing their gap analysis, they decided that a small-town environment would suit them better, and they wanted jobs that would involve the retail industry. In deciding what product they wanted to sell, they chose coffee, which they both loved.

The couple then set two major strategies. First, they wanted to move to a small town filled with educated and creative people. Second, they wanted to open a business that would deal with coffee, a business that had the potential to develop, grow, and lead to the formation of other businesses. Thus, they wanted these two strategies to lead them to careers in the entrepreneurial path.

On a separate sheet of paper, write down the major strategies that address the issues you identified in your gap analysis. You should involve your family in this process, just as Don and Judy worked together. Make sure your strategies address the fundamental issue of whether you will stay in your current career path or transition to another.

Also, review your strategies to ensure that any major issues from the following categories are in your plan: personal, relationship, career, and financial. Specifically, be sure to address issues such as children, housing, time with family, investments and retirement planning, promotions and job transitions. But be careful not to set too many strategies, since this could either dilute or overload your efforts. In general, three to four strategies are sufficient. Judy and Don strongly believed that by accomplishing their two main strategies, all the areas of their lives would be improved.

Once you have mapped your strategies, review your opportunities, threats, strengths, weaknesses, and future expectations. Do your strategies take these issues into account? If not, modify your strategies so that your plan will be more personally customized to meet your unique situation and your vision for the coming years. Also, review your strategies in light of the exercises in chapters 2 through 4; make sure your strategies address skill development and are compatible with your values, emotional health, and any initial thinking you included in developing your list of goals.

You may also want to set your strategies aside for a few days or weeks and reflect on them. It took Don and Judy several months of thinking before they had fully defined and committed themselves to their strategies; taking the time to make sure these strategies are right for you is a wise step. The next section will help you make sure that all of your strategies work together; it will also help you plan to bring each one about.

A Strategic Framework

Once you have set your strategies, it's time to take a step back and make sure that they are in line with your life purpose. The following four steps will help you:

First, decide on your career path. Now that you've analyzed your strengths and weaknesses, reflected on your opportunities and threats, considered possible trends that could affect you, and put together some strategies, take a moment and make sure that the career path you've chosen is right for you. You might want to reread the appropriate section in chapter 1 pertaining to this career path to ensure that your traits are consistent with successful people in that path.

Second, determine what skills you'll need to develop, and make a development plan for each. Look over your weaknesses from this chapter's exercises, and reread your notes from chapter 4. For each skill you need to improve, state specific ways in which you plan to do so. Make sure that these skills will be adequate to empower your success in your new career path.

Third, plan how you will build your network. No matter which path you believe is right for you, you'll need talented people to help you get there. Decide who your network should include, and arrange to meet with them.

Fourth, combine this information to formulate a step-by-step plan. This step involves charting your course for the future, making sure to do the most important steps first. These steps become your tactics to help you achieve each of your strategies.

Let's illustrate the steps above by using a hypothetical example. A man decides to take the entrepreneurial

Reflect on the career path you've chosen.

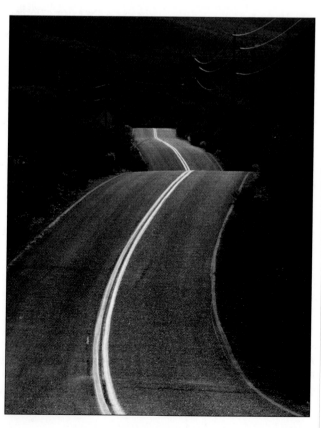

path as a real estate broker. After analyzing his strengths and weaknesses, he recognizes his need to improve his accounting skill. In addition, he wants to focus on commercial real estate, so it will be important to know executives of medium-sized companies (the commercial group that buys and sells most real estate in his area, which he learned from his research). Putting all this together means working toward his degree in accounting while also working toward his real estate license. At night, he begins attending meetings frequented by executives in his area, including rotary and chamber of commerce meetings. By the time he finishes his degree and earns his license, his network is sufficient to allow him to transition to his ideal job in his ideal, entrepreneurial career path.

Take as much time as you need to plan how you will reach your ideal job. Don and Judy used this method to achieve their strategies.

Don and Judy set several tactics under their first strategy of moving to a small town with educated and creative people. First, they decided to drive up and down the California coast until they found a town that "felt right." Second, they began asking their family and friends for recommendations. Third, they began reading demographic research about small towns in the West.

For their second strategy, they set two tactics. The first was to fully investigate coffee by researching it from a business perspective—learning about importing and exporting, roasting techniques, and the nature of other small-town businesses. Second, they began researching small businesses in general, reading books on business and marketing plans and working with small-business consultants.

By breaking down their two main strategies into several tactics, Don and Judy made their plan more actionable. In time, they accomplished everything they set out to do. They moved to the resort town of Cambria, along California's *central coast. And they opened a business called "The Coffee Den," which is soon to expand to a second location. They are also beginning to sell their own line of coffee beans and are looking at other ways to branch out their business. And they recently accomplished their other main goal: marriage.*

Your plan has already taken a great deal of time and effort, but chances are you'll need to revise it continuously. You've set numerous strategies, targeted industries and companies, decided on an organizational environment, and devised a self-marketing plan.

How do you feel about your plan? Is it workable? Have you set the goals high enough to motivate your efforts? Is there an acceptable level of risk involved? How can you improve your plan? Are there weak points that could potentially limit your effectiveness?

Implementing Your Action Plan

You should now focus on the implementation of your plan. How are you going to accomplish all this? What specific tasks will you accomplish—and when? You want your plan to make sense, to be "do-able."

Review your tactics and prioritize them in a meaningful order. To do this, first pick out those steps that must be done first. In the case of Judy and Don, they had to pick a town before they could write their business plan, so their implementation plan had to take this into account. Write out your tactics in an order that seems reasonable. Their final action plan is presented below.

At this time you should develop your implementation schedule. It may never be perfect, but a good plan implemented right away is better than a perfect plan that takes too long to get off the ground.

As changes occur in your life, environment, or industry, you'll need to make adjustments to your plan. As you monitor your progress over the next few months, you'll be measuring and analyzing the soundness of your strategy and tactics. Using these steps has allowed you to develop a vision of what you want your career and life to look like. This effort should help you build excitement for your new life, as you move ever closer to achieving your goals. This process, of course, is not an end in itself, but simply a means to help you adjust or change your life for the better—to start living a life that you love.

We now move to chapter 6, an exciting study on how to better package and market yourself to prospective employers, clients, or investors. It will help you win new and exciting opportunities that you may have previously been unaware of. You are well on your way to changing and improving your life by reinventing your career.

Judy and Don's Action Plan

Tactic ▼	Due Date ▼
1. Read books to research the coffee business	August 1
2. Investigate possible towns in which to live	September 15
3. Pick a town	October 31
4. Hire business consultant and finish business plan	December 15
5. Give notice at work; move to new town	January 3

Chapter 6

Self-Packaging and Marketing

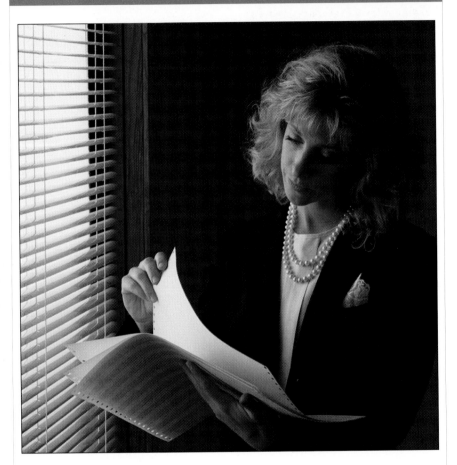

C hapter 5 helped you "put it all together" and decide which career is right for you. The purpose of this chapter is to help you get there. Whether you decide to pursue the corporate stalwart, entrepreneur, special achiever, expert, or facilitator career path, this chapter will help you get there through self-packaging and marketing techniques.

Marketing yourself is a complex step that requires perseverance, self-confidence, and just plain guts. Yet it doesn't have to be overly uncomfortable. By using a clear system to "get the word out" about your availability and desire to work in a certain career path, you'll probably find that the process will be relatively easy.

One of the most common mistakes people make in marketing themselves is to become impatient and not give the process enough time. A recent survey of the unemployed who had been looking for corporate jobs indicated that the average time spent job hunting was just *three hours a week*—and this is for people who literally have all day free!

This chapter will give you the conceptual tools you need to get started and will present a self-marketing process that will help you get results quickly. In addition, the process will guide you and help make sure that you put in the required time.

Before the Search

Next to putting in the time, the most important step in marketing yourself is to know *exactly* what you're looking for. Many people are laid off, quit voluntarily, or panic when they see their income base decline. They feel the need to *do something, anything* to get work. The result is often a haphazard, poorly coordinated effort that produces only frustration and fatigue.

In this first step, reflect and define your objective. The value of this book is that it condenses millions of career options into clear career paths to assist you in your search. Which path do you feel is right for you? In what way do you want to express yourself with-in this path? These are the most critical questions.

This book's purpose is to present the five career paths and to help you decide which one is right for you, to give you basic insights about which careers you should consider, and to give you some help in marketing yourself in preparation for the 21st century. But you may need to perform additional job research and personal introspection beyond the exercises in this book. Here are some additional steps you may want to consider:

- Take personality inventories such as the Myers-Briggs test.

- Assess yourself through interest inventories such as the Strong-Campbell test.

- Interview people in specific jobs or industries you find interesting.

- Define which transferable skills you most like to use.

- Examine salary surveys for specific jobs.

- Take university courses in entrepreneurialism, marketing, and other business-related areas of interest.

Knowing which career path is right for you—or at least having a good idea—will provide a framework for whatever other research you need to do. To complete this step, define as precisely as you can what you're looking for in your career. Here is how Tim Machado began this process.

Tim worked as a project manager at a major computer company in Silicon Valley. Yet he felt that his career wasn't quite measuring up to his desires. The situation was becoming so stressful that he dreaded going to work and he knew that he needed to reinvent his career.

Tim worked through some introspective exercises and realized why he didn't fit in his company. Implicit in the informal rules that made up his work culture was the notion that entering into a managerial position was the only route to "progress," and Tim just didn't want to follow that path.

He finally came to understand that he was most suited to the expert career path. Tim enjoyed working toward the pursuit of knowledge but felt that he would need to undergo more educational training before he could claim to be a real leader in his field.

While continuing to work in his job, he pursued and completed a master's degree in computer science at Stanford. He then applied for several doctorate programs and was accepted at the University of Washington. He quit his job, moved into campus housing, and took a job as a teaching assistant. Although he took a substantial cut in pay, Tim never felt happier. He was finally taking the steps toward his ideal career.

Like Tim, you might not know exactly where you want to end up, yet knowing which career path to

A career counselor can help you hone your search.

follow will empower you to take the right steps.

The remainder of this chapter will focus on helping you position yourself for the career that you've chosen. So if you haven't yet devoted enough time into figuring out exactly what you want to do, now is the time to make this decision your top priority.

If you believe you need additional work to help you get to your ideal career path, you might start by reading the latest edition of *What Color Is Your Parachute?* by Richard Nelson Bolles; *Life Skills: Taking Charge of Your Personal and Professional Growth* by Richard J. Leider; and *Wishcraft: How to Get What You Really Want* by Barbara Sher. You might also consider contacting a professional career counselor who can help you delve deeper into your personality, specific interests, and aptitudes, as well as advise you about salary ranges for jobs you're considering. You can find career counselors in most phone books under "Career Counseling" or "Employment Counseling."

Once you've finished any additional career work you need to undertake, you'll be ready to pursue either standard full- or part-time employment, employment on a onetime basis, or employment on an ongoing advisory basis. The next sections discuss how to pursue and win whichever of these is right for you.

Traditional Employment

This section will be particularly relevant to people who decide to pursue traditional full- or part-time work, usually people in the corporate stalwart career path, many experts, some special achievers, and a few facilitators. Many facilitators and almost all entrepreneurs will decide to begin their own ventures or work as sole proprietors.

The most important step in finding traditional jobs is knowing where to locate them. More than 80 percent aren't advertised, and most jobs that do appear in a "Help Wanted" section of a newspaper or trade journal are entry-level positions. Many others are standard professional or semiprofessional positions, such as accountants, purchasing agents, salespeople, computer programmers, and engineers.

Reinventing your career is a creative process and will probably point you toward jobs that aren't standard. Chapters 2, 3, and 5 helped you decide what you love to do, and if you listen to your heart and instincts you'll probably pursue jobs that are specialized and considerably above entry level. Thus, newspapers and trade journals aren't particularly valuable resources for you.

The key to finding specialized and advanced jobs is through *networking*. Chapter 4 took you through some self-assessment exercises to determine your current level of proficiency in networking. You might want to review that exercise again to better understand your networking strengths and weaknesses.

To improve your networking ability, it's important to master three skills. The first skill is *giving your "story" in less than a minute*. Your story includes exactly *what* you're looking for, *why* you think you can do well in this area, *how* you got to be in your current situation (currently working but ready for your next promotion, looking for work, etc.), and *when* you would like to make this transition. The key to your story is in coming up with language that is factually true and that you support emotionally. Your story isn't just a line; it's a summary of who you are—where you've been and where you're going. It's like your business card; it's what people will associate with you. So spend some time developing your story until you're comfortable with its language.

The second skill in networking is *mastering how to get value-added referrals*. The premise of this skill is that each of us knows several people who might be able to give us feedback and job assistance, but most of us

Many jobs aren't offered in a newspaper.

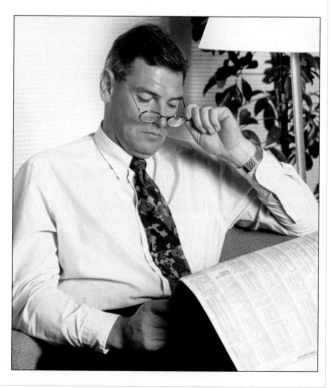

don't know *enough* people. The way to increase the size of your personal network is go to those people you do know, get whatever advice they have to offer, and then ask them for the names of other people you can talk to—either because these people are hiring or because they might be able to provide additional valuable advice.

This second skill overlaps with the first. Your objective in meeting with someone should be to tell your "story," yet make it clear that you also value their input, advice, and criticism. By showing appreciation for what *they* have to say, you're increasing the chances of being referred to their colleagues, friends, and contacts—the essence of networking. If it doesn't happen in the natural course of the conversation, you might just say: "Your input is very helpful. Is there anyone else you know who I could talk to? I really think I need more advice." You'll increase your chances of getting referrals by:

- *talking to people at the right level.* If you're looking for a job in the expert career path in a research and development department, it's probably a mistake to try to get interviews with Fortune 500 company presidents. Consulting with R&D managers will probably get you better advice and increase the chance of referrals.

- *doing your homework before the meeting.* By giving you referrals, people are putting their credibility on the line, and they're more likely to help you if it looks like you've already answered basic questions about the field you'd like to work in. People looking for corporate stalwart jobs in high-tech companies, for example, should understand the chain of command and the political structure of the organization *before* meeting with someone from that company.

- *positioning yourself as an "up-and-comer."* A few people will give you referrals out of the goodness of their hearts, but not many. The majority will only help *you* if it somehow helps *them.* By coming across as a rising star in your career path and your industry, you position yourself as the kind of person who might some day be able to "return the favor." Positioning yourself includes intangibles like having a successful and optimistic attitude, as well as tangibles such as providing "leave-behind" material (we'll discuss this later in the chapter).

The third skill in networking is follow-up. The basic idea in this step is that after you speak with the referrals you get, you need to go back to the person who initially referred you. Ask for additional referrals, if you believe this will help. But, at the very least, you should send thank-you notes to all individuals that have participated in the networking process. And in many cases it's very appropriate to phone the person and let him or her know how your job search is progressing.

What holds most people back from effective networking is the simple fear of rejection—that no one will talk with them, that they won't get any referrals, or that they'll receive referrals but no job offers. It's important to realize that fear won't go away by trying to think differently. It only goes away, in most cases, by taking definitive action. So if you believe that traditional employment is right for you, and you are feeling fearful, just start networking. The fear will probably diminish. This is what happened to Matt Shapiro.

Matt had always feared the consequences of losing his job. He had worked for years at a defense plant as an aerospace engineer. Then, after the Cold War ended, all 1,200 people in his division were laid off. Matt's worst fears had come true.

In outplacement counseling, Matt was advised about the probability of getting another job as an engineer—and the news wasn't favorable. His wife encouraged him to consider starting his own venture. Matt accepted the challenge and decided to become an entrepreneur.

He enrolled in a college class in entrepreneurialism and sought advice from a retired executive in the SCORE program at the Small Business Administration. He decided to start a new firm that would provide engineering advice to large companies that had downsized their own engineering divisions. Matt started the company and hired some of his old colleagues as subcontractors. The business was marginally profitable, yet Matt wasn't happy, because he found the stresses of always trying to line up the next contract just too overwhelming. Matt turned over the daily control of the firm to one of his colleagues and began interviewing for general management positions. He found that his new contacts had given him a strong network of people who considered him very competent. Within two months of his job search, Matt accepted a position as chief operations officer at a software company.

Thinking back, Matt reflected on how difficult his transition from the defense contractor to the software company had been. But by forcing himself to get to know people, Matt had overcome his fear. He no longer worried about what would happen if he lost his job, because deep down he knew that everything would be fine.

In Matt's case, career reinvention resulted from a lack of choice: he had realized that the aerospace engineering industry was shrinking and that it just didn't have enough jobs for all the qualified people. And he was able to transcend his fear by starting to look for his next opportunity. If your company is downsizing, your situation may be very similar.

Onetime Assignments

You may not desire traditional employment. Many experts would rather take a onetime consulting assignment to earn money while learning about a new issue in that industry. And many special achievers would rather work as independent contractors, focusing on consulting, selling, or producing other key results. Mel Solway is an achiever who makes most of his living from onetime assignments.

Mel spent over a decade as vice president of administrative services for Fidelity Federal Bank. Preferring the freedom to pursue his many interests, Mel formed CBS Consulting with a colleague, and now provides guidance for corporations in a variety of areas.

With a broad background in facilities, insurance, inventory control, printing, purchasing, real estate, risk management, security, and warehousing, Mel was well prepared to provide legitimate expertise to a wide range of clients. And it wasn't long before he began receiving numerous calls from colleagues requesting his assistance with various projects.

Like Mel, most people who contract onetime assignments enjoy the freedom this type of lifestyle offers. Yet there are two other key advantages that you may want to explore. The first is that people like Mel earn more on each job than most full-time employees doing similar tasks. By using effective marketing techniques, you can earn more—in some cases, a lot more—than by obtaining full-time employment.

The second advantage is that onetime assignments are often easier to obtain. Usually, you won't have the same interview and application process, since companies can terminate contingent workers much easier than they can full-time employees.

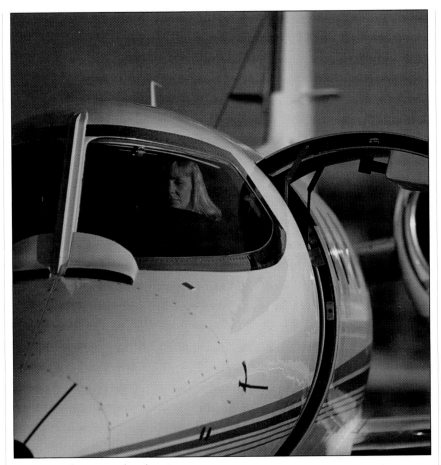

Contract employment can be a lucrative venture.

While some companies are trying to restrict temporary and contract workers, it's still relatively easy to get hired into these positions.

The real challenge in obtaining a onetime assignment is just knowing what is available. The key to knowing about what's out there is, once again, your ability to effectively network. The vast majority of these jobs aren't advertised (only about 2 percent are), and those that are advertised are often entry level. You might want to look through the last section of this chapter, as well as review your notes in the chapter 4 discussion on networking to evaluate yourself and plan ways to become a better networker.

The process employers use to select candidates for onetime employment is significantly different than for full-time jobs. With full-time positions, the goal is often to find someone who is available; except for top corporate positions, this usually means looking for people who are either unemployed or who are working but might be lured away with a better offer. For onetime assignments, though, the goal is often to find someone truly exceptional—a real leader in the field. So to obtain these positions, it's often necessary to perform more indirect marketing.

Your goal in these indirect marketing efforts should be to position yourself as someone who knows a lot—or who has done a lot—in a specific area. And you need to position yourself with people who could potentially hire you. This means identifying these people, finding a way to contact them, and following through. For a few industries, cold calling may be effective, but for most industries you'll need to use more subtle methods. Here are some suggestions:

- *Write an article in a magazine, newspaper, or journal that is read by people you would like to work for.* Writing an article is a long process; it includes thinking of an interesting idea, pitching the idea to an editor, writing the manuscript, and editing what you've written. Because this process takes so much time, you have to be careful to write articles that will truly help you. This means spending a lot of up-front time to find magazines that the right people read. Many magazines will tell you about the demographics of their readership if you ask, but you can usually get a good sense of the reader's job level on your own simply by looking at the articles.

- *Circulate articles you've written.* If you've written articles on solving specific problems, or case studies that highlight how one company or person did something exceptional, you can use the article again and again. One way to do this is to write letters to potential employers and include a copy of the article. This strategy shows a potential employer that you're knowledgeable regarding a specific issue. Another approach is to try to get the same article published in another journal, newspaper, magazine, or company paper (make sure you obtain reprint permission if you don't already own the rights). You probably won't make much money by circulating an article, so evaluate the potential job benefits before investing a lot of time.

- *Give speeches to groups.* One of the most effective ways to circulate your name and reputation is to find groups filled with people who might want to hire you to speak to them. Such groups might include chambers of commerce meetings, Rotarians, Kiwanis clubs, Toastmasters International, professional association meetings, networking clubs, and so on; most of these groups will include members who regularly hire people on a onetime basis. Most people fear public speaking and so will shy away from giving speeches. Yet this situation creates many opportunities for people who can break through stage fright and present effective presentations. Many groups will welcome speakers who provide a specific talk that will interest the group members. And by mentioning your line of work, and then leaving brochures, business cards, or pamphlets behind, you can use speeches as a way of showing potential employers what value you could add.

- *Become active in professional associations.* Professional association meetings are good forums to meet people and establish mutually beneficial relationships. Make sure your networking skills are strong before investing time in these meetings, since they are often time-consuming and professional association dues can be quite expensive.

- *Let previous employers know about your interest and availability.* One of the best sources of employment on a onetime basis is a person or a company you used to work for. This is an advantage since the people making the hiring decision know your abilities and aptitudes and are accustomed to working with you. This can give you a real edge if you exploit the opportunity. You can do so in a number of ways: make regular "keep-in-touch" phone calls with decision makers in firms you used to work for; keep abreast of the opportunities and threats facing your old employers, and in your conversations with them point out how you can serve as a resource; send them copies of articles you've written; and remain active in professional associations frequented

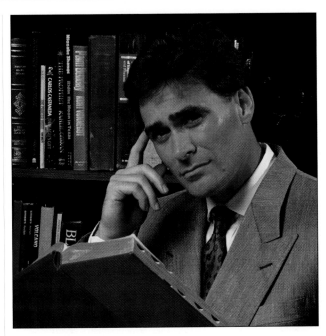

Research or write an article for a widely read professional journal or newsletter.

by your old employers. Try to position yourself as someone who has learned and grown significantly since you stopped working for them, so that they won't think of you as someone who hasn't progressed in your field.

• *Start your own newsletter, or use a stock newsletter.* A more innovative yet time-consuming approach is to start a newsletter targeted to potential employers. It should contain a mix of information that will be helpful to the people who might hire you, as well as information about your credentials and experience. A more costly but speedier approach is to buy a stock newsletter and place your name on it.

Since indirect marketing efforts take time to become operational, most people will need to do something else to earn an income while writing articles or giving speeches. To effectively transition to working on a onetime employment basis, try to spend as much time as possible doing things that will enhance your experience or credibility—perhaps teaching at community colleges or in university exten-

sion programs, or working in traditional employment in a related field.

Employment in an Ongoing Advisory Capacity

Many experts, some facilitators, and a number of special achievers may desire employment in an ongoing advisory capacity. This work involves providing technical or procedural help to an employer, or moral support to top decision makers. Often this type of work involves being put on a retainer, so that the client reserves a certain amount of your time, often at a reduced rate. Jerry Lindberg works as a career counselor, often on a retainer basis. The story of how he gained significant expertise and marketed himself is typical of other people who work as advisors.

Jerry works as a career coach on retainer for several clients. The story of how he became a career counselor offers many lessons for gaining employment on an ongoing basis.

It started for Jerry in 1972, when he enrolled in a professional course

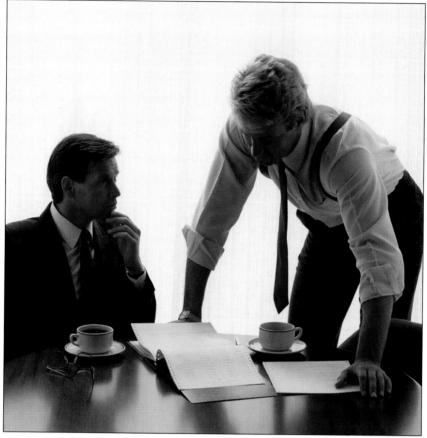

The "expert" at work: career counseling on retainer.

on financial investment. He believes that financial investment is inseparable from other major life issues, especially career and family. After graduating from the program, he used word-of-mouth marketing to reach a wide range of clients. Most paid him on a project basis.

After nine years, he was near total burnout. Jerry describes a morning when he woke up and hated what he was doing so much he couldn't go to the office: "I just couldn't do it anymore—I became incapable of continuing in that line of work," he says. He spent six months doing an in-depth analysis of his life and his overall strengths and weaknesses. During this time he met a counselor/psychologist who began training him to include his overall career as part of his coaching skills. Over the next few years, he enrolled in a variety of training programs and was mentored by some of the leading people in the field.

At first, Jerry began volunteering his services as a career coach to people who needed help. His techniques were so powerful that many who once needed help were empowered to turn their lives around and became very successful in their careers. In time, these people referred other professionals to Jerry, who soon established a lucrative career coaching business. Today, all his clients come to him through referrals. Jerry notes that it took a great deal of pain to reach a point where he could make a living as a career coach.

Today, most of Jerry's clients keep him on retainer. Some pay him a specified amount each month; others pay each time they use his services, up to the amount specified in the contract. Others pay up front for extended services. Jerry's key in making ongoing advisory employment work is to be flexible toward the client's needs. Yet in order for his services to lead to breakthroughs for his clients, he emphasizes working with them for an extended period.

Like Jerry, most people who obtain ongoing advisory employment have already proven themselves by having achieved specific and impressive accomplishments. In Jerry's own words, they've already exhibited their success as "superexperts," worthy of the trust that advisory employment implies. Naturally it follows that this type of work is usually more difficult to get than either traditional employment or work on a onetime basis.

More so than the other types of employment discussed in this chapter, advisory work is often performed by people who are part of an "inner circle" in their field. Depending on the specific field, these are the top experts, the most well-known facilitators, the top executives from the corporate stalwart path, the entrepreneurs who created the most famous ventures, and the achievers who can point to the most successful results.

This is not to say that everyone hired on an ongoing basis is at the top of her or his field. Many are not. But most are seen as being more capable, more competent, and more reliable than other people.

Pursuing employment in an ongoing advisory capacity can be a lifelong venture filled with specific jobs, each more high-profile than the one before. Many people in the expert path will build their careers using this model. Doing it right requires obtaining more and more prestige, solving more and more complex and difficult problems, and continually developing your skills. For this kind of employment, skill building and self-packaging are the keys to staying in demand.

Specific marketing strategies for this kind of employment are similar to those for onetime basis employment, but are at a higher level (you may

want to review the previous section). There are numerous helpful suggestions specific to ongoing advisory employment. They include:

• *Write a book, or several books.* Milton Rosenau, who runs his own management consulting firm in Texas, tells of one of the best ways to obtain advisory employment: "Arrange a meeting with someone who can hire you," he advises, "and wait for the question that always comes up—'why should I hire you?' Then you answer, 'because I wrote the book.' Then take out the book and set it on the table." Impressive stuff!

• *Give keynote speeches at professional or technical conferences.* Most conferences bring in one or two "big names" to give the keynote speeches. Giving such a speech will put you before many top decision makers in a specific field and will give you significant exposure. Often people are selected to present the keynote speech because they've written widely read books, been elected to a high office in a professional association, held a prestigious job, or achieved a major breakthrough in a technical or business area. Thus, you may be selected to do so only after you've spent significant time in a field and have successfully marketed yourself. Still, this is a worthy goal to set—and you just might surprise yourself at how quickly this goal will be realized.

• *Start with small companies and clients.* By using some of the strategies discussed in the previous section on onetime basis employment— writing articles, giving speeches, and starting a newsletter—you may become sought after to do advisory work for small companies and clients. This can become a great stepping-stone to future work with more prestigious clients or for obtaining work at higher rates of pay. Thus, if advisory work is your goal, you may have to start small and then grow.

Whichever type of employment is your goal—be it traditional, onetime, or ongoing—there are several issues on which you need to focus. The next section looks at the first of these issues—the resume. We will then turn to interviewing and a discussion of leave-behind material.

Resumes and Beyond

Many people who are laid off focus first of all on their resumes. However, this is often a mistake, since they haven't yet decided what type of job they're seeking. Even if you won't be applying for a corporate job, resumes are still important because they're often requested if you're bidding on a specific job, joining a professional organization, or giving a marketing speech. Thus, it's advisable to have an up-to-date resume, even if you don't think your career transition will involve formal job interviews.

The consensus of many employment officers and job experts is that, while resumes are important, they're often overemphasized by people trying to market themselves. As discussed earlier in this chapter, it's important to know *exactly* what you're looking for. If you've taken the time to analyze what type of work would suit you best, the process of putting together a resume becomes quite simple: it presents what you want to do and demonstrates that you have the qualifications to do it.

If you need to generate a resume, there are some excellent books to help you get started. These include *The Damn Good Resume Guide* by Yana Parket, *Knock 'Em Dead: The Ultimate Job Seeker's Handbook* by Martin Yate, and *The Perfect Resume* by Tom Jackson. For our purposes in this section, however, we'll assume that you

have already prepared your resume. Our focus here will guide you in performing a "resume check" to make sure that you've avoided the five most common mistakes people make in creating their resumes. By focusing on each of these, you can make sure your resume will serve you effectively. They include:

1. *Keeping your resume broad, so you won't be excluded from any potential jobs.* This approach falsely assumes that potential employers looking through resumes will follow up with any applicants who even remotely fit their criteria. The reality, however, is that most people who look through stacks and stacks of resumes have the luxury of waiting for "perfect fits," and so the screening process usually involves weeding out all those resumes that don't exactly fit the open positions. The best advice therefore is to focus your resume as much as possible; while it's true that some people will screen out a more job-specific, focused resume, this approach increases the chances that the right people won't.

This advice holds true for both traditional and nontraditional jobs. Even in cases of professional associations looking for speakers, or employers looking for advisors, a focused resume increases your chances of showing that you're the perfect fit.

2. *Exaggerating a little, or a lot.* Some people feel insecure about their qualifications, and alter details here or there: *Supervisor* becomes *manager*; *manager* becomes *director*; *the third-best salesperson in the state* becomes *the top seller in the nation*. While these edits may seem small—and may be easy to justify to yourself—there are two potential dangers. First, these modifications may be easier to spot than you think. Many seasoned employment officers and job experts can quickly identify resumes peppered with untruths. Second, the exaggerations may catch up with you: You may land a job for which you're not qualified and thus

be doomed to failure, or you may invest a lot of time in one potential job only to be filtered out when your references don't check out. The best advice is to phrase your experience in the best possible way while being completely truthful.

3. *Double-talking and in-speaking.* Many people don't consider their potential audiences when they design their resumes and include technical language that will only be understood by specialists. In many cases, resumes are first read by executives or professional executive search consultants—and many such people aren't technical experts. Another common problem is that job seekers don't know exactly what they want to do, and their writing becomes as unclear as their career objectives. A classic example of double-talk includes: "Objective: to work for a progressive and innovative firm in a position of increasing responsibility." This roughly translates to "I want to work for a company that pays well and will promote me quickly," or "I don't really know what I want to do, but I want to get paid a lot anyway." The best way to cut through double-talk and in-speak is to focus your job search efforts and tailor your resume for each person you send it to.

4. *Using verbose wording, lots of pages, and little white space.* Some people are so excited by their experience that they're certain everyone else will be, too. Thus, they paint a wonderfully vivid picture through lots of words. The problem? The person reading a lengthy resume probably isn't that interested and will find the wordy language reason enough to disregard the resume altogether. Most career experts suggest that you get to the point quickly, use bullets rather than full sentences, and assume the reader will spend about 30 seconds on your resume.

5. *Focusing on activities, rather than results.* A sure giveaway that a resume is in trouble is when many sentences or sections begin with the word "Served," as in:

Served on several committees analyzing procurement policies.

This translates to "I spent time in meetings," and few people are hired to sit in meetings, unless they bring a strong expertise to the table. Don't focus your resume on how you spent your time, but rather on the outcome of the time spent. As much as possible, quantify your accomplishments, as in "Increased sales in my region by 25 percent in one year," "Won the top sales award for XYZ company in 1990 by outselling 200 other salespeople."

"Massage" your resume until it safely jumps over all these pitfalls. Once it does, you're ready for the next section, which will help you use your resume as a powerful self-marketing tool.

Using Your Resume

Once your resume is ready, you're prepared to start marketing yourself. And this is where many people fall into yet another career pit—they use methods that probably won't get them the kind of results they want. Richard Nelson Bolles, author of *What Color Is Your Parachute?*, presents research on the best and worst job-hunting methods. The least effective include using computer bank listings (96 percent failure rate); answering local newspaper ads (76 to 95 percent failure rate); going to private employment agencies (76 to 95 percent failure rate); answering professional and trade journal ads (93 percent failure rate); and mailing out stacks and stacks of resumes (92 percent failure rate). The most effective method by far is networking, and while it's hard to quantify its success rate (since most people network slightly differently), some evidence suggests that it *works* for about 86 percent of those who use it.

One of the most powerful networking systems for getting the right kind of employment fast is to combine informational interviews with a good resume. This method is built on the so-called "axiom of networking," which says that the more people who know about you, the results you can achieve, and your career objective, the more job opportunities you'll have. Thus, one of the keys to getting your next job—regardless of the employment or career path you think is right for you—is to show off your resume, which should quantify these points about yourself. Of course, you have to do so in a manner that does not appear arrogant, abrasive, or obnoxious.

Arguably, the best way to accomplish this goal is to seek resume advice from people in jobs similar to those you'd like to hold. You probably already know someone in this category; if not, you probably "know someone who knows someone," or you can find such a person by using the networking methods discussed above.

Once you locate the referral, schedule an appointment for a meeting, making it clear that you're trying to transition into a new career and that *all* you're looking for is advice. Most people won't turn this down, since you're paying them a great compliment by asking for their opinion. In the meeting, present your resume and ask for tips on making it better; most people will give you some advice. Then, toward the end of the meeting, ask if the person knows of anyone else who might be able to give you advice. Once the meeting is concluded, make any changes the person recommends and then send him or her a clean copy. Repeat this process with any referrals the person gave you, or with other people you know.

There are several advantages to using this method. The first is that your "good" resume gets "better" through lots of feedback from people who work in jobs similar to the one you would like to hold. The second is that your resume gets in the hands of many people who might be able to help you;

when they hear of openings, they'll probably think of you. The third is that you get the chance to meet many capable, accomplished people one on one, and these meetings will help you to further focus your career objectives and strategies.

Even if no job offers result from this exercise, you'll nevertheless emerge knowing many more people and having a resume you can use to get other opportunities, such as speaking engagements, articles published, or membership in prestigious organizations. But chances are this method alone will get you offers and, ultimately, the type of job you're seeking.

Interviewing

In all likelihood, your networking efforts will pay off with people phoning you to schedule interviews. When this happens, it's time to shift career gears from "getting the word out" to "finding the right opportunity."

There are two common mistakes people make in interviews. The first is trying to read the interviewer's mind to tell her what she wants to hear. This is a mistake for several reasons: First, it's impossible to know what the person wants to hear; second, in many cases the person wants to hear something that will quickly exclude you from the running, which will simplify their life by having one less candidate to keep track of; third, the interviewer usually isn't the one who will make the final decision (in many cases, the ultimate decision maker wants to hear something different from what the first interviewer heard!); and fourth, your goal shouldn't be simply getting an offer but instead finding an opportunity that is truly right for you.

The second mistake many people make during the interview process is looking at every question as a hurdle to get over; an ideal interview, according to this thinking, is one in which you don't make any big mistakes. The better way to think of interviews is as a forum for you to "tell *your* story," as described earlier in this chapter. By the time the interview is over, you want to have left a strong impression on the interviewer that you are the ideal candidate for the position. Thus, when the person asks questions like "why do you want to work for us?", answer in a way that will leave the impression that you are the right person for the job. This actually means answering the question "why are you right for the job?"

It's also a good idea to prepare answers for the most common interviewing questions. These include "Tell me about yourself," "What is your greatest strength?", "What is your greatest weakness?", "What can you do for us?", "Why do you want to work here?", and "Do you have any questions?" Good advice is to answer each of these in a way that will help position you as the one to be hired. If you feel you need specific help in preparing for interviews, read *Sweaty Palms: The Neglected Art of Being Interviewed* by Anthony Medley, *The Perfect Interview: How to Get the Job You Really Want* by John Drake, and *Make Your Job Interview a Success: A Guide for the Career-Minded Job Seeker* by J. I. Biegeleisen.

Marketing Packets and Portfolios

In today's economy, it's important to distinguish yourself from other job applicants by giving potential employers a way to remember you. One method is to create material that you can leave with the person after the interview, such as portfolios, fact sheets, articles you've written, or articles written about you. These materials can also be used when you give speeches, bid on consulting jobs, or

as follow-up material in your networking efforts.

This section describes two of the most common and important types of leave-behind material and discusses how to make these materials work for you. The first type is a *marketing packet*. This includes a description of what you do, examples of what you've done, articles you've written, and a list of your services. This kind of packet is especially useful for people in the expert and facilitator career paths, as well as for special achievers working as consultants in management, marketing, finance, or other business specialties.

An effective marketing packet will, in a concise, abbreviated fashion, give potential employers "the inside scoop" on your skills and abilities. Therefore it is essential that you give careful consideration to the kind of impression that you want to make.

Putting together a marketing packet is a deceptively simple task. The easy way to do it—collect some of your articles, a testimonial or two, and some extraneous text about your services—probably won't get you a great result. The more effective way to accomplish this task results from executing a full marketing plan, which forces you to define your target market segment, the aspects of your business that differentiate you from your competitors, and exactly how you should position yourself.

Bill Cohen, a Los Angeles–based management consultant, author of more than thirty books on business and management, and a well-known lecturer, needed to create a marketing kit that effectively condensed his accolades into one readable document. The result was "Cohen's Maxims," which he often hands out after speeches or gives to specific clients. The one-page "Maxims" lists key business-related terms such as "compensation," "duty," "leadership," "responsibility," and "success," and then briefly defines them within the context of Bill's own personal business credo, underscoring his strong work ethic and personal commitment. Bill's kit clearly indicates that his practice is built on his unique set of values.

Beverly Kaye's needs dictated the creation of a different kind of promotional kit. She runs Beverly Kaye and Associates, Inc. in Los Angeles and is an organizational consultant who specializes in career development, management training, and human resource planning. Since her business exists primarily on her reputation, this fact sheet emphasizes her accomplishments in an up-front yet professional style. It also summarizes the services of her business while highlighting her many qualifications. Kaye's kit includes an impressive list of clients, titles of books she has written, a partial list of trade publications in which her articles have appeared, lecture and workshop credits, and honors and awards received for her work.

The second common type of leave-behind material is the *portfolio*. Portfolios are especially important for people who work in the special-achiever career path, including artists, mechanical engineers, writers, landscapers, architects,

and so on. This leave-behind material is a visual aid that tangibly demonstrates what kind of results you can bring to a person or organization. A copywriter's portfolio, for example, would typically include print advertisements in which the writer's work has appeared (or storyboards if the work was for television), as well as a list of past clients and campaigns worked on.

To put together an effective portfolio, start by recalling exactly what type of work you're looking for: traditional, onetime, or ongoing. Then take a step back and ask yourself which of your accomplishments will help you get your desired employment. Finally, put together a preliminary portfolio. The most important step is getting feedback and constructive criticism on how it can be improved. Some job hunters have submitted their portfolios to people using a process similar to the one described in the "Using Your Resume" section.

This chapter presented a basic overview of how to market yourself in preparation for a new career, even for a transition to a new career path. Chapter 7 will focus on negotiating salaries and contracts and on getting yourself set up in your new career.

Chapter 7

Negotiating Compensation and Contracts

hapter 6 focused on improving your personal packaging. If you worked through all the sections, your resume should be more concise, more powerful, and more representative of your true self. You should now be ready to market yourself in more innovative and effective ways. These improvements in your personal packaging and promotion either already have or soon will provide you with new and exciting career opportunities.

Your time spent in career reinvention is about to pay off, but you'll also want to ensure that you're properly compensated for your efforts. Now is the time to think about negotiating

your salary and benefits (in the case of a traditional job) or your contracted rate of compensation for other types of employment.

This chapter will cover principles for not only negotiating present and future compensation but also establishing win-win employee contracts that leave both parties satisfied in both traditional and contract employment. By and large, most corporate stalwarts/experts will pursue traditional employment, as will some special achievers. On the other hand, facilitators will likely prefer contract or contingency employment, in which they will be hired for a stipulated time period to accomplish specific

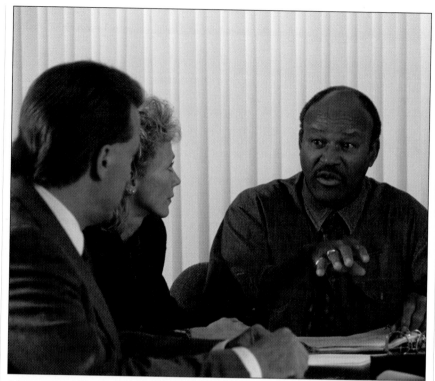

Bringing your skills to the table: negotiating a salary agreement.

objectives (some special achievers also fit here). Whichever type of employment you choose to pursue, this chapter can help.

Overview: Gauging Compensation

One *Wall Street Journal* report noted that 40 percent of job seekers accept starting pay at a lower level than they could have been paid. Why is this? Has this happened to you?

Job interviews are bad enough, but discussions about compensation tend to make cowards out of the fiercest lions. Fear, anxiety about losing one's job, and uncertainty about their true monetary value are all factors. What is the employer willing to pay? Will they pay market value? Or will they insist on giving you less—perhaps requiring that you prove yourself first?

You know you want the job. The position is either a good fit, an opportunity to get your foot in the door of a good company, or simply puts an end to the desperation to get back to work. Or maybe this is the first job of your planned career transition.

Whatever the case, the employer usually has the advantage—especially in large markets like New York, Chicago, or Los Angeles, where literally hundreds of candidates apply for every opening. It's also difficult to sway a decision maker if the position isn't critical to the company's operational success.

So you may experience feelings of despair when the company offers you 10 to 25 percent less than you'd hoped for. What do you do? You need a job, but receiving less-than-adequate compensation at the job onset can affect your long-term financial stability, perhaps costing you hundreds of thousands of dollars over a lifetime. If you face this dilemma, this chapter will provide you with the answers you need.

Steps to Gain the Upper Hand in Negotiating Compensation

The key to successfully negotiating compensation is to be adequately prepared before you "approach the table." The next six sections should give you an idea of what to anticipate in a typical negotiation session.

Be Your Own Agent

Without an agent, you're stuck doing your own negotiations. It's an idea that hasn't caught on yet, but just as professional entertainers and athletes have personal agents to negotiate their contracts, you'd be better off having someone else negotiating your compensation.

Why such an outlandish suggestion? Because, as the person performing the services, you're too emotionally close to the deal. It's hard to be objective on issues that are so near and dear to us.

Obviously, our expectations are high as we envision and anticipate receiving a generous employment package. Unfortunately, blind expectations cause us to actually limit what's ultimately possible. So the ideal situation would call for using an impartial third party as our advocate. Unfortunately, this practice isn't customary, unless you work through an executive recruiter. If you find yourself in one of these categories, the process will probably be easier for you. But if not, what should you do?

You need to become your own agent. To do this, you have to "step outside" the situation. Most of us have the ability to see other people's problems clearly, to offer legitimate solutions from the "outside." You have to

see yourself in the same manner—as a third person. This will keep you from becoming too emotionally tied to the outcome and will ensure that you negotiate a better deal.

Do Your Homework

No matter what you're negotiating— a real estate purchase, a new car purchase, a salary or contract negotiation—you have to do your homework. What's the going rate for that position or for that kind of employment?

Salary levels vary by profession, industry, region, job title, educational level, certifications achieved, budget responsibility, number of reports, and unfortunately, by gender. Industry salary levels are available from industry associations and public libraries. Hourly rates for other types of employment vary by the type of services you offer, the amount of time you will serve a company or person, and numerous other factors.

Have a reasonable range scoped out before you begin negotiations. If your asking price is based on objective data, the employer has trouble saving face if his offer is significantly lower than average.

Select the Right Venue

Most interviews and salary negotiations occur at the employer's facility, but it's not always a good idea to conduct salary negotiations in person. If the company really wants you, it might be a good idea to keep them at arm's length for awhile.

After the initial interview, communicate by phone or E-mail. Let them court you. Allow them time to build up eager anticipation. If you make them wait, and they really want you, they may drive the price up to force your commitment. Of course, you have to be careful with this approach: You may think they really want you when in fact they really wanted the person who turned them down.

Keeping abreast of industry averages will help you gauge appropriate compensation.

It's also a good idea not to consider the offer until you have it in writing. The written offer should specify the rate of compensation, any special terms of employment, basic details on benefits (in the case of traditional employment), and other perks. Although the salary may initially sound good, there may be an unpleasant surprise in the form of uncompetitive benefits.

In the case of contract employment, there are only two main variables: hourly or daily rate and length of time. In some cases, you may be paid by the project, in which case these two variables are collapsed into one. If you find yourself negotiating this kind of employment, it's even more important to select the right venue—and then take it slow. Unlike traditional employment, you can't negotiate for better benefits to help compensate for a lower salary.

Respond to the Compensation Question

Before you negotiate base compensation, you should have a good idea of what the market will bear and what you're willing to accept. When asked how much you're interested in making, be very careful as to how you respond. If the figure is too low, the prospective employer may think you're not at the competence level they're seeking. They may assume that you didn't ask for more because you never made more; and they may think that you've never made more because you're probably not worth that much. Thus, they reason, why should they hire you? And they may decide not to!

According to most job experts, the best answer you can give regarding your desired rate of pay is to quote the industry average and inquire as to their intentions. "How much do I want to make? Well, the industry average is $82,000 a year for this position. Of course, that's only the average rate, and I believe my history of achievement demonstrates that I'm worth much more than that. What's the salary range you've established?"

This response answers the compensation question with objective evidence and throws the question back to the potential employer to state his or her objective range. The issue is no longer emotional or scary and has simply become a discussion.

In the case of contract employment, the other chief variable is the length of time the employer will regain your services. If you're in the expert or special achiever career path, it's common for employers to say that they will extend your stay if you do a good job. Get as much of this as possible in writing before you start work. Otherwise, your work may be exemplary but the job will nevertheless not be renewed if the company shifts direction or announces staff reductions.

Negotiate Items

So what would make you happy? A chauffeured limousine or a country club membership? Well, not everyone's a top executive, but there's still plenty of options on the table. Titles are important. So are bonuses, stock purchase options, 401(k) plans, medical and dental coverage, life insurance, vacation, cellular phones, severance packages, and so on. For many salaried and ongoing hourly jobs, you may be able to negotiate many of these items.

Before doing so, spend some time researching the company's policies. For most publicly held companies, this information is available in official publications. For small, closely held firms, your best research may come down to phoning the human resources department or asking a current employee.

Once you know what is and is not negotiable, you're in a position to try to get as much as you can. One of the best negotiation strategies is to find some weak spot in the salary offer—such as paying the national average for a position when the company is located in an area with a higher cost of living. Once you spot the weak link, offer to consider the position if the company adds in whatever negotiable items are important to you.

Respond Appropriately to an Offer

Never, never, never say "yes" to the first offer. In general, you should allow yourself a day or two to think it over. Things always become more clear after a good night's sleep. Furthermore, most companies expect you to make a counteroffer, and you should be aware that, without an attempt on your part to renegotiate, your perception and credibility may jeopardized.

Prospective employers want to feel confident that they're hiring a savvy and knowledgeable businessperson, someone who understands their value in the marketplace. Thus, your counteroffer should at least upgrade the salary range you've been offered.

Even if you decide to accept the company's offer, it's important to consider the future before you begin your new assignment. This means that your ultimate goal is negotiating your future promotions and raises before you complete a single day of work, although this isn't always possible. And with today's turbulent economy, it probably won't be any more common for the next five years. Nevertheless, in some firms, such a deal can still be made. Again, the best advice remains: Research your company and see what fits the particular business culture.

Jim Wilk, senior vice-president of human resources and administration for Health Systems International, offers this advice when negotiating salary and benefits. "The most important salary negotiation is the first one. Get certain understandings up front. You should negotiate a salary review after the first six months, and get them to promise you a promotion if you accomplish certain objectives. Negotiate compromises. Shoot for a promotion every six months. Be flexible, but try to get the future in writing."

Contract employment is simpler. Most people who work from one contract to the next have less to gain and less to lose from a single job. Thus, you may feel freer to accept work. But take the same careful approach in trying to negotiate the best possible deal.

Other Factors to Consider

Initially, you will probably feel elated about joining a company. You look forward to the additional pay, if that's the case. If you've been unemployed, you're no doubt happy to be back to work. Nevertheless, a certain amount of apprehension over new surroundings, people, and requirements is only natural.

There's also no guarantee that the job is going to work out for you: The interviewer may have misrepresented the position; one of the employees in the department may have been passed over for promotion and is now trying to sabotage your success; or someone in another department may take a disliking to you and try to "take you out." All of these potential scenarios may be concerns of yours, so you really have to commit to making a change—and it should be because you feel certain as possible that you'll fare better at the new company.

The best reason to take a job is that it serves your long-term goals. In today's economy even corporate stalwarts will probably change companies several times. So each job you take must prepare you for the next opportunity.

Should You Accept a Pay Cut?

You're supposed to move forward, not backward. So why would anyone accept less money than they were previously earning, or less than they feel they're worth?

One possibility is that you're trying to get into a good company and you're willing to settle for less to get your foot in the door. This can be a risky strategy, but it's worked for some.

Just because the interviewer is willing to discuss the possibility of rapid growth and advancement does not constitute a promise on the employer's part. Nevertheless, it's often heard as a promise that eventually results in hard feelings if the promotion or raise doesn't materialize. It's therefore crucial to ask yourself if you can afford to take less money temporarily.

Sometimes people want to change industries and are forced to take a temporary lower wage. Other times people move to a different region of the country where the wages are lower. The worst scenario is when you've been out of work for a long period and you feel compelled to take whatever you can get.

The decision about whether to accept lower pay comes down to a value judgment and should be made with your overall future in mind. You may feel forced to take what you can get, or you may see it as an opportunity in the making. But no matter how it looks, take the time to research the company, the position, and the people: At least your decision will then be an informed one.

What about Employment Contracts?

Many people who have worked exclusively in traditional jobs have never signed an employment contract; however, with litigation mounting over employee terminations, employment contracts may soon become in vogue. And although most companies hire employees under "at will" arrangements, litigation cases and costs continue to escalate.

Changes in the economy are prompting an increasing number of people to consider contract work rather than traditional employment. Again, this increases the chance that

Employee contracts can be beneficial for both sides.

you will some day be faced with an employment contract.

Contracting for employees can create a win-win situation for both parties. Employees benefit if they're goal-oriented, and they can earn further raises and bonuses by achieving agreed-upon performance objectives. This is especially profitable for high achievers when their company has a flat-rate raise policy. Employers benefit because they can ensure that employees are focusing on results that increase the company's bottom line. Performance objectives are an excellent means for evaluating staff performance and deciding whether to retain an employee's services.

If an employee achieves or surpasses her or his objectives, management will probably renew the contract and increase compensation as appropriate. If, however, an employee fails to meet objectives, management can choose to renew the contract at a lower rate of pay or not renew it at all. A good contract should also indicate what severance and outplacement services the employee will receive if terminated.

Stay Committed to Your Life Plan

Regardless of the circumstances, you must strive to stay on course with your life plan. Is this step in line with your goals and life purpose? If not, why are you taking it?

Do you consider your new job or position a temporary move until you get something better, or are you taking a calculated gamble that you'll move up quickly? It's important to stay true to yourself and not let fear or emotion distract you from your life plan.

You're Well on Your Way

You've come a long way in a short time. Chances are that this book is causing you to think differently about your life and your future. You've done a thorough job of analyzing yourself and your ideal work environment. You've selected a career path and perhaps a new profession. Overall, you're now better informed and ready to embark on a fuller, happier life.

Now that you have progressed to this point in reinventing your career, you need to look ahead to what the future holds for our expanding global economy and what this means for you.

In chapter 8, we'll discuss how the changes in the next millennium might create interesting challenges and opportunities for completing your career plans, and we'll describe major social, economic, and technological forces that might affect you and your career.

We'll explore such topics as the expanding information superhighway, the aging of the workforce as baby boomers head toward retirement, telecommuting and the virtual office, opportunities in direct marketing, and the changing international trade scene. By focusing on these trends, your career will be better protected from potentially negative influences, and you'll be one step ahead of the game in reaping the opportunities the next millennium holds.

Chapter 8

Navigating the New Millennium

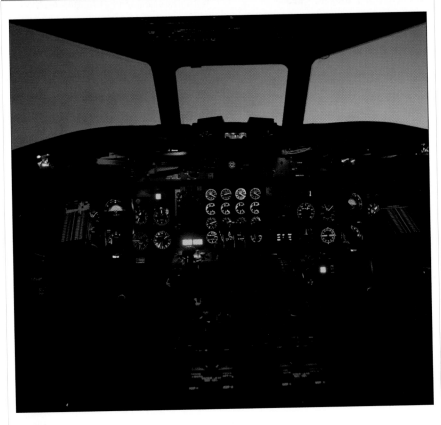

In the brief period it took you to review the first seven chapters of this book, you've hopefully gained some self-awareness and now possess the tools necessary to create a new future.

Life can be fresher and more exciting. It's possible to enjoy your life more than ever. You've now learned how to create the life that you love. Let's briefly recap what we've covered.

In chapter 1, you learned about five career paths that have materialized from the rapid, massive changes in our economy. There are thousands of specific career possibilities in each of the five paths we've discussed. By understanding each path, you have acquired an overview of the entire economy and can envision new possibilities for your future.

Chapter 2 provided you with a new analysis tool to help you evaluate the current state of your career. Having gone through the process, you are now much better informed about your current status and future potential.

Chapter 3 helped you to prepare for the life you'd like to live. You've identified lifelong personal preferences, your natural strengths, and your ideal work environment.

You also set specific goals in several areas of your life. Rather than allow you to limit yourself, you were encouraged to set "monster goals," goals that require effort and courage to pursue. To help ensure that this was a productive process, you measured your level of contentment by testing your emotional health. You also learned to turn your inner voice into an ally rather than an impediment to your progress.

After this, you specified your values for every segment of your life. Finally, you put it all together to identify one unique package—yourself! You understand what career path is right for you, and you know what you're capable of achieving.

In chapter 4, you evaluated basic skills and principles that, if carefully fostered, will help ensure your success. You learned how to take better care of your health. You also evaluated your communication skills and planned improvement steps.

You took a fresh look at networking and learned a new way to apply its concepts. You now think more creatively than you did, and you learned ways to generate powerful ideas.

In this everchanging world, you must not only anticipate change but also learn to *create* it. And you can. You're now ready to help lead your field through the beginning of the next millennium.

Chapter 5 helped you to put it all together. You documented your chosen career path, and a life plan is in place. You're now fully in control of your future—and it has clarity, focus, and energy. You have a fairly clear image of what you hope to be doing with the rest of your life. And you're prepared to identify future opportunities and potential threats.

In chapter 6, you learned ways to market yourself in a competitive world. You're now set to package and promote yourself as a high-quality product. No matter what career path you've chosen or what specific career you've targeted, there are great opportunities out there— and they're yours for the taking!

Chapter 7 provided ideas on how to earn an income commensurate with your chosen career. You learned how to prepare yourself for salary negotiations and how to plan for the next raise or promotion.

In chapter 8, this concluding chapter, we will explore the major social, economic, and technological forces that will affect your career over the next several years. Topics will include the continuous flattening of organizations and the implications to corporate jobs, the expanding information superhighway, the aging of the workforce as baby boomers head toward retirement, the home as office (telecommuting) and its special challenges, increased opportunities in network marketing, and the changing international trade scene.

The Changing Face of Corporations

As we move into the next century, we can expect considerable changes to alter the way companies do business and employees succeed in their careers. These changes are sure to significantly affect you and your role, regardless of which path your career takes. Thus, your objectives should include perceiving these changes as positive and seeking workable solutions to these changes.

The first trend is the continuing wave of mergers and acquisitions in corporate America. Industries such as health care, media, telecommunications, banking, railroads, automotive, retail, pharmaceuticals, computers, and defense have been merging at a frantic pace. But this phenomenon is not unique to large firms: Mergers are also increasingly prevalent with funeral homes, management consulting groups, and environmental engineering companies.

You may find it surprising that large mergers have occurred for over 100 years. In fact, mergers that took place in the 1890s and 1920s were

The future of your industry: What's next?

more significant, relative to real Gross National Product (GNP), than the highly publicized merger mania of the 1980s. Between 1895 and 1904, 1,800 U.S. companies merged, creating 157 megafirms.

A new merger wave has swept the 1990s and is expected to continue in the years ahead. In 1994 we experienced a record-breaking year with 348 large mergers totaling $272 billion. A new quarterly record of $137 billion was set during the third quarter of 1995, and the current pace is projected to reach a record $411 billion. We're all aware of recent activity involving AT&T, Time Warner and Ted Turner, and ABC with Disney. And the experts forecast that the deals have only just begun.

Business pressures are forcing companies to live by the credo "merge or die." These pressures include the need for industry consolidation, emerging technologies, evolving markets, and preparation for entering the 21st century.

Sales executive Michael Close sees mergers as an opportunity: "There are only a few times in your career when a window of opportunity opens. You have to take advantage of it. The cream always rises to the top. After all, you never know about a person when times are good. You only learn about them when times are tough. That's when you find out who the true leaders are."

The American people fear that mergers will create huge monopolies, which, in turn, will shift the concentration of wealth to these large firms. And economists debate the benefits and the drawbacks—for example, higher corporate profits against higher consumer prices. It's an issue that future presidents and congresses will continue to deal with. On one side of the issue, corporations continue to try to remain competitive and protect themselves against foreign competition, while on the other side the justice department seeks to enforce antitrust laws that protect smaller companies.

The new globalization can help you rethink your corporate boundaries.

Onlookers wonder if the merging companies will remain stable. Will my service be disrupted? Is the company going through turmoil? If so, is it strong enough to navigate through the storm? Will there be sufficient resources? Will the really strong players exit the scene? These are some of the tough questions that investors, shareholders, and customers are asking about mergers, and it will most certainly affect *you.* So what protective strategies should you adopt as unemployment rates continue to rise? Chuck Braden knows.

Chuck is a retired bank executive that now serves on five boards and runs his own management consulting firm. He's also heavily involved in the active merger and acquisition scene. His advice for workers today is to frame their lives around tried and true principles such as balance, integrity, and commonsense. "These will serve you wherever you go, and a good reputation will precede you if you follow these guidelines," he says.

"Set a good example and work hard. Choose to be a leader, not run with the pack. Be different. Find a way to set yourself apart. You also need a well-balanced life at home and at work. If you put in 8 to 10 hours a day, plus drive one hour to work, it doesn't leave you time to do the important things. You have to have your life in order to succeed. And this is especially important during mergers."

But what if you do lose your job? Chuck advises, based on his own experience, "I always had several things going, like different investments, to lessen the impact in case I lost my job. I urge others to do the same. In unstable times, you always have to be prepared."

As mergers and acquisitions continue, there will be fewer top management opportunities. At first this may look like bad news for people desiring the corporate stalwart career path. But, as globalization continues, there will be many opportunities for people willing to take on foreign assignments. And as firms come together, increasing opportunities will exist for people skilled in coordinating and merging functional systems—primarily in such areas as finance, accounting, human resources, manufacturing, and operations. Such opportunities could lead to rapid up-the-ladder advancement.

The merger wave should create significant opportunities for many people in the expert and special achiever career paths. As companies reduce their ranks of full-time employees, people who can work under contract will be in great demand. In particular, experts with specialized, in-demand knowledge in such areas as biotechnology, computer science, and international marketing can do well by positioning themselves as substitutes for traditional employees. And special achievers willing to take advantage of subcontract labor assignments may find themselves making much more money than could ever have been feasible in a salaried position.

The downsizing that results from these mergers and acquisitions is opening up many new career possibilities for those on the facilitator career path. Some people have found a niche by selling "yellow pages" of outsourcing and outplacement firms, as well as people willing to take on work as subcontractors in specific industries. Others combine the skills of analyzing what functions to outsource with a knowledge of which firms can take on the extra work. Others work as brokers, selling businesses to people wanting to leave the corporate world.

If you are—or aspire to become—an expert, facilitator, or special achiever, you can position yourself to take advantage of these changes. *And you should start today.* Become active in business-related associations, take on some outside work as a subcontractor in your field, perhaps even write articles that will be seen by prominent members of your business community. Accept jobs that will give you exposure. Above all, meet people—lots of people. And keep in touch with the people you meet.

Third-Wave Companies

Not only are companies flattening, but many are becoming more democratic—that is, more willing to allow lower-level workers to participate in making key day-to-day decisions. In turn, employees are gaining more satisfaction, meaning, and self-esteem from their work. This trend in corporations is the second important factor that will impact careers in the next few years. As world economies become more interdependent, people and governments are reexamining their values and their purpose for living and working.

In his insightful book *The Third Wave*, Alvin Toffler described past changes in the world's economy as economic eras, or "waves." The First Wave was the agricultural revolution of the 19th century. The Second Wave was the Industrial Revolution, which emphasized mass production and growth and encouraged individual achievement, competition, bigness, survival of the fittest, and hierarchical management.

The Third Wave began when the United States embarked on an information economy. It emphasizes team accomplishment, cooperation, flat and lean organizational structure, mutual interests, and participative management. Whereas the Second-Wave company may pollute the environment in the name of higher production and profits at all costs, Third-Wave companies are environmentally conscious. They recognize not only the futility of trying to survive on a planet that is continuously undergoing the ravages of pollution, but they also recognize the tremendous economic, political, and social ramifications of abusing the environment.

One of the goals of Third-Wave companies is to quickly meet the needs of customers or adjust to economic trends. This is generally achieved by either transforming products or the organization itself. These organizations, by necessity, are flatter and more flexible than companies from prior eras. Nothing is permanent. Everything is likely to change. Nothing is considered too sacred, because the company's survival may depend on its ability to make rapid changes.

Jim Wilk, mentioned in other chapters, understands this trend very well and offers advice for making the most of it. "You have to take risks," he suggests. "Look ahead—what are the trends? Let go of outdated concepts. Ninety percent of what you learn in a company is useless, because everything is always changing. I believe in preparing my people for the year 2010." To succeed in tomorrow's world of Third-Wave companies, then, you need to be quick to adapt.

Management in Third-Wave companies encourages creativity. In turn, employees feel motivated by the opportunity to grow and make a difference. Risk taking and innovation are supported and encouraged. A prime objective of Third-Wave companies is to utilize resources where they best serve the company's interests. Although we could elaborate on several other distinctions, the important point is that companies will no longer operate as in the past. For many Third-Wave managers, such a massive change in culture necessitates a total change in outlook. "Attitude adjustments" will need to complement evolving company needs.

If you're a corporate stalwart who wants to stay within the traditional models, you'll have fewer opportunities as a result of eliminations of non-value-added positions through mergers, acquisitions, downsizings, and restructurings. But if you're willing to make lateral moves, stay flexible, and continually improve your skills, you can be successful within this environment. For those willing to grow and improve their skills as economical changes warrant, opportunities will be greater than ever. But the future is grim for people resistant to change. As Jim Wilk described it, "For those who can make improvements, there will always be a job. But don't rely on old accomplishments; instead, take and apply new concepts. You have to keep up with the trends. You have to practice lifelong learning."

The entrepreneur can expect more opportunities. In fact, the largest percentage of business growth has been occurring on this career path, and is expected to continue. Government regulation, on the other hand, is predicted to enter a decline. Keep in mind, however, that as more small businesses start up, competition is likely to increase proportionately.

Experts' roles in academia may be declining due to increasing budget cuts for research funding. Yet as companies continue to downsize and outsource, corporate opportunities will abound for top experts in different fields. Not only will opportunities increase but corporate employees who do not keep abreast of trends and who ignore the cultivation of new skills will be cast aside, thus opening the way for experts in specific fields to "do their thing." For experts deriving their income from research grants, marketing and networking skills will become more and more important.

More people will become achievers, as specialization in the newer technologies becomes more common. But these same new technologies may make some career choices obsolete (real estate and life insurance agents as well as car dealers are representative cases in point). With improvements in telecommunications and increasing use of the Internet, the services performed by these middlemen may no longer be necessary and will be viewed by companies

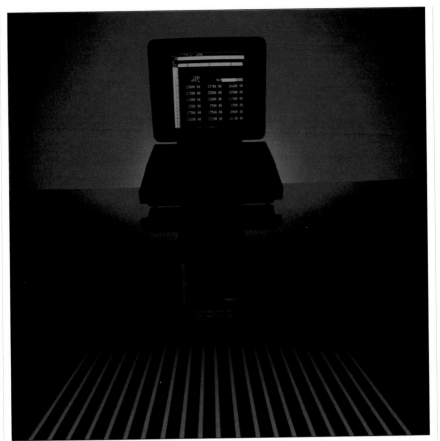

Cyberspace enlarges the corporate playing field.

and customers alike as "dead weight." But, in contrast, achievers who can add significant value to companies and customers will be in greater demand.

Facilitators will need to continually increase their contacts and learn more about the people they serve. As with the other career paths, adaptability and creativity will be vital. In particular, facilitators will need to keep up with changes in the Internet, as more people interact via this medium. In fact, there are remarkable opportunities for facilitators to become Internet guides for people in virtually all careers and fields.

Surfing the Net

The information superhighway will soon become the standard by which we conduct commerce—advertising, banking, and direct sales. Currently, over six million Americans "surf the net." Corporations are adding websites at a steady pace, recognizing it as a powerful source of new ideas, communication, and innovation.

The Internet, the third factor that will greatly alter corporations and careers, currently allows individuals and companies to send messages and mail, advertise and search for products, and locate new jobs and business opportunities. Whereas industries such as medicine and education should benefit, middlemen and retailers who don't adapt may be left out.

Realistically, most industries will realize some change, including the altering of competition and economies of scale as we know it. Literal "virtual companies" will spring up around the world, as our global economy becomes a global workforce.

A company located in New York, for example, might hire a programmer from Toronto without even meeting her. Many entrepreneurs have already offered their products over the Internet, making deals both countrywide and worldwide. A law firm in London could utilize the services of a legal specialist from Berlin. An achiever in the investment banking business could arrange a deal in Los Angeles without leaving his home in Atlanta. And a facilitator will help put all of these deals together by acting as a clearinghouse. The Internet makes all of this possible today, and you'll see these trends increase even more dramatically in the years ahead.

Aging of the Workforce

The fourth factor that will affect your career involves the aging of a unique group of workers, and a very different group taking their place. The aging of baby boomers, currently the predominant leaders in our workforce economy, will create major changes in the economic landscape. From a human resource, marketing, or health-care viewpoint, the maturing of the baby boomer generation will have profound effects.

Marketing experts feel that baby boomers will create quite a challenge in the years ahead. As this group becomes more fractionalized, targeting them will become more difficult.

According to Mike Gallagher, a seasoned financial expert on the health care industry, "You can see by the demographics [the aging of the population] that a big 'wave' is coming our way. We need to analyze technology, service needs, and availability to predict what will work, and how we can capitalize on trends."

One anticipated trend is an increase in the number of grandparents and grandchildren. Currently 30 percent of the population are baby boomers. After a peak in 1997, the number of baby boomers will decline steadily over the next 30 years, with only a 19 percent baby boomer population remaining.

As the next generation dominates the workforce, you're also likely to see significant cultural changes in company attitudes and behavior, as the "baby busters" predominate. Born between 1965 and 1983, these baby busters have different expectations and values, particularly in regard to work, careers, and relationships.

As a group, busters aren't threatened by the changing trends mentioned in this book. They thrive on change. They value flexibility. It's as if team management was created with them in mind. Busters feel a need to respect the philosophy of the organizations for whom they work, and many won't tolerate a company that's not environmentally conscious. Of course, it's too early to predict their full potential, but one thing's for certain—as a group, they are quite different from boomers and the world they create will be just as unique.

These characteristics will encourage the movement away from corporate positions and toward the other four career paths. Not only are busters more inclined to prefer the other paths, but companies are also beginning to wise up to the realities of having to rely on this generation. Those busters who do stay within the corporate arena will largely do so in Third-Wave companies, where their needs for team-based, environmentally conscious management and a flexible learning environment will be ensured.

Telecommuting

The current trends toward working from home in a small business, or telecommuting with your corporate

Telecommuting is experiencing an upsurge in popularity.

job, should increase significantly in the years ahead. This is the fifth factor affecting companies and careers, and it will continue to change the world in the next several years.

Over 20 million Americans operate home businesses. John Naisbitt, in *Megatrends*, predicted that home-based businesses will add increasingly to the nation's economy. In conjunction with this, as of a few years ago, approximately one out of three companies had a plan for allowing employees to telecommute. The number of telecommuters is expected to continue to rise.

Most telecommuters appreciate the flexibility, and a good number find that it lowers their stress level, although it is often a difficult transition. Contrary to the skeptics' view, most managers have noted an increase in productivity from those who work at home. Companies have also noted that it helps to improve employee retention, reduces overhead, and lessens congestion and air pollution due to reduced traffic. Again, advances in technology make this possible.

Telecommuting also creates a significant impact on corporate life and allows companies to utilize cheaper labor overseas. It again emphasizes the need for people in all career paths to remain flexible with their job duties, to adapt to new working environments, and to quickly learn new skills.

Network Marketing

Network marketing, the sixth factor that will help shape careers as we enter the next millennium, has become one of the largest growing sales methods, currently surpassing almost $15 billion per year. Made famous by Amway and other similar companies, network marketing works by having "independent representatives" (people who are not direct employees) sell products and also recruit other sellers. While many people find network marketing distasteful—and associate it with "pyramid schemes"—it is nevertheless a large force in our economy that is expanding every year.

Network marketing efforts lead to approximately 15 percent of consumer sales. And a larger percentage of consumer sales of other products include some network marketing elements, such as MCI's "Friends and Family" program that encouraged people to have a hand in signing up the people they call most often. Network marketing is a growing force in the economy because it works without traditional advertising, which is becoming increasingly expensive. Recent studies reveal that as the number of advertisements increases, the effectiveness of each individual ad is lessened. Network marketing is a cheap, reliable alternative.

With the aforementioned changes in technology and the trend toward network marketing, companies will tend to lower their overhead by eliminating high-priced sales positions. Many unemployed salespeople will likely become independent representatives of various products, seeking to take advantage of their skills. People in the facilitator career path will be in high demand to serve as brokers, sales managers, and trainers (showing how to sell "simply by using one's Rolodex"), and strategists helping to bringing companies together with consumers around the world. Experts focusing in consumer trends, pricing strategies, and market research will also be in high demand. And facilitators will be called on to bring all these parties together.

International Trade

There is much concern among American workers that recent trade pacts with other nations may eliminate jobs at home. There is likely some credence to this, although many details of the GATT agreement still need considerable fine-tuning. Whatever the outcome, international trade will continue, and this is the seventh factor that will affect almost every career.

As previously mentioned, our new global economy allows people and companies to sell their services to any person or company on the planet. Because of continuing enhancements in information technology, several new markets are emerging as never before.

The Clinton administration has identified Argentina, Brazil, China, India, Indonesia, Mexico, Poland, South Africa, South Korea, and Turkey as the primary nations that have developed their infrastructures and moved toward privatization. Over the next 20 years, these countries should account for more than 40 percent of all global imports. Not only are these countries a major part of the U.S. trade strategy, but they can be an important part of your career strategy as well.

New technologies and markets create opportunities for people in all five career paths. Not only will new markets stabilize corporate jobs, but entrepreneurs, experts, achievers, and facilitators can also benefit. But with increased competition comes the need for increased skill levels and higher quality performance. This gives the larger, more established firms an advantage. Because of their broader range of resources, the threat exists that larger multinational firms might drive the smaller firms or sole proprietors out of business. Yet increasing trade is good for people who display flexibility, willingness to learn new skills, and commitment to innovation and quality.

The changes coming with the new millennium are indeed exciting. As with all changes, some people will adapt and thrive. Others will respond with denial and resistance, resulting in fewer opportunities for advancement. It is our sincere hope that you will use the knowledge in this book to capitalize on the coming trends—in both your personal and professional life. We wish you the best fortune as you embark on your reinvented career.

Index

W

Credits

Authors

David C. Logan teaches organizational communication at the University of Southern California and serves as a consultant in organization development and reengineering. His clients include Fortune 500 companies in the aerospace, health care, and entertainment industries.

Bryan Kritzell is a manager in the materials and administration division of a major health care company headquartered in Los Angeles. He has published over thirty articles on business and management topics and has developed widely used training programs in management, personal development, and corporate outreach.

Photos

All photos provided by PhotoDisk, Seattle, Washington.